THE

ROAD OF

A NATURALIST

WOOD ENGRAVINGS BY PAUL LANDACRE

The
Road of
a Naturalist

DONALD

CULROSS

PEATTIE

G.K. HALL & CO.
Boston, Massachusetts
1986

Library of Congress Cataloging-in-Publication Data

Peattie, Donald Culross, 1898–1964.
  The road of a naturalist.

  Reprint. Originally published: Boston : Houghton Mifflin,
1941.
  1. Peattie, Donald Culross, 1898–   2. Natural
history—United States.   3. United States—Description and
travel.   4. Naturalists—United States—Biography.   I. Title.
QH31,P17A3 1986   508′.092′4 [B]   85-24946
ISBN 0-8398-2890-X (pbk.)

ACKNOWLEDGMENTS

THE author acknowledges gratefully permission to quote in this volume from articles that have appeared in the following periodicals: *The Atlantic Monthly, The American Magazine, Bird-Lore, The Chicago Daily News, The Chicago Naturalist, Cosmopolitan, The Country Gentleman, Esquire, Frontiers — A Magazine of Natural History, Natural History, The New York Times, The Reader's Digest.*

CONTENTS

1

TO THE MOJAVE · *PAGE* 1

2

SURVIVAL ON THE DESERT · *PAGE* 21

3

DEATH VALLEY, CHRISTMAS, 1849 · *PAGE* 39

4

EARLY ON THE WAY · *PAGE* 51

5

ROVING REPORTER · *PAGE* 66

6

SAGEBRUSH · *PAGE* 88

7

A HOUSE THAT WAS HOME · *PAGE* 109

8

WYOMING IN THE EOCENE · *PAGE* 123

9

YOUNG MAN NOT OF MANHATTAN · *PAGE* 138

10

A CABIN ON FISH CREEK · *PAGE* 158

11

MY TOWN · *PAGE* 178

12

THE LONG GOOD–BYE · *PAGE* 194

13

DOWN FROM HIGH PASSES · *PAGE* 219

14

FALLING WATER · *PAGE* 237

15

HOW THE DROUGHT BROKE · *PAGE* 254

16

SINCE WALDEN · *PAGE* 273

17

ROAD WITHOUT END · *PAGE* 294

THE

ROAD OF

A NATURALIST

1

TO THE MOJAVE

THE car, a flying home enclosing us man and wife, descended out of the mountain pass in a rush upon a waste on fire with sundown. Unleashed for the long stretch, the motor took up a loyal thrumming. The wind at the lip of the window lifted its coyote whimper that it keeps for the Mojave. This was a strange sunset, even for the desert; dust or clouds had diffused it till it stretched all around the sky. There was no quarter of the earth that was not engulfed in conflagration.

A last rim of snow upon the San Gabriel Range flashed light like a signal for help. But the dark came on swiftly. We think of night as descending from the sky, but it is, of course, born of the earth. It is earth's own shadow, and it wells up from the hollows and cups and pits of the planet. Like rising flood waters, it last of all engulfs the high places; the snowy peak went out like a doused lantern.

We bored into an enormous twilight, and up around us the desert began to raise the outpost sentinels of its sole forest force. An armless figure or two rose over the scrub, then a group of sentries in static gesticulation against the retreating day. The Joshua trees are the only wood upon this part of the desert. They stand, devoid of any grace of spreading foliage, sparse and apart, their leaves like daggers thrust into their rigid limbs. They looked in the dusk, as we came speeding through them, fantastically like the remnants of some decimated host that had been stripped and hacked for punishment.

By day there is such distance here as can hold immense mountain ranges and keep a space between them that looks astronomical. There is such aridity that the melting snows from the mountains, and the few thin, braided rivers, are soon lost in sands. Once they found their way to dead seas; now they die themselves before they can push on so far.

But by night the Mojave is no longer merely vast. It is boundless, and when, as on this night, the sky is roiled over with clouds, the darkness is absolute. It gives me the terrifying sense of vacuum that I have felt in swimming at night. I am genuinely afraid in a dark sea. There is no horizon, no certainty of any shore. So it is on the desert when there are no stars. Perhaps, I thought, it is like this to know that you are dead.

But we the living had companions in this outer space. Once the two eyes of the car met the eyes of a coyote, rolling with a hydrophobic glare as the tapetum caught the headlight blaze and threw it back. Once I saw the slinking tail quarters of a kit fox. And often there were the little scuttling shapes of chipmunks, and jackrabbits with ruby eyes and foolish ears big enough for any rumor, panicky refugees that jumped away in a crazy crisscross.

The road forked; ahead the car lamps picked up the cochina dolls that top each one a gatepost of the ranch. Passing between them, we saw that, since no windows gleamed in the scattered adobes, the people at the ranch were all asleep. But we knew our way here; we knew the hospitality that would have left unlocked the door of the adobe house we liked to call our own.

A star or two, where the clouds rifted, glinted as the car's lamps winked out. By their light we crossed the sand to the door; it spoke a welcome, giving to my push. So we found again that calm interior which is a home to us because it is made of natural things that are home to the spirit of man. Its 'dobe walls were two feet thick, to keep out summer heat and winter cold, and lofty enough for thoughts to rise in quiet dignity, as smoke was rising within the tall chimney bulge from the fire that dwindled on the hearth. The beams that held the roof were redwood. The broad doors, facing each other across the room to let a draft go sweeping through at noon, were hasped with hammered iron; their thresholds were level with the earth. Climate and tradition both were suited here in comfort, and so was I. I stirred the fire and threw on it one more log from the stack of juniper lengths that must have been cut in the mountains and hauled here to lie waiting in their shaggy brown coats of bark, to give us light and heat, the crackle of fire's willing service, the pungent smell of the woods brought home.

This was the first halt on what, that night, felt less like a holiday journey than an evacuation from a battlefield eight thousand miles away, but brought right up against the eardrums, the eyeballs, by today's methods of spreading the news. Foresight is one thing, terror another. It will make none of us safer to believe that the human race is foundering — not in the four-hundred-year shakedown of the Graeco-Roman civilization, but with the two-minute sinking of a torpedoed liner. After so much of talk like that it was time, I thought, to discover what evidence might lie in the great silences of my country. Of the desert, and the forests holding their ground by quiet roots, and the Rockies that are the backbone of America. While my wife knelt to blow upon the fire, I bent down and disconnected the radio in the room.

Yet on the way to sleep I still had to listen to all I had stifled in that box in the corner, the oratory, the persuasion, the clipped excited bulletins. They echoed with confusion in my tired head, unearthly loud in the deep calm of the desert. By the smouldering log, I saw that she slept, with arms tossed upward in surrender. A flicker of light caught in the lantern which hung from the beams became the focus of my insomniac contemplation.

Where, in all this, does the naturalist come in? What use as defence is there for what he knows and does? Or had he best be beating his typewriter into a sword, and scanning the skies for parachutists with his bird binoculars?

I punched my pillow higher. It seems to me, I argued — against some enemy viewpoint — that he is by pro-

fession a defender of just such human values as men die
for. The purity of science is as precious to the cause of
liberty as the manuscript of the Constitution, and more
so; only by the ethics and intellects of free scientists can
it be held aloft. Love of the living world's beauty, seldom
alluded to by the naturalist though he is pledged to it as
loyally as to science, is an unwritten franchise in the rights
of man. Nature is an ultimate sanctuary for sanity and
goodness; American nature is a first national principle.
To it I am dedicated.

Get on with your job, then, was the obvious advice to
give myself.

But my trouble was that I couldn't go on with my job,
as one can who knows he keeps a small but necessary cog-
wheel ticking round on time, with the comforting feeling
that if all do as well, we may still keep the clock from
stopping. For I haven't got any job of this routine and
essential nature.

Technically, I suppose, I could be written down as one
of the Unemployed. On credit cards I can never give a
business address, which always looks bad to credit men,
especially when I add that I have no independent income.
Nor do I teach my subject to classes, nor research it in
the laboratory or in the field under the aegis of some institution; nobody sends me on expeditions from which I
might bring something back alive for study, or dead for
exhibition. If, even, I were engaged in a ten-year survey
of the food habits of the coyote, in order to decide whether
conservation would best be served by extirpating or pro-
tecting coyotes, I could count on that ten years as a
period when I was, conventionally at least, considered a

useful member of society. Of course my findings would possibly be published in a jargon too incomprehensible for criticism except by a few men speaking the same limited scientific dialogue. And then, after all, it might hardly matter whether western farmers and stock men should exterminate the coyote, if by then he was howling in white moonshine over the rubble of our bombed cities.

Perhaps in that end of the world, the faithful student of coyotes could find some comfort in the fact that his project had been worthy and his conclusions abstractly right. But I am not a delver in research. Nor am I a confident moralist reading in Nature's gospel a text from which to preach heavenly purpose; I do not see the wild as a garden benignantly planted. All that, though Wordsworth still is a good poet, is 'out'; it never was good science, and it is trite now even with the unscientific.

I could not hear her breathing, but I heard another sound. We were not alone in the big 'dobe room. Someone else was trying, with a faint scrabble, to find his way out. Giving up the woodpile, he made a bold essay across the hearthrug, a noiseless flicker of shadow, eyes glinting fearfully with that same light which was all I had to see by.

And I saw my business plainer, the kangaroo rat a part of it. For we are all part of Nature; and now in the night, attentive to the grand enduring whole, I heard that the guns in my head were silenced. I heard instead the sound of sap creeping up, of the wind in a plover's wing as it beat northward to nest. Life is the battle in which we all fall, yet it is never lost. My station on this field is as interpreter; my present journey was for news from the front,

of that America which was here before the Americans
came.

Every morning, since the great new freshet of blood
began to soak into old earth, I had wakened with a start
of dread. Then came implacable realization to stop the
heart a moment; the heart labors on thereafter, shouldering its burden of grief for the suffering.

So now I woke, in the pre-dawn of the desert. Here was
the world again, with a high tide of human thought and
action going out, sucking down the weak and unwary by
its dark undertow. Already, lying slack, I felt that tug.
The deep self-doubt that anything I might do or think or
stand for could meet the challenge of this time, pulled me
sickeningly down.

With all my forces I struck out against that current.
The gray light was growing, showing the stalwart ruddy
beams that braced the ceiling, the tall bulge of the adobe
fireplace, the stack of logs beside it where the kangaroo rat
had hidden from his own fears. My wife lay hiding from
the light in the toss of her hair. But I was hungering for it.
Habitually I wake with the light; I like to do this; I would
not willingly have my bed where I could not see the sunrise, or the stars if I should rouse in the night. I can tell

time by them in a rough way, and so I know how long I have to wait until the dawn birds sing and the adventure of living begins again.

For a naturalist is a man who can hear a bird calling right through his deepest sleep, and deliberately wake himself up to listen. If it is a known bird, still he listens reverently, attentive for all the fine points to be found in the call of even a familiar voice. One has never heard a grosbeak's spring song too many times. And a man, you know, has just so many May mornings in his life. So few, rather.

There had been days when I had wakened in this room, winter mornings, which were birdless and without a note of life in them. Only the sound of the wind, finding in the house corner an opponent to which to give tongue.

All the wide West lies open as an instrument to the wind. In Arizona, Nevada, Colorado, New Mexico, and desert California, the voice of the wind is seldom still. It is not heard as a rushing sound like the torrent in the eastern forests. In unforested country it is most audible at door or window, in a chimney or a mine shaft. There it goes telling old tales, making new promises. In other, softer terrain that whimper would be a pathetic sound, but there is nothing pathetic in the West. Even at Virginia City, or at Casa Grande, where there are vanished people and departed grandeurs to recall, there is no snivel in the story. Gold-rushers and their jades are not touching, and Indians, as they do not shed tears save ceremonial ones, do not ask them.

You could say rather that the wind of the West is historic. And it suggests perpetually that the story is not

over. The Indians are gone, or subdued; the cattle feuds
are ending; the stagecoaches gather dust in museums, and
the wild bonanzas will not come again. But the winds are
still born and die here on the Mojave. The desert heat,
the winter snows, the cactus and the canyon abide and
will be reckoned with by all who come this way. There
will be, for ages to come, adventure in the West. Not the
old kind, not any sort one can safely predict. But whatever it is, it will not be the removed, vicarious or seden-
tary adventure of crowded living and dying. It will still
have wind in it, and sand or snow, mountains, cattle, gold,
and trees. The wind talks of these things. It is not only
remembering them. It is prophesying.

Now it sighed down our chimney, stirring the ash. Soft
exhalation that it was, it was America's own breath, and
it quickened mine with a patriotism whose colors are the
goldenrod and the reddening sumach and the green of a
Douglas spruce branch against blue sky.

I did not ask, God knows, to die for my country, but to
live in it for a cause large enough to survive all causes.
No use, in days when one ship of state after another went
hull-down into the sucking tide, to cling to any loyalty
not great enough to fit the day when men shall pledge
united loyalty to all other men.

There is no other final victory for mortal man to hope
for. We are conscript at birth and at our first wail doomed
to die. So are all things living, and more than we can decipher from the rock have been wiped out utterly. But
who, on a summer morning in the woods when every leaf
and blade is spread to the full, and every grub is plumping
himself out on the juices of them, till it becomes a banquet

for the bird that snatches it — who then will doubt the strength of his allies in the long fight of all to live? Nature is more than a refuge from human chaos, more than fresh

air for smoke-filled lungs, and quietude from ears in torture. It is the common way of living, and as such it is our touchstone.

If it has no pity, yet it has much of it a warm heart beating with first feelings like our own. Even unfeeling, it spreads out a banner of hope. I never saw those colors ripple so gaily to the wind as on the April morning that, having come late to this adobe as on the night just past, I opened my door in early sunshine and stepped out.

The desert, I saw, was in bloom.

Not every spring does the stone roll back like this, but only when the rain and the snows and the sun combine fortuitously to decree it. I had not seen the miracle before, road-runners though we had been for years, criss-crossing the southwestern wastes in all directions, across the Antelope Valley and down into Death Valley, beside the Salton Sea and over the Yuma dunes, across Nevada sagebrush, Arizona mesas, alkaline playas of the Amargosa Desert, spaces of the Gila Desert where solid things have the unreality of mirage. I knew occasional flowery spots, brief blossomings licked by blast of wind and blaze of sun; I knew the secretive blooming of the desert shrubs, in flowers without petals, or lonely corollas falling beside some seepage of water in the high clefts of the hills, where even the bees, you'd think, would not thread their way to find them. Dusty, wiry, naked but for thorns, resinous, bitter, sparse, the desert brush and cacti are admirable for enduring where they do at all; they are, like the scorpions and centipedes and rattlesnakes of their environment, much to be respected. In a sort of dead and silvery and almost invisible way, they are even beautiful, as the ghosts of Tamerlane's Tartars might look, if one had an hallucination of their passing in a blur of heat and whirling dust.

But here to my feet, that April morning, swept a radiant

populace of flowers, sprung overnight, it seemed to me, from what had looked barren soil. As anyone will cry out involuntarily at an unexpected sharp pain, so there was no stopping the laughter that rose in the throat at the sight.

The desert flora at all ordinary times is grandly, confidently monotonous, made up of certain hardy species little varied over an area as great as the two Virginias plus the two Carolinas. That is the norm, the always present uncompromising reality, in season or out. But this other, this dazzling profusion of color and dancing shapes, this unexpected smile breaking over the Mojave's stern face, was all herbaceous, made of delicate annuals. The sea of bloom was only ankle-deep; many species were not an inch tall, though with flowers sometimes two inches across. In this fashion the beautiful little rose namas, the desert stars like English daisies, desert-gold, tiny-tim, and humble gilia with its petals the color of moonlight on frost made a dense carpet that it seemed heartless to tread upon.

Above this close undermat danced a second tier of flowers, goldenglow and white tidy-tips and desert dandelions with heads of canary yellow. And, pervading the sunny waste with fragrance, rose sprawling sand-verbenas, lavender as they are pink. There was a lupine blazing here and there throughout, a taper of royal purple. There were the scabiosa sages, salvias really, that the Spanish settlers called *chia*, whose brilliant blue two-lipped flowers leap out of a tiny spiny sphere of bracts. There were desert mallows, with their crumpled dusty leaves and flowers varying from vivid apricot to deep grenadine.

But most profuse, most constantly in motion on their

hair-fine stems, most innocently frail, were the blue gilias.
Some were clear white, some lilac, some true blue, some
with yellow eyes, some tall, some dwarf; what looked like
many species was only one variable kind, *Gilia Davyi*.
When the wind blew, and these children of the desert
danced, their fragrance was blown quite away; when the
sun baked perfume from the sand-verbena, the gilias' odor
was smothered. But when I brought them inside the cool
adobe room, I became aware of a tender perfume stealing
into my thoughts, getting into my dreams at night. Every
day, every hour, you saw the gilias, but you never got
used to the sheer improbability that anything so dainty
could be put forth from the Mojave. Indestructible,
thorny, bare, the creosote bush and salt bush, the burro
bush and rabbit brush are the natural sons of the desert,
warrior sons, like Homeric soldiers naked but for spear
and shield, thorns and bitterness. But just as a savage old
man might beget gentle daughters too, so the Mojave
sends forth blue gilias, once in many years a million of
them, like this.

Above the two tiers of flowers there rose spindling ex-
amples of a third. Here and there, for instance, a slim
wand of lilac larkspur. Or thistle sage, kingly tufts of
cottony silver thick with long mauve salvia flowers the
longer for their orange anthers. And an aster with
lavender heads in bold clumps of twenty blooms and
more.

In all, those April days yielded to my vasculum some
seventy-five species. Large as this number sounds, it is
not a greater variety than would be found at a corresponding stage of seasonal development anywhere else; what

brought delight was the sheer abundance of the bloom, the feeling that we were besieged by an army of little flowers. The bees were drunk with them; they came in thousands from only the Mojave knew where. I saw the humming-birds flash by in such a state of excitement that they looked as if they had been shot sideways out of a cannon with a twisted bore. They seemed unable to settle their scattered brains on anything; they went so fast I couldn't follow them with my glasses to identify which of California's many kinds of hummer they were. We used to wonder, at the ranch, how far this flood of rare flowering washed across the desert floor. You couldn't tell; you only knew it went on to the rim of the horizon. And you knew it was brief. It must be loved while you had it, like the song of the thrush in the southern states. Something that each morning you dread to find gone at last, whelmed by the advance of summer heat.

Resting from the sweat and blindness of collecting in full sunlight at noon, I would lie on my back in the adobe room, on the cool of the tiles, and let the flowers dance before my closed eyes. And their biologic meaning was borne in upon me. Desert plants do not follow what we consider a normal cycle — green in summer, and dying back to some perennial root in winter. For when it is calendar summer here it is biologic winter; the leaves drop and everything dies or wears the look of death. It is also, biologically, winter in autumn as well as in winter when snow lies on the desert. But spring is not only spring but summer and autumn in swift succession. And of all desert plants the best equipped to deal with this climatic ex-travagance are these little annuals, these fragile exquisites

so prodigal of their scant waters. Swiftly indeed do they
wilt. They not only wilt, they die, completely, the entire
crop — only to survive as seeds. As seeds, a year later or,
if conditions oblige, ten years later, they will sprout again,
and in from two to six weeks rush to full flower, become
pollinated, set seed, distribute seed, and die again. Such
is the life of an annual, and of all forms of life history the
annual is the best for desert life.

For, like the seventeen-year cicada which is a grub all
those years underground and enjoys but a few weeks of
aerial life as a winged, singing, mating adult, the swift
vanishing spring desert flora passes the greater part of its
time as dormant seeds. Only irregularly and most briefly
does it escape as a flower, before the continuous stream of
life is caught inside a seed again, indefinitely to wait. So
the champion desert plant is not the tough creosote, the
malicious cholla, not the Joshua tree or the sage, but seed
as tiny as gilia's. For a seed is not just part of a plant; detached, it is a complete plant, with a plantlet folded inside,
a supply of food, an infinitesimal supply of moisture.
Boxed in its shell, it defies drought, heat, cold, poisonous
alkaline soils. Only water has the password to open its
prison.

Now I began to notice seeds everywhere. The deliberate
big harvester ants, who can both bite and sting so fiercely,
were bearing away seeds of all sorts of plants, as fast as
they fell, in industrious braided lines. I saw chaff outside
the untidy nests of pack rats, and I presume that all of the
desert's tremendous rodent population of gophers and
kangaroo rats, ground squirrels and field mice are in part
dependent on seeds; birds too devour them. As they are

the secret and triumphant desert flora, so they are the
hidden larder, the basic food supply.

The heat, and still more the light, were often insup-
portable as the days crawled lizardlike across the desert.
I wore a huge peaked sombrero of lightest straw, and
smoked glasses, sandals and white ducks and a rag of
shirt. And still I was often so giddy I felt I must drop
flat or die. Black and red dazzled before my gaze, and I
measured the distance to the roof of the adobe cottage
with the eye of one who has to swim back to shore farther
than he is sure he has the wind or muscle to make it. The
rime of snow on the San Gabriel Range looked mockingly
cool, and distant as the moon. Finally I cowered under
the redwood beams, writing up notes, pressing specimens,
reading; and only went out at dusk.

It was then that I discovered that the desert dandelions
and Mojave asters and many other flowers close up at
night. And another flora, nocturnal, steals into bloom.
All day long one lax and weedy plant had looked dead,
its flowers withered. But by twilight this wild four-
o'-clock secretly opened its rose-pink calyces and emitted
a faint odor. Where I had tramped the burning blossom-
ing swells and hollows at four and seen nothing of it, a
flower called evening-snow suddenly appeared at dusk.
Leaf and stem are mere sand-colored threads; flowers are
twirled up by day into a pointed bud absolutely invisible
in the glare. But fifteen minutes after twilight's fall,
millions of them open, with a soundless silken uncurling
of their petals, and lo, they are white gilias, the color of
starshine. As they expand, a delicate fragrance takes the
air.

The West is a kingdom of evening primroses; though I knew many species, still I was unprepared for the dune primrose I found in the desert dusks. Its crepuscular flowers are large as those of a wild rose when they open, but insubstantial as spider floss, great mothlike petals languidly expanding as if still oppressed with the long siesta of the day. They are white, but as soon as you pick them they turn pink, and in ten minutes they are faded and cannot be revived. They seem to have just the turgor in their gleaming cells requisite to sustain life only if they are not sun-smitten or touched by human hands. They are so secret that they cannot survive the appreciation of a fingertip, and they hold their sweet breath until the approach of darkness.

In mid-April I had left the ranch, wanting not to see this rainbow fade. Early in May a friend wrote: 'Come back; there is another flora on the way.' It was easy to quit my desk at that, and make the four-hour motor journey to the desert. Gone was the first candor of the early flowers, and in their place had come a gaudier, coarser, stronger flora, corresponding, I suppose, to that of eastern summers. Yellow buckwheat was everywhere, and another flower, called alkali goldfields, had replaced the coreopsis. A ranker, branching dandelion took over from the desert dandelions; the weedy rock pink was in bloom, and the desert trumpet too; deep rose cups glowed on the beaver-tail cactus. It was the season now of *el barbasco*, the fish-poison spurge, of spiked stillingia spurge also, that gushes a spurt of milky juice upon the hands in revenge for being picked. And where the sunlight blazed the fiercest, where the hard sands reflected its intolerable

glare, there burnt up from the ground an almost stemless
chalice of fiery orange. It is something to look a desert
mariposa in the eye.

You find mariposas all over the West; they change
height, change shape and color, as you trace them from
the mountains of Colorado, over the Utah soda plains, up
and over the High Sierra, down into the Great Central
Valley, and where they climb the coast ranges and descend
till they dance on the brink of the cliffs of the Pacific.
They change names too — fairy lanterns, Mormon lilies,
cat's ears, *Calochortus*. They are lilac and pink and white;
they are like frail tulips delicately penciled and painted;
they are like fritillaries, nodding half closed. But nothing
you ever saw of them prepares you for the desert's one
species, for that intense cup of flame holding in reserved
candor the geometrically elegant display of its organs.

In the hot, late May that is the desert's brief lease on
summer, the ground was thorny with kinds of gilia now
inhospitable — prickly gilia and calico flower. Underfoot
was spiny-herb, all ridges and spikes, symmetrical on a
plan of three. And a relative that looked as if it had been
cut out of tarnishing metal by Euclid; at the center of its
saucer of bracts you find what appears to be a clutch of
tiny seeds; they are really the larvae of a blue butterfly.

In the innocent phase of spring there had bloomed an
astragalus, very like a lupine, but straggling, crazy,
clouded, its pea flowers sickly pink. This is the locoweed
of the cowboys. Now its bloated pods, that popped between my fingers, were blotched and scrawled in madder
with a meaningless alphabet; in this could be read only
madness and death for the horses that crop it and fall
victim to its deadly chemical, selenium.

The paper-bag bush, too, had gone to pod, just a few of its purple mint flowers left, where I had seen the humming-birds at pollination. The hop-sage was turning red, as if with autumn tints; the color of the fruits upon the Mormon tea was trembling between purple and pink; bronze was overcasting the salt bush foliage, and out on the desert burned the last unholy glories of its ultimate flora — nicolletia with off-shade yellow-pinks and mustardy green-yellows and a skunky odor that simply would not wash off the fingers; also a brassy-colored dyssodia with a name which means ill-smell, thrice and four times deserved. The desert at last had bloomed itself out; it had exhausted the gamut of beauty and, like a decadent, found beauty in the repulsive.

Now I had come again, when by the calendar it was June. In Illinois the prairies of my childhood would be flowing under a fresh wind, timothy and daisies and fox-tail grass blowing all one way in long rooted ripples. In Maryland the Queen Anne's lace was dancing under apple trees that make wide pools of shadow. In Cambridge the old lawns would be green. Mid-June, the day after school closes — youth's moment. But the desert and I were past that. I would not even look at the brittle dusty straws that were the stubble of the blue-eyed jillies. Life was going off the land; even the meagre foliage of the shrubs was dropping, leaving naked thorns. The wasp's larvae were beginning to come out of the inflated stem of the desert trumpet, where their mother had laid them when that stem was succulent and bore flowers. It was so paper-thin and brittle now, that it broke at a touch; no sound was in its parched throat, no humming reveille in the trumpet. There was nothing anywhere, from the foot of the San Bernardinos to and beyond the Colorado River, but heat and wind, and sand upon the wind, and blinding light. The color had seeped out of the world, the laughing tints, the fiery hues that followed; now there were the enduring ochres and grays, the washed-out rusts, the silvered stalks, the horizons dancing with heat waves. The desert had forgotten its one relenting tenderness; it had gone back to the vast inertia of being desert, as dryly and sternly itself as an old squaw. Even at ten thousand feet the snows on the San Gabriels were going; they too were but winter's intercession. They were not eternal. The dew was going from the mornings, each day a little less, until at last there was no sip for a linnet; the song of the orioles was silenced in the Joshua trees, the birds were hatched; the brown pouch hung empty.

2

SURVIVAL

ON THE DESERT

OUR tall still room, within the coolness of adobe walls two feet thick, was a fortress ringed around by an enemy glare, gold bright in the morning and by noon white gold. The windows, curtained to slits, watched that implacable blaze of space as far as the mountainous horizon, and found no break in it. Only the strict contorted shadows of the Joshua trees, bearded and shaggy prophets bent at every joint with the look of protest against pain. Other trees branch serenely, the white pine in a whorl, the elm in lofty umbrella form, the willow in a deep hospitable V-shape, the oak in natural alternate forks. But

Joshua trees take a contorted way to grow, because they can grow in no other.

Every fantastic down-bending, each crazy side thrust, is an escape. There is a weevil whose adults live on the sap of the Joshua, its grubs fattening on the flowers and heart. Such destruction do they cause of the tree's central shoot that the plant, instead of taking a straight upward course like other yuccas, puts forth lateral branches to compensate for the damage. These too the weevil nips and heads off, so that the Joshua tree branches again and again in no predictable way. Even bloom obliges it to grow writhingly, for if a bough flowers, then growth in that bough stops and branching begins there. It is a tree that seems to stand rooted in some inborn torment.

So, cantankerous of outline and stingy of shade, the Joshua is not a very congenial tree to a man. But you make the most of companionship when it is limited. Getting to know and like these yuccas on the desert, I discovered how much there was to find out about them. For the Joshua tree is the Mojave's enigma. No one knows how it is able to attain tree stature on a desert that does not otherwise support trees. No one can tell how old the Joshuas are, for they do not give us true annual rings by which to count their years; instead they produce false concentric rings that prove nothing, and thus conjecture is left to run wild about the age of a giant among them, surmising anything from three hundred to four thousand years, with the first guess the more probable. No one knows when next these trees will unite in a great flowering year, for like all yuccas the Joshua is irregular and spasmodic in blooming. Every year a few bloom; only at infrequent intervals a forest of them comes almost unanimously into heavy white blossom. And finally, lacking fossil evidence, no one knows the Joshua tree's racial antiquity; what grows on the desert returns as dust to dust. Archaic as they look, Joshua trees are not, I think, a picture of the past, like redwoods and ginkgos. In their position as quite advanced members of the distinctly progressive Lily family, they more probably foreshadow the forests of the remote future, when the planet may be desiccating, and from plant families not now dominant may emerge a resistant covering of green things adapted to deserts of continental proportions.

Some people do not like this glimpse into the future. The first American to see Joshua trees was John C. Frémont, heading his motley company in 1844 in search of the mythical river of Buenaventura. Where now the desert wind blows a gale every day from noon to midnight around the house corners of the town of Mojave, Frémont came upon a forest of embittered-looking Joshuas, and did not hesitate to pronounce them 'the most repulsive trees in the vegetable kingdom.'

Clustered in a thin band along the desert bases of the southern Sierra from the lonely Little San Bernardinos blazing far in the south, to the deep Owens Valley with its lost lake in the north, the Joshua trees stood unseen and unadmired for another decade. The Whipple exploring expedition struck the Mojave River from Arizona in 1854, and with it was good old Doctor Bigelow of Boston, botanist, landscape artist, physician hero of the cholera epidemic. He was the first man ever to introduce cheerful planting into cemeteries, and to him the Joshua did not look out of place on earth. He collected its fruits and, getting hold of them, the botanists back East began making up Latin names for that improbable thing out there on the desert.

No one could tell them anything about its flowers, those rare infrequent flowers that must have come before the curious fruits. Another twenty years went by; Doctor C. C. Parry, who found out how much botanical discovery there was to be made on the Mojave which people called a waste, was the scientist first to come on a Joshua tree in flower.

And what flowers, each cluster the size of an ostrich egg, the petals like creamy leather, a quarter of an inch thick! They seem never quite to waken, but from their drowsing, nearly closed lips they exhale an odor no one can be found to praise.

Unless it is the smoky little Pronuba moths, who come to the blossoms, mate there, hover and hide and perform small extraordinary rites without which no Joshua tree would stand and brandish arms at heaven. Some sixty years ago the spotlight fell upon Pronuba. Let us watch the act. The bull's-eye lantern is in the hand of that cheerful eccentric of a science full of eccentricities, Charles Valentine Riley. He is a young man still, State Entomologist of Missouri; the Pronuba that he is tonight observing is a female. Thoughtless, guided by the sure hand of instinct, her eggs fertile within her, she runs to the top of a stamen of the yucca flower that is her stage, bends its pale-gold, pollen-laden anther down to her, curls her tongue about it to hold it while with her tentacles she scrapes the pollen from it. This she kneads into a pellet with her forelegs, patting it and rolling it, and when it is a ball three times the size of her head, she picks it up between her forelegs and her body and flies away.

The spotlight, an all-seeing eye, follows and finds her on another yucca's flower. Here for a moment she rests. Suddenly she takes a swift exploratory run at the bottom of the flower around the columnar stamens, climbs them, and, backing, straddles two of them. So she raises her tail against the great six-angled pistil which rises gleaming creamy white between the stamens. Then from her tail she thrusts out her ovipositor, a thing as delicate as a thread of silk but sharp as a needle, and sinks it into the pistil. As the egg passes down the ovipositor, into the ovary of the flower, her body quivers. So intense is her preoccupation, so devoted every instinct, that she does not stir when a penknife clears the heavy petals and two of the stamens away, when the light of the lantern blazes more fiercely down on her, and the hand lens is brought gleaming within an inch of her head. Egg after egg she lays, after each occasion running ceremoniously to the bottom of the stamens and once more climbing them. Again and again she carries pollen to the top of the pistil, to its receptive stigmatic surface, cramming it down, forcing it into the pollen chambers with her tongue. The hot light beats upon her; the lens follows wherever she goes; nothing deflects her dutiful industry, the laying of her eggs among the ovules of the flower, on some of which her grubs are to feed. In reciprocity, she has cross-pollinated her children's host. Only by the agency of the Pronuba moth can a yucca be sure of setting seed.

This night's work, carefully recorded in Riley's now famous pocket notebooks, established the complete symbiosis, or mutual dependence, between yucca and Pronuba. The Joshua tree has other intimate associates. I found one such, a quick-dodging, splay-footed wriggle more tail than lizard, when I ripped open a half-rotted branch fallen upon the ground. There, or under the Joshua's bark, or deep down at the base of its daggerlike leaves, these night lizards lurk by day, and they are never far from Joshua trees o' nights. For they live on termites, and the termites live on the Joshua tree, tunneling long galleries down its contorted stubborn length, crumbling the fortress from within.

Now, though termites eat wood they cannot, all alone, digest it. A termite needs a friend, and even a termite has one. Within its alimentary canal dwell colonies of flagellate protozoans. These one-celled animals break down the cellulose of the Joshua tree, as the termite slowly devours it, into compounds available to the termite system. As each baby termite begins life seriously, it becomes infected with the flagellate protozoans, as it must or die. And flagellate protozoans must find some termite in which to live and prosper.

Thus is the web of life spun, on the desert as in cities.

Take another strand woven into the tough fibres of the Joshua tree. It leads you back a million years or more. I picked it up one day in the natural history museum of my little home city, when I stood beside a sober paleontologist gazing with reverence upon the exhibit in one of the specimen drawers he had carefully pulled forth for me. It consisted of dung. Dung taken out of a Nevada cave,

million-year-old dung. Dung of the giant ground sloth,
Nothotherium, a great hairy fellow who in his day could
rear up and grasp with his forefeet the top branches of a
Joshua tree, the better to eat them, my dear. Which is
not conjecture, but the result of a meeting of great minds
over this dung. My friend was a sloth man, one of the
only three men qualified to speak on prehistoric sloths in
our enlightened land. He pronounced the dung to be
sloth dung. But it was a paleobotanist who, with mi-
crometer and slide, had determined that what the sloth
had for dinner that day a million years ago was a bite off a
Joshua tree. This is science. Chastened about my own
frivolous place in it, I went away from the hushed museum
room housing the sloth dung, because I could not laugh
there.

Now here is a land, a vast faunal province the size
of two or three eastern states, distinguished from all the
rest of the continent by its aridity, its thirsty wastes, its
drying winds, its water-sucking heat. And it is an ax-
iom in biology that where there is no water there is no
life. The very word desert means that it is deserted by
living things.

Yet the Mojave is populous with a life all its own. First

to be noticed are the jackrabbits, mule ears pricked in
perpetual apprehension; pack rats and wood rats are not
hard to see. When the ground gives way beneath your
foot, some little householder may find his roof caved in,
a kangaroo rat, grasshopper mouse, pocket gopher or
ground squirrel. This is the very kingdom of lizards; the
crested lizard darts across the sand at a footfall and then
turns, raising himself up like a small angry dragon to stare
the intruder down; the hotter the day gets, the more the
leopard lizard frisks; under the stones the gentle geckoes
lie. At twilight the night lizard wriggles out from his
Joshua tree, and over the cooling sands the snakes slip
forth. The dusky sky is swept by little pipistrelles and

chittering lump-nosed bats and, as the light goes, the long wings of Texas nighthawks sheer the gloom, the white bar just visible on the underside of the murky plumage. In the enormous unbreathing calm of the darkening Mojave can be heard their faint purr, like an engine left running somewhere, and the mewing call by which they speak to one another. Far off rings the call of a burrowing owl, two notes that signal solitude.

Desert dawns are full of the chattering song of the bold cactus wrens, so out-size for their clan that they belie their wrenhood, of quarrelsome kingbirds and sweet-voiced Say phoebes. Industriously and secretively the horned larks forage in scattering little flocks among the scrub. There the roadrunner goes racing, a great raucous fugitive fowl who looks as if he had been in a cockfight and lost half his pride, and usually has the corner of a lizard hanging from his mouth. And that mild-mannered plodder, the desert tortoise, pokes and scratches over his own business.

No water, no life; it is the law. When the West first was opened, the government sent out costly expeditions to chart the desert's waterholes. But for countless ages the animals have known them; the biggest, thirstiest creatures frequent them. Even geese and herons passing over the Mojave on migration know lonely oases; doves will fly fifty miles for a sip of water, since fifty miles is not an hour's journey to a dove. The small birds know spots where the few sips of water may be had which will suffice their tiny systems for the day. Even the dew film is important to a host of minute creatures. As for the tortoise, he provides for periods of drought by carrying about a pint of water with him in each of the two sacs under his shell.

The startling fact is that most desert animals go without drinking. Some of the small mammals probably have never had a drink from the day of weaning till their death. They derive their moisture from their food. The owls eat the pocket mice and find the water in the mice; the mice eat the plants and the plants, as usual, are the base of supply. It is enough, since the tiny desert beasts perspire little or not at all, and lose very little water from the kidneys.

But the water content of the seeds eaten by pocket mice, of the dry wood consumed by the powder-post beetles, is something so slight as to be imperceptible to human sense, almost inconceivable, indeed, to the imagination. Any animal that can keep alive on what we would call bone-dry food must have some trick of elaborating water within its own system. This is just what is done by countless species of desert creatures. Their water is called the water of metabolism.

It is one of the easily forgotten facts in the equation of combustion that an end product of fire is water. When you burn or oxidize organic product, the chemical sum of adding oxygen to the formula comes out as heat or energy, carbon dioxide, and water. Most of us animals, beside breathing out the carbon dioxide and using the energy to fight, think, work, or play, eliminate the water more or less polluted with poisons. Not so the economical desert dwellers. The tiny modicum of water produced by breathing-combustion is kept pure and circulated round and round inside the powder-post beetles as, with a faint sound like crackling flames, they reduce the desert shrubs to sawdust.

As the desert days open, blaze, and wither one after another, you become not so much inured to their elemental violence as overcome by it. Embattled by sun, wind, and drought, the desert, after all, is no more a place of utter peace than it is lifeless. These last snows on Old Baldy, and the hot breast of the Mojave sands, war perpetually to establish the temperature. The still, shimmering breath of the desert rises at morning to skies palely blue and pure. Its first long sighs lift the odor of sand verbena to the nostrils and carry bird song to the ears. That early breeze, sweet and cool, bestirs the heavy desert drowse like the trade wind in the tropics, that they call 'the doctor.' The brightening glare seems easier to bear; under the tiled veranda of our 'dobe, I am at first refreshed, then cooled, finally chilly.

Noon brings the strong fresh forces of the snow-bred airs sweeping down upon the blazing dust. By one o'clock the wind is complete master of the desert. It is rising and falling in great puffs of strength, a stiff breeze even in the trough of its billows. Every door and window in the adobe is creaking and straining; the blows of the wind upon the

roof set even those great redwood beams to thrumming;
the thrum is answered in the deep walls, and a subdued
tremble goes through the floor. The angles, eaves, and
slits all whistle and wail, a song that drops and soars.
From within, I see the scrub outside fighting and bowing
in the wind, and even the Joshua trees, though offering
less resistant surface than any other trees I have ever
seen, roll their upper torsos and bounce their blunt boughs
up and down like elbows in a jig. So that, if the house is
like a straining schooner, the desert is like a sea just beginning to whip up in response to the gale. Only the mountain ranges, like some far-off coast, remain unmoved.

Braving the blast of gusty heat, I roved the staring
wastes to make acquaintance with what else was abroad.
I heard the raven's hoarse syllable, uttered, it seems, with
difficulty from an unused throat. It is laconic and sounds
obsolete, something left over from speech learned long
ago from the vanished Mojave Indians. I saw the raven
shadows before I saw the birds, black and slow in the brilliant azure just above me.

There was another bird I followed through the chollas.
In his long down-pitching swoop from one gaunt Joshua
to the top of another in an upward flight like that of a
trapeze artist who just doesn't miss his perch, I saw the
white patches on his wings break out, plain as an unfurled
pattern. But I did not know him till, turning his head in
the strong light, he showed the mask of black velvet across
his eyes, and the slender curve of his bill. The shrike is a
bird with a bad name, the name of 'butcher bird.' Long
before I ever saw one, I had been taught that, like the
butcher who hangs a pig's carcass on a hook, the shrike

impales its kill upon a thorn, but alive. This crucifixion singled him out, so my Fifth Reader said, as the one black-heart among the gentle tribe of small birds.

I have seen the dingy shards of grasshoppers dangling from hawthorn prongs, and known the insects did not dash themselves there by any accident. In winter I have seen field mice thus ganched upon the hooks, hardly at all decomposed because they were so hard-frozen. But, though in California you may notice a shrike on every section of telegraph wire, looking deceptively like a little mocking-bird, I never saw its tortured prey struggling alive upon the thorn. For the shrike generally eats his meal at once. If he is too full for that, he kills against a leaner day, like any provident soul, and hangs his food as the farmer hangs his flitches. He kills simply out of hunger, without hate, without sentiment of one sort or another. To be sentimental would, in Nature, be suicidal; if there is no compassion in it, neither is there any persecution. You cannot find in Nature anything evil, save as you misread it by human standards. Anger blazes in a fight between two bull moose; anger then is a plain preservative measure, like fear which is the safeguard of all living. Together, these primary emotions bare the fang, they tense the muscles in the crouching haunch. You may call that hate, if you will, but it is brief and honest, not nursed in the dark like ours. In all of Nature, which fights for life because it loves life, there is nothing like human war.

We alone are responsible for the existence of cruelty, in the sense of maliciously inflicted pain. This is one of man's inventions — of which so many are already obsolete. Nature is too unimaginative to have thought it up, and too practical to waste time with it, since the pain of another creature is of no use or pleasure to any in the wild. In this present agony of mankind, men talk, shuddering, of 'going back to the ways of the beasts.' Let them consider the beasts' way, which is cleanly and reasonable, free of dogmas, creeds, political or religious intolerances. Let no one think he will find in Nature justification for human evil, or precedent for it. Or, even among our natural enemies, any but fair fighting.

After sunset on our last day at the ranch I walked out into the desert. Shadows gathering in the wide sandy miles below this yucca forest persuasively created the image of a sea. Light was thinning; the scrub's dry savory odors were sweet on the cooler air. In this, the first pleasant moment for a walk after long blazing hours, I thought I was the only thing abroad. Abruptly I stopped short.

The other lay rigid, as suddenly arrested, his body undulant; the head was not drawn back to strike, but was merely turned a little to watch what I would do. It was a rattlesnake — and knew it. I mean that where a six-foot blacksnake thick as my wrist, capable of long-range attack and armed with powerful fangs, will flee at sight of a man, the rattler felt no necessity of getting out of anybody's path. He held his ground in calm watchfulness; he was not even rattling yet, much less was he coiled; he was waiting for me to show my intentions.

My first instinct was to let him go his way and I would go mine, and with this he would have been well content. I have never killed an animal I was not obliged to kill; the sport in taking life is a satisfaction I can't feel. But I reflected that there were children, dogs, horses at the ranch, as well as men and women lightly shod; my duty, plainly, was to kill the snake. I went back to the ranch house, got a hoe, and returned.

The rattler had not moved; he lay there like a live wire. But he saw the hoe. Now indeed his tail twitched, the little tocsin sounded; he drew back his head and I raised my weapon. Quicker than I could strike he shot into a dense bush and set up his rattling. He shook and shook his fair but furious signal, quite sportingly warning me that I had made an unprovoked attack, attempted to take his life, and that if I persisted he would have no choice but to take mine if he could. I listened for a minute to this little song of death. It was not ugly, though it was ominous. It said that life was dear, and would be dearly sold. And I reached into the paper-bag bush with my hoe and, hacking about, soon dragged him out of it with his back broken.

He struck passionately once more at the hoe; but a moment later his neck was broken, and he was soon dead.

Technically, that is; he was still twitching, and when I
picked him up by the tail, some consequent jar, some me-
chanical reflex made his jaws gape and snap once more —
proving that a dead snake may still bite. There was blood
in his mouth and poison dripping from his fangs; it was
all a nasty sight, pitiful now that it was done.

I did not cut the rattles off for trophy; I let him drop
into the close green guardianship of the paper-bag bush.
Then for a moment I could see him as I might have let
him go, sinuous and self-respecting in departure over the
twilit sands.

Out on the desert, nightfall puts an end which is
merciful to the summer day. This last night was clear;
a vast cool sense of space diminished earth to something
nearer its relative proportion in the universe. For the
stars were out, populating all heaven with their separate
radiance.

Their shine tonight upon the upturned faces of my
friends was gentle. But how, we wondered, can people
dare seriously to believe in astrology? Have those so confident of Saturn's co-operation in their affairs ever really
looked at Saturn? It's one thing to catch its twinkle with
the naked eye, and another to peer into the astronomer's

little mirror and see the ringed planet hung out there in all its giddy and enormous indifference.

There is a ten-inch telescope out here at the ranch, set up by the generous young editor of Victorville's weekly paper. My first look through it, one black January night when the desert sky was frosted over with drifts of stars, was distinctly more impressive and exciting to me than a peep through the sixty-inch on top of Mount Wilson. There you are one of a crowd, with somebody behind you coughing and nudging. And you are permitted to see just what they choose to show you — usually Saturn or Jupiter. You can't say, 'Let's have a look at Sirius!' and have them swing the mirror around for you.

My friend beside me in the winter night allowed me to call the tune. I demanded to see Venus, Jupiter, Saturn, and Mars, and was promptly gratified. We just looked in the sky, located our star, and pulled the instrument into place, free hand, hunting with the lower power, as in a microscope, focusing into high. The Mount Wilson instrument is clocked to swing against the rotation of the earth, keeping the object in view. A great convenience, but not comparable in excitement with this amateur instrument in which one searched for Saturn and found it, rings a-tilt, tearing out of the field of vision. You had to chase it, like a hound of heaven after a celestial jackrabbit. Nothing so gives you the consciousness of astronomical speed and momentum as this simple phenomenon of earthly rotation.

I cried then not for the moon but for Canopus, the second most gorgeous luminary in all the visible universe, queen star of the southern hemisphere, to be seen in

America only in the south, and in the winter months, when it just rises, skims low in a brief arc and early sets. Though Sirius is apparently brighter, that is due to its nearness, eight and six tenths light years away. Canopus is so far away that the distance is immeasurable; it is so brilliant that its candle power has never been ascertained. In the telescopic mirror I beheld it as an object from which great tongues of curling, leaping flame flashed indecipherable signals of blue, red, purple, yellow, and white.

In actuality, of course, this too is a purely terrestrial and optical illusion. The beauty of Canopus was all due to the earth's envelope of atmosphere. Outside our mortal dusty sphere, Canopus must be a horrible, blinding searchlight stabbing through a black and icy void. Realistic astronomy is the most terrifying of all sciences. Philosophically, esthetically, it is only endurable for me in a ten-inch reflector.

That night, as I peered and asked questions and chattered my teeth in the bitter desert wind, all the time I could hear the howling of the coyotes. It is a sound that begins with a few sharp barks, rather like the whining splash of a horsewhip in the air, and is followed by a long, tremulous, singing quaver. By repute this is the loneliest of all earthly sounds. But not after you have been looking at the cold, relentless, lifeless fact of Saturn, or the threat of the 'horse's head' in Orion. A coyote sounds then like a brother; he is living; after his fashion he is talking, communicating, even singing. It was good to know that wolves were close at hand, hot of breath, with beating hearts, and mortal hungers like our own.

3

DEATH VALLEY,

CHRISTMAS, 1849

So HERE upon the Mojave, under the indifferent stars — our sun the most ruthless among them — I had found ample measure of comfort both for body and for soul. I had found a native populace also, plant and animal, living in equable balance; not heat nor drought nor thirsty wind dismayed them. For us these elemental dangers were rendered less than distressing by the provisions for ease at the Rancho. The deeply sunken well, the domestic power plant, the air-cooling unit in the dining-room, the electric ice-maker, the pool of fresh serenity that was our room — these deceived us all into thinking life on the desert the most agreeable of conditions. We rather took it for granted that we were as well adapted to it as the gophers or tortoise. We bred a large and sunny complacency among us.

Lying under the stars, listening to a Sibelius symphony rolling out across the night sky like the northern lights, I thought about this; I considered how little, after all, I knew the desert. I was muffled away from it by comforts, thank heaven. Not so the first of our people to come to it. They knew it in all its unmitigated reality. There are still men who die here on the Mojave, of thirst or heat or hunger, when they stray too far from the straight roads. And the Mojave is not the most relentless of our deserts. There is always some hope in its high air. More exceptional, more terrible is low desert. Wastes without outlet, whose floors are well below sea level. Such are the Salton Sink, and Death Valley which earned the name it bears.

When I went to Death Valley a few years ago, it was out of a naturalist's curiosity to see what sort of life abides in that spot with a name like a curse. Nature out of her vast variety has provided forms that prosper even there. A hundred and forty sorts of local birds have been listed; plant life has found wide-spaced, precarious footing. But I brought few specimens out of that moon-pale trough between the Panamint and the Funeral ranges; what I carried back with me was a little more knowledge of man's place in Nature.

It was the fate of the Donner party in the snows of Sierra passes that turned the Valley Forty-Niners far to the southward of the gold fields. Into southern Utah they came trekking, with fine fat oxen, with meal sacks under the seats, and banjos plunking and children waving flags. But by the time they had crossed waterless Nevada, the oxen were bags of bones falling by the wayside; strong men were deathly sick with drinking bitter water; the children wailed. The Indians cut off the stragglers and back-trackers, and the wavering band, lost and heartsick, without food enough to turn back, was driven toward the trap that had been preparing through the ages.

They came beholding what travelers will see ten thousand years hence, in a land that cannot change — the crumpled strata striped with green of chalcedony and unearthly cupric blues, porphyritic reds and black of lava. There sparkle gypsum crystals, and rise minarets of tufa and sculptured talc, and the levels gleam like lakes with chloride and borate and carbonate. The weary migrants passed dead craters and cold cinder cones, and plucked their way through sliding dunes.

Compared to this surrounding waste, the Valley can seem fair, at a glance. A valley, to one who does not know the vast scorching valleys of the West, sounds sweet. It means to us, in the East, meadows and smoking chimneys and brooks that children love. Toward twilight, with the purple shadows rushing out of the red Panamints to cross the playa in a stride, even Death Valley looks like Canaan. It conceals its sterility in veils of color; it tells nothing, from the heights, of the bog pit at its bottom where even the iodine bush, jointed and bloated and drunk with poisonous salts, creeps no farther on the coruscating soda crust.

Part of its fatal allurement was that there was at least a little water, a little grass in the Valley — enough to bait

the unwary. So the Piutes, watching, saw twenty-seven
canvas tops, twenty-seven rumbling arks bearing their
freight of tenderfoot flesh, roll down to Furnace Creek.
The Indians, who had fought a pitched battle with the
whole train the day before, went up to the shade of the
mountain pines and ate sweet pine nuts, and watched like
vultures from an eyrie. They would have to fight no more;
they knew their Valley, and death was on their side.

However the Valley appeared, from the eastern passes,
to the spent travelers, it must have disillusioned them
swiftly when they camped beside the springs and found
them bitter, and the sick oxen tried the hard brush, and
bellowed with hunger.

The total roll of these folk will never be known now, in
the state of the records. But we hear of the 'Jayhawkers,'
under Doty, who were young gold-rushers from Galena,
Illinois, and of the 'Georgians' under Colton. There is
Captain Towne's party, and the Martin party; the Wade
Family, and the Reverend Brier and his wife and little
children, and the Bennett-Manly party, with its tender
hostages to fortune. But no one leader commanded all.
The gold-rushers and the family men put different values
on their lives, and held opposing stakes as highest. In
common they had perhaps nothing but a fatal error in
judgment — Death Valley. Each at some trickle of a
spring, some waterhole no bigger than a farm bucket,
some seepage in the quicksands, they held the councils of
despair.

And they saw that they must slaughter some of their
oxen for food; and for fire to roast the meat, they must
burn some of their wagons. On Christmas Eve of 1849 all

over the plain blazed those fires. The canvas threw up
tattered hands of flame in the fierce upward draft; the
floor boards snapped; the big wheels, hewn out of stout
ash and shagbark hickory and goodly burr oak from the
eastern forests, slowly burned till they cast their warped
iron rims. Wood from home, life stuff of shade trees, going
to ashes on the treeless stones. And the singeing smell of
the slaughtered oxen rose like an Old Testament appeal,
to a sky that seemed to know no God. Tough meat, slimy
with emaciation, a banquet from which the starving
turned in disgust, offal washed down with poisonous coffee
water. Some ate ravens, rather; some ate snakes and
lizards; some soaked a few hard crackers in the drink.

Christmas dawned. At home, in fertile Illinois, with the
clean snow on the picket fences of Galena, they would be
cooking goose. In Georgia, turkeys were a-baking in out-
door kitchens. Iowa children were reaching for rosy apples in the bottom of their stockings. Neighbors would be
coming in, stamping snow from their boots, shouting
'Merry Christmas, Merry Christmas!'

Among desperate men, it is every man for himself, and
each party in Death Valley took a different course. It is
easy now, in the light of better knowledge, to see their
manifold mistakes. Over their heads the nutritious mes-
quite beans clicked in the slight breeze, dangled and
swayed — and were left untouched. In the high canyons
there were pools of fresh snow water. Up there the Piutes
were feasting on piñon nuts and mountain sheep. And —
so obviously, as now it seems to us — the whole train, perhaps ninety armed men, besides children and wives, should
have moved out together. They would still have known

near-starvation, and thirst no less. But the whole Georgian party would not have been massacred by Indians, nor of 'eleven young men in light marching order,' only two have been spared by the Piutes. Sharing their pack-animals, they might at least have carried the sick and failing, the children and women. As it was, they separately departed, and separately suffered, died, or staggered to the shores of the Pacific.

Last of all, by the Circe lip of a spring, lingered the Bennett-Manly party. Seventeen souls they were: four children, two women, four hired teamsters thinking first of themselves; the rest all men responsible, tense, gaunt, divided in council. They alone had not burned their wagons; it was the thought of their women and children, the tools, the 'fixings from home,' that held back the torch. While the wagons stood and the cattle lived, they still had transport in the wilderness, beds above the ground, the privacy and shelter of a home for every family.

So they drove their shaky oxen at the passes of the Panamints, and those scorching flanks of rock flung back wheel and beast. They turned and drove straight down the Valley, and heard the children gasping for water, and saw the oxen froth and stagger. Then they drove back, to the sulphurous springs, and slaked their thirst with hot poison. The biscuit failed, and the cool nights shortened. the blazing days grew longer. Even the tule reeds withered in the heat.

There was another council, while the children slept and the women sat apart, sewing, pretending never to wonder or doubt or fear.

And the decision was to send for help. The two strongest young men, Manly and Rogers, were to set forth, afoot, for the Spanish settlements on the coast. That was two hundred and fifty blazing, mountain-barred miles, without maps, without known waterholes, known passes, nothing certain, except that there were Piutes abroad. Two hundred and fifty miles to go, two hundred and fifty to return, with horses, it was hoped, and food, and knowledge of a road for the wheels, and water for all. With grim ceremony one ox was slain, and seven eighths of its unwholesome flesh was placed in the scouts' packs, with two spoonfuls of rice apiece, and two of tea.

At dawn they left.

No sooner were they gone than fresh disagreement broke out. Two young men, scoffed the doubters, to walk to the coast and back — five hundred miles! Who could believe they would ever return? If they died, who would ever know it? The longer the lost waited for rescuers who might be corpses on the side of the trail, the less chance they had of getting out alive. Or, if the scouts lived, what prevented those two from catching the gold fever, and rushing north to the fields? Neither were married men, with hostages in camp; both were young, unseasoned. If they jumped their duty, not one survivor would there be to pursue them with the nemesis of outraged humanity.

The four teamsters shook their heads; they would have no foolish faith in fellow men. That night they deserted. All four took their share of the provisions and decamped. Arcane and Bennett, their employers, pleaded in vain that this left the camp the more exposed to the Piutes. The drivers put their own scalps first. They took their due, and showed their heels. We need not blame desperate men. But there is nothing to thank them for.

Earlier each night set the wintry Orion; slowly the Dog Star, glittering in blue purity, slipped down — the losing chase of the brief desert winter. Suddenly, inhumanly, the desert spring was upon them, no familiar lovely thing of windflowers and hepaticas in tenderly budding woods, but a fierce and sudden flowering of shrubs that must have been nameless to the desolate sojourners. Sea-blight and salt bush, shad-scale and arrow-weed, greasewood and desert rush and iodine weed, they blossomed in their cryptic, sun-bitten way, even as they withered, as if thereby they tried one desperate throw on life.

The two Earhart men and an Earhart son left next. They took their share of what was left; they took their rifles, and their strength; they took their lives in their hands, and their long chance, and packed.

The ducks went over, and the herons. The little hummingbirds darted backward from the withering corollas of the desert flowers, and departed on tiny wings. The swifts could fly, a mile a minute, over hot wastes where a man could not make three miles an hour. The rough-winged swallows, the Audubon warblers, yellowthroats and chats, titlarks and tiny gnat-catchers — all could depart; all knew the way. With their little beaks they could find water between two mountain stones. With a homing power like a magnet in their breasts, they could take their way to cool lands, to green woods, and living brooks. The rock wrens and the canyon wrens, the sage thrashers and mountain bluebirds watered the air with rapture, while the children's tongues were swelling, and their ribs showed through their flesh.

Next departed Captain Culverwell. Within a few days he crawled back, dying, into camp, and expired before the eyes of the rest.

Where are you now, young Manly, brave Rogers? Dead on the Mojave? Dead in the Panamints, with your scalps in Piute belts? Or panning gold on the American River? Or with the women and the grog of San Francisco?

Yet still Arcane and Bennett, family men, desperate but trusting men, believed in Rogers and Manly. They believed because they couldn't bear, any more, to look at their children undressed. Mrs. Bennett sat beside her little Martha, watching her die day by day. Mrs. Arcane held her baby on her lap, her back to the sun to thwart the shadeless blaze. One can see the glitter of her fashionable brooch, in all that metallic waste, as it quivered on her breast. And the droop of Sarah Bennett's shawl from her shoulders.

The men raised clenched hands, and let them fall by their sides, since there were only thorns on which to beat them. At night, over beyond the spring, in the willows they must have muttered together:

It's a long time, now, Asabel. What do you think? . . .

We could move on, Arcane, a little each day, before we have to kill the last ox. . . .

And leave the springs, with the children like this? . . .

Yes, I'm coming, Sally. We're only talking politics. . . .

The desert blossomed with wild verbena and golden gerbera. The song birds had left; the ravens bickered, the hawks and the falcons quartered the dazzling playa. The men walked no more beyond the tules. They lay panting under the canvas tops that had been taken off and spread and propped as tents. The children could not find their tongues to cry. Count of the days was lost; they passed in a hopeless blur.

A shot rang out. The men roused themselves, stirred slowly to action. Another shot. Arcane crawled forth, and stood up. Out of the bushes ran Rogers and Manly.

'The boys have come! The boys have come!'

Men and women ran to meet them, with the embrace of the drowning. No one could speak. When Manly saw little Martha, he turned away.

That night, in low level voices, Manly and Rogers told the trials that lay ahead. They had started back with horses, but the beasts lay dead. They had packed food till, staggering, they could carry it no farther, and had cached it on the way. There were cliffs down which the wagons could never go. There were deserts beset with the dreaded 'jumping cactus,' and wastes of broken rock as far as the eye could see. And days in succession without waterholes. The oxen would some of them have to be eaten on the way. But the humans might just make it, with God's grace, if God remembered the Great American Desert.

The supplies were picked over and over. One necessity after another was thrown away, as the owner remembered that he might have to carry it, if the oxen died. Toys were flung aside by the children — to be found twenty years later, unweathered in the arid wastes. Pots and kettles, shoes and hats, were abandoned, and the wagons set with the torch — one last signal to the unfeeling skies.

So that what with packing and sorting over supplies, and sewing up the canvas tops into bags to hold two chil-

dren apiece, one bag on each side of old Crump, the gen-
tlest ox, it was late in the morning and hot, when camp at
last was broken. Mrs. Arcane, for her trip across the
Mojave, put on her most fashionable flowered bonnet.
The little girls were dressed in their best pantalettes, and
the babies in their coolest lawn and clean tuckers. Men
pulled their stoutest boots on, and set broad hats over
parched, determined eyes.

At the top of the pass the emigrants looked back at the
scene of their sufferings and despair. The men took off
their hats, and shouted, 'Good-bye, Death Valley!' It
was the first time the words were ever spoken, but it has
borne that name, and will doubtless bear it, forever.

Six of the eleven oxen gave their lives for their masters, before the travelers crossed the desert, broke through the coast ranges at Saugus, and suddenly saw heaven open before their eyes. Green fields, fat cattle cropping flowers, their udders running with cream. Great live-oaks, and sycamores prodigal of lisping shade. The clatter of clean-running brooks, and the hacienda of the San Francisquito Ranch, where other emigrants had found help. Words of sympathy in a Christian tongue. Food, water, and white beds.

These Valley Forty-Niners were not professional soldiers, like those who gave such an exhibition of ugliness and panic in the Valley disaster of 1871. They were not 'desert rats,' such as have so often died in the Valley — old prospectors who knew their chances, and had no stakes to lose but their own hard-bitten lives. These were our people, common people, small-town people, farm families and home-seekers, women who followed where their men went, and young men good as their word. They made all the mistakes of tenderfeet, and suffered as only tenderfeet can. But they did not crack under horror or agony; they rose up in their everyday courage, and by their homely virtues found their way out of the Valley of the Shadow.

4

EARLY ON THE WAY

THE smell of creosote bush went with us all
the way from Victorville to St. George, Utah. It smells, if
you think about it, like hot varnish, like the inside of a
commuter's train. But what you feel when you smell it is
the Southwest. The sunny emptiness, the wonderful
nothingness between range and range, the naked splendor
of morning there, the unpolluted glory of sunset, the
night's immensity. What little foreground there is to the
desert by day is blacked out after dark, and there is left
only the poetry of speed and wind, of the ribbony road
rising and falling. As outrider, went a full moon overhead.
The jagged inky outlines of the bordering ranges looked
cut out of metal; the herbage was brushed with silver; the
Mojave was a vast bubble inside which we floated.

There was a light now and then in the ranges, planetesimal; there would be a roof there, a man, perhaps a woman too; once the headlights, pointing up the sandy ruts, caught a board lettered *The Wife and I Ranch*. Swept together by distance and perspective, the scattered lamplit windows of a town became an indistinguishable glittering cluster like the Pleiades, and as far out in space. It grew, as we rushed upon it, to a hiving of golden bees, a gas station and half a block of bald plank façades, and was swallowed by the night behind. From the horizon an airplane beacon clawed heaven with long nails of restless light; the car lamps picked up out of vacancy the marching towers of the power lines. A demon power, they suggest at night, like the Prince of the Power of the Air of which the Bible speaks, bestriding the wastes on his great steel legs, the reins of his might hung slack in loops from skeleton tower to tower, as if such were his strength he need not draw them tight.

Enclosed thus in the car speeding through darkness, I get detached from orientation. Not unpleasantly, as a drug cuts one loose, not drowsily; I simply find myself anywhere I please on the stream of life when I cannot see its banks. I remember the trick I had when I was small, of being in two places at once. The one where my scrawny, bronchitic body would find itself was stone-cold and dirty gray, so I would mentally adjourn to the other. Of the first time I actually found myself there I can recall nothing except that I was standing alone in a country that was green and blue and red. The red was the deep cuts in the clay soil; the green was pine forest, and blue was mountains and dreamy melting distance. In that place

I felt warm and vigorous; I could no longer hear Lake
Michigan shouldering up its ice and stones to smack them
on the beach, nor the thrumming of the old furnace, or my
father's desolate coughing. I was free, and explored where
I pleased. I was rich, with a piece of quartz in my pocket,
and there was sunshine on my hand.

It seemed to me as a child that I had two lives, and when
I was living one the other was insubstantial and shadowy.
One thread ran through them both; it comes to me, out of
earliest years, as the steady sound, like the drumming of
rain, of a typewriter. I heard it over my head as I played
under the table; I heard it in my naps, and often at night I
went to sleep to it. It was the sound of my mother at
work. Over both the crowded city life and the lonely one
down in Carolina, prevailed that admirable woodpecker of
a machine.

Thus, before I knew enough to think about it, I learned
that a writer does not get his work done by waiting for a
divine fire to quicken him, while he tries to find a chair that
is the right height, a pen with a point he likes, a room without noise, and people who understand what he is doing and
appreciate it. My mother began to be professional in a
day and a family where talent was acceptable in a woman
only as a pretty accomplishment. She had been taken out
of school after the sixth grade, to be useful in a home full
of younger sisters; at sixteen she sold her first writing, and
bought books with the money.

She was red-cheeked then, and already brilliant with the
vigor that lasted her long life. The new young man at the
dance who asked to be introduced to her was as alien to his
home environment as she to hers. The dance was a waltz,

The Beautiful Blue Danube, and Mother totally forgot the boy who had squired her here; she let Father take her home.

My father belonged to only one of my two lives, the crowded, the stimulating city life. Out of a narrow, even a dwindling Scottish line he came, with his step light as a cat's, his mustache and his beard cut like a Gascon's. His was the most encyclopedic mind I ever have known. Yet his schooling broke off early in high school, when he went to work. For almost fifty years he worked for newspapers, turning out editorials of a rare charm and delicate fancy while the stuttering telegraph battered on his eardrums. His life long, he never signed a word he wrote; I remember the evening he showed me some of his poems in an anthology, over a whimsical pseudonym. To him the product was everything, personal credit nothing. In the old galaxy that brightened Chicago newspaper nights — Eugene Field and Teddy McPhelim, Charlie Dennis, Henry Justin Smith, Harry Smith, and the Powers, John Mc-Cutcheon, Bert Leston Taylor and Jim Keeley — he was the lightest wit, the kindest friend, the man who found anybody a job and let everybody take his scissors (a hanging crime, around a newspaper office). Nobody who saw him dining at vanished De Jonghe's or at Vogelsang's, pouring French wine in the glasses of his guests and topping the last story, no one who heard him whistling bits from *The Pirates of Penzance* and *The Bohemian Girl,* had any idea that he clung to life with a grip terrifyingly light. That, indeed, he did not open his hands and let it go, only for the sake of his children. None but his family knew his tortured nerves, his hoarded breath, his disappointment in a life that was nothing better than Chicago and bills and putting coal on the ravenous old furnace. When he wanted to go to the Gilbert and Sullivan operas and couldn't afford to, he bought tickets for us. All his days he dreamed of Paris, of the boulevard cafés, and carriage rides in the Bois, book-rummaging on the Seine banks — a legendary Paris of *Trilby* and *La Vie de Bohème, Sappho, La Dame Aux Caméllias*, of Offenbach and Eugénie; he sent his boys to Paris when I was fifteen. What I remember earliest of him is how my mother would tell me to watch for him, at the black frosty window, and how at last I saw him struggling through the drifts, his thin body buffeted by the bitter lake wind; I knew him in the blustering dark by the elegance of his gait, and would run to tell Mother so that she would open his bed for him.

On his tombstone is cut: 'Journalist, Wit, and Gentleman Unafraid.'

My mother chose the words. She had kept him alive till seventy-three by her own passionate vitality. It burned like two tiny candles in her sea-colored eyes. Or perhaps she did it by laughter; their marriage rang with it. There was mirth around her like a scent; there were always people around her, or stories of people. Interesting conversation was as much a necessity to her as bread; she fed multitudes with her magical loaves. She could create not only feast but festival from nothing, pinning on a rose for her children, pouring the sparkling wine of her daily adventure. She could fight like an Indian; she could make anyone her friend. The stone above her grave next my father's reads: 'She ate of life as if 'twere fruit.'

It was she who would reach into the grimy midwinter

misery of my city life, and pluck me out of it, and take me
to that far-off country where winter was no more than long
frost crystals making forests under the red mud. A land
where a hidden bird called 'Peet-o, peet-o,' and another
flashed into sight red as a banner, over a brook that chuck-
led to its stones. In our cottage, where the fat-pine
kindled her fire, my mother's typewriter went clickety-
clack. I came in out of the beginning of spring, bringing
her pine-saps, a fistful. I had found them under leaves, and
they smelled of carnations, inside their dead brown husks,
and were cold as fungi to my fingers.

Another year (I think it was my eighth), I had the luck
to catch the measles, and got earlier into my chosen life,
for the longest stay there. I was still shaky, and wore
dark glasses to protect my eyes, when I got on the south-
bound train. The station porter as he went hurrying along
the boards was calling the magic words, 'Big Fo' Train!
Big Fo'! Pullmans in the reah!' I knew those smoky,
poky old green and varnished Pullmans now, and the
three times you had to change trains on the journey. And
I knew that, come the second morning, I would tear off the
blue glasses and see in all their shining clarity the swinging hills, and hear the rivers' roar rise under the trestles as
we crossed them and come right through the double windows. Then the wheels curve into the giant horseshoe that
lets you see the waggling tail of your own train; the engine
gives a long call to the echo in the passes, and you are
there.

But we went farther, up and up the mucky red clay road
that sucked at the horses' hoofs and the rocking wheels of
the yellow surrey. Between the boles of tulip trees and

armored pine I saw the world of people fall away, grow
small, grow hazy blue, forgotten. In seven months upon
that isolated summit of the Appalachians I began to discover a world older and greater. It is the world now of my
established habitation, my working days and holidays, and
it lies open to all men, in valleys as on mountains, by any
road you choose to enter it.

Each day, up on that mountain-top, I saw nobody, and
each day again there was no one to see. I was lonely, and
complained of it, and knew at last that I did not care.
For I had a brook that to me was as alive as an animal; it
slipped with an alert silence over sands where glinted what
was gold or only fool's gold; either was as bright. Red
tritons nimbly got away again out of my hand. The turtles
let me hold them, but they went inside themselves and so
got away too, after all. Squatting with my chin between
my knees, I built dams in the brook until my hands were
cold as the running water; I built stone cities on the ledgy
shore.

The brook said nothing about where it was going, but
when I followed it I heard the shouting and the singing
even before I got there and beheld the foamy plunge of the
great fall down the mountain-side. That most eternal
movement, wind of a waterfall, stirred the glistening laurel
leaves all down the sheer steep even on a still day, and I
had a sense of hallelujah and rejoicing as far back into the
woods as I could hear the cataract.

Somewhere up here there was a cave with bats in it; I
could not find the way to it again. I often went, though, to
the springhouse that held an odor, under its odor of moss,
of cold essential granite, a core smell of deep down. I would

go back to the log cabin where my mother wrote all day, but I did not linger indoors, for she had not let me bring any books but *Alice*. One I was given up there, by a kind elderly gentleman who seems to me to have walked into my life to bring it. It was written by a young man whose melancholy portrait I admired in the frontispiece. He said to me:

> O thou whose face hath felt the Winter's wind,
> Whose eye hath seen the snow-clouds hung in mist,
> And the black elm tops 'mong the freezing stars!
> To thee the spring will be a harvest time.
> O thou whose only book has been the light
> Of supreme darkness which thou feddest on
> Night after night when Phoebus was away,
> To thee the spring shall be a triple morn...

And now I knew the mayflower and trillium by name, and the Carolina wren and the cardinal, all the singing birds except the one who sang alone in the rain, lifting his voice and letting it fall in a long silver whistle. I knew the smells of plants I could not name; I had a small hatchet and made trails in the woods, hacking sweetgum and spice bush and sassafras, sheering their pungent bark so they bled odors that I got by heart. There amid the glittering leaves I stood a long time listening for the thrush to sing again. Slowly the notes came ringing through the woods, a mile away and bell-clear. I could finish the young man's verse now, out of memory:

> O fret not after knowledge. I have none,
> And yet my song comes native with the warmth.
> O fret not after knowledge! I have none,
> And yet the evening listens. He who saddens
> At the thought of idleness cannot be idle,
> And he's awake who thinks himself asleep.

From this high vantage point, this mountain holding me up to the sky in its sure back, I could look out and discern the foreground of a continent. Northward from the Narrows rose Sugarloaf, higher than I, and beyond lay the Chimney Rock country, bright green and dark green with forests, all the way to the Black Mountains, highest of all; there, I knew, the thinner air was heady with balsam and spruce. I had none here but the dried needles in my little pillow. Southward lay the Valley view. Far down there stretched the fields where people lived; I could make out the small white dome of the county courthouse set amid them. Away rolled the red clay land, hazy pink turning to blue, toward unseen ocean and a city by the sea called Charleston, inhabited by Confederates in gray. Standing on a rock above all this I heard a silence deep as any sea, and saw the turkey vultures trim their sailing wings upon it. Once in a week there was a sound from that land fathoms down below, the sound of church bells. One trail led east, out to the mountain's rim. From what I called my sunrise rock I could see morning, and the reaches of Rutherford County. And sometimes I could catch the labor of a train down there when it struck high country, and the wail of its whistle as it plowed its lonely course through blue distance.

My sunset rock, lying out to the west, gave on the uptossed crests of near-by mountains that as the color faded took on the tints and insubstantial quality of bubbles. Sometimes the clouds rolled in below and hid even these heights, and on my loftier mountain-top I rejoiced that, while men put up umbrellas down below, my world was lifted higher, into the sun. Sometimes I saw the storm coming straight at me, in a slant banking threat across the sky, to break in pattering tumult on the cottage roof. At night I slept, resting between the mountain's shoulders, waking only if the men were out after 'coon or possum; far away I heard the yells, the shots, the dogs baying, and I imagined the light of the torches licking up the pine trunks and how they caught the treed thing's eyes in a sudden furious glitter.

Fret after it or not, knowledge comes. I did not mind the lessons in my school life, when its gray wintry waves closed over me again. Some of the teachers in that public school I have been grateful to ever since, though they got small thanks then from me, I suppose. A mill district bordered on our suburb; every room of my school held six rows, each ten seats deep, with all the seats filled by German, Italian, Polish, Irish children in constant vendetta among themselves, united only against Teacher. A mother is able to love her child even when it is stupid or naughty; a public-school teacher has to handle the stupidity and naughtiness of sixty children not her own. We were never naughtier than to the comical, fat, piping teacher who flushed readily and was easily diddled by even the smallest girls. But one day I stopped day-dreaming out of the window and began to listen to what she was saying. She was telling us about a creature named Ameba, its movements, its pursuit of its prey, its sensitivity that was still unconscious. She had no microscope, no lantern slides, no demonstration material. Her restless listeners rejected a lesson not in the books as one too many. But in the back row by the window a startled mind took its first step in biological thought.

The knowledge which I did not wish to learn was taught me by my schoolmates. Abe was a little Jew who stuck close to me on the playground in the hope that I would protect him from the Polish and Irish boys. Every day they goaded and tormented him more. But from the hour he came to school Abe had plainly expected to be persecuted; he slunk so, that first day, that he attracted attention to himself. And he was always trying to start a swap for something in your pocket with something out of his.

Then one time when he was beginning to run, they began to chase him; I saw the flying stones hit his head. They caught him and jumped on him; a heel pressed on his mouth and blood came out. I can't recount that I did one thing toward defending Abie. I stood rooted, shaken to my soul, paralyzed, at the spectacle of unjust violence so completely successful. I had never seen a mob in action before — just a crowd pushing good-naturedly at some big rally in the downtown streets, or a circus audience roaring with laughter over the clown's plight when he got caught at the tail of the band wagon and smoke came out of the seat of his pants. I had never before heard howls of laughter at someone else's genuine misery — misery inflicted by the laughers. Nothing in my whole life had prepared me for this sight.

Being spanked by a parei t never struck me as an inva-
sion of the soul's dignity; you were lucky to have a father
to do it. But they were holding Abie while others kicked
him. And though I did not like him much, I was so shaken
with impotent hatred of the Polish boys that all I could do
was stand by, like a good 'Ought-Hundred liberal, and by
neither quitting nor entering the mêlée, register on the one
hand my sympathy with Abie and, on the other, the isolation of my own interests. Some other Protestant boys
came up. They agreed with me that it was a disgusting
spectacle. But we were only four or five against about
thirty or forty; we'd be getting our noses bloodied hope-
lessly for Abie. I saw it was essentially an emotional affair
between the Jews and the Catholics; the Polish boys, when
we asked them why they rubbed Abie's face in the dung
where the big draft horses pawed and pulled the coal down
the ramp to the engine room, had answered that Jesus
Christ wanted them to do that. The Irish boys stood
aside from the last ignominies. They were ashamed of
their fellow Catholics now. They didn't think you ought
to be talking about Jesus Christ like that, not around
Protestants and dung. They told the Poles to keep their
mouths clean. The Poles snarled back a stream of com-
mingled religio-sexual obscenity, to show how dirty they
could talk if they pleased.

I didn't speak of the incident at home. I felt I had to
spare my parents. They believed in American democracy;
they were sure I went to 'a fine democratic American
school.' Why, my grandfather, who fought in the Battle of
the Wilderness and lay wounded at Fredericksburg, who
was the first settler in this part of the city when it was

nothing but dunes and oaks and sloughs, had stamped his
cane in the Education offices till Ella Flagg Young got a
schoolhouse up out here for Jim Bushnell's kids and the
Fair children, and his. I couldn't let my family know
what really went on at school, out in the world.

I couldn't ask for help to square the facts as I knew
them about Poles and Jews and the Irish. My father was
briefly but brilliantly eloquent about the oppressed nations
of the world, among whom he numbered Poles, Irish, and
the African Dutch. My mother's head trembled when she
talked about the Czar and the Cheka. She had told me
about Kosciusko, and I had read *Thaddeus of Warsaw* and
With Fire and Sword; a drawing of Paderewski's sorrowful,
sensitive young face hung over our piano, and I loved the
Revolutionary Polonaise. Adoring a good tale, my mother
trailed a perfect string of Irish friends; often and often I
had heard them toast *Sinn Fein! Sinn Fein!* in her Scup-
pernong wine, and I knew who the 'Dark Rosaleen' was.
As for Jews, there was never even a joke about them told
in our house; if one was our guest, we were more carefully
polite; by way of training in good citizenship, I had been
taken to see *The Melting Pot*.

But now I had also seen the blackness of the human
heart, which I then and for long after considered smaller
and more vicious than the soul of a driver ant. I grudged
man any place in Nature at all. Nature was the other, the
unhuman, the beloved. It was the waterfall that, white
and incorruptible, leaped from my distant mountain-top;
it was the blue space over the rolling crests into which my
thoughts took flight in longing.

Till with time I forgot to remember how I used to lie on

my back on a rock under the hemlocks, watching the buz-
zards soar up and up, moment after slow spiraling moment,
with never a wing flap. Not for years did I go south again.
I was not homesick for it any longer; sometimes, as I grew
too tall and my wrists shot out of what was still a new suit,
I thought it was because I could no longer feel that sweet
nostalgia that I was sad. But the present, the populous life
was triumphing. I wasn't a child with playtime any more;
I was headlong in the business of growing up. I was six
feet in my seventeenth year; I was an adolescent in first
evening clothes, whose after-dinner sip of Benedictine
burned his vitals, and I stood very thin and stiffly in my
costume of manhood, a broomstick made of green wood.
The opera was *La Traviata*. I had such health now, I was
so much more innocent at seventeen than at ten, that I
could revel in the musical glitter draped over prostitution
and tuberculosis. I knew every note that was coming;
with a voice now well established in the deeper register, it
was the coloratura rôles I hummed when I was gay. But
now I was too happy to be gay. Rapt, I sat looking not
at the stage but at the glister of pink taffeta, pink ame-
thysts, in the box beside me, and the big pink feather fan
that played, with a skill borrowed from the *diva*, over a
half-bared childishly thin shoulder where the brown curls
lay. And still, for all my own impatient pulses, I would
have said that Nature was too good for men to be a part of
it.

But the years of common lot that I have so far lived are
quite enough to teach any man that, whether he would
have it so or not, he is Nature's child and prisoner.

As we sped cutting through the southern corner of

Nevada, the long darkness streamed away behind us like the years. Tired, she leaned her head against me; I laid my hand upon her shoulder where once curls had lain.

But what is still the agonizing unsolved knowledge, I said to myself, is how men, sometimes so near the angels, can be such a stain upon the fabric of this indivisible life. If there is no answer, I thought, there is no bearing it.

The moon had gone ahead of us, and now was slipping out of sight behind the inky ranges; the night was nearly over, but when you are two it is not too hard, after all, to travel in the dark.

5

ROVING REPORTER

THIS was Mormon country; this was Utah, state shaped like a brick with the corner nicked off, dusty state with a half-desertic floor and bold brick-tinted ranges running as we ran, under a hard blue sky. Yesterday that baked red color had burned its grandest in the lofty walls of Zion. They enthrone invisible presences, tall as unlawful deities out of Deuteronomy, painted like New World savages for war; there was a silence among those seats of the mighty as loud to my ears as the silence after trumpets.

In today's hot wind of passage, we paralleled the fresh alluvial green winding along the Sevier's course. Elsewhere range land showed its elbows through sparse cover. This was not frankly desert, like the Mojave, not real bad-

lands, not the Utah I first saw some years ago from the rails
of the Union Pacific cutting northwestward across it. I
stood then on the back platform of the flying *Overland*
with the knowledge that I had got into new terrain, not
easily to be mastered, pricking in my thumbs. It had been
night when we passed through Wyoming, which therefore
kept its secrets, and the day before I had still been certain
of my way, in the outrageous, gorgeous, corn-weather heat
of the Great Plains of Nebraska. I understood those
flowers and those birds, those people and towns. Then
when I awoke there was snow on a rugged red face strange
to me, the face of Utah. The gigantic ranges behind Ogden
were capped in glittering hoods of snow, as the train crept
over the Harriman cut-off that bridges Great Salt Lake.
To the west the lower ranges were lost in inky rain clouds;
the somber saline waters extended into desolation. For
miles a gull on strong slant wings followed the train some
twenty feet above the rails into the badlands that lie to the
west of the lake.

Badlands are bad enough for the farmer or cattleman
who so names them. Intractable to the plow, inhospitable
to cattle, they offer nothing practical to be done with them.
But the naturalist calls them not bad at all; like bogs, everglades, or bleak alpine passes, they are good going pre-
cisely because they are hard going. What you bring out of
them will be nothing you could have found near home; I
got what I count riches on the desert. In Nature the only
barrens are the cities; these are all a howling wilderness
where neither lion nor jackal dare set foot.

So, I remember, every growing thing that fled past me
as the train sped toward the Nevada line seemed waving

at me to stop. But it is not so easy to flag the *Overland*. It paused to pant a moment, somewhere that was nowhere, and I got the brakeman, when he swung down to signal, to gather me from just below the railway a bit of that strange smouldering leafless thing that had been flashing me a signal of its own, all across the salt flats. I took it back into my car, dug out from my book suitcase Tidestrom's *Flora of Utah and Nevada*, spotless and crisp with newness, found that what I had was samphire, and scrawled my first note on the margin of that book.

Now, summers later, in the hot heart of Utah, I was putting down new jottings in the excellent Tidestrom, my knees dusty with a handful of wild roses, violet beardtongue, wild blue flax from the roadside; they withered swiftly in the warm breath of our speed.

It is one thing to ramble across country with a vasculum over your shoulder, investigating bank and dale, collecting duplicates and triplicates, peering for discreet small growing things in grass and moss. It is another to botanize on the wing. This, if you have a trained eye and some background, is racy fun, even in broad new country such as the Northwest was to me. Out here it is made easy by the fact that a few forms like sagebrush or creosote bush, greasewood or burro brush, repeat themselves for fifty miles on end. Then there's a flash of something that you know for new, and almost know for what it must be; with a long skidding protest the wheels stop, and I walk back along the highway.

There in the suddenly still warm air it blows, a Pentstemon, of course. Even at sixty per, I ought to recognize — but didn't I? — that look, stance, habit, that particular pitch of color radiance.

In the car, with my wife driving, I determine the species, usually without much trouble from one field book or another of the slant rank propped by my bird glasses on the ledge of the rear window. If, for identification, technical dissection looks necessary, the plant goes in the vasculum to wait until tonight. Or even, it may be, until some chilly twilight next winter when the children have decided that Father's worked enough and that the rug before his study

fire is the softest. Once they break in, I might as well take down for them a pile of Seton's *Lives of Game Animals*, Audubon's *Birds*, Ditmars on snakes, the tall volume of orchid plates in color. And get out those specimens, unmounted still and not all of them identified, that I collected on last summer's journey. Flat and dry between sheets, a tall spire will bear flowers faded to the color of a June day ending. *Pentstemon cyananthus* — I named up that one when I picked it. I jotted down a note then, I see — 'near Gunnison, Utah. June 25' — next its description in Tidestrom.

This particular *Flora* is a sterling government publication that I suppose no commercial publisher would have undertaken. If he had risked it, he would have charged me five to ten dollars for it. I got it for nothing, and my thanks are due the excellent James Smithson, natural son of the first Duke of Northumberland by Mrs. Elizabeth Macie of the Hungerford family of Studley. By the terms of his will, which suddenly and inexplicably left his fortune to the United States for the founding of the Smithsonian, that institution must distribute its publications free to all men who require them, wheresoever situated.

It is remarkable how many of the books back there under the car window — and they are the careful pick, for this trip, of a scientific library that fills many shelves at home — bear a government imprint, or the stamp of some university press. I'd never come to Utah without my *Range Plant Handbook*, a thumping volume put out by Forest Service in Washington, with a wealth of good drawings and color plates. That book on Rocky Mountain trees, displaying handy little distribution maps and telling drawings on almost every page, emanates from the University of Iowa. The one next it, on California shrubs, has just been published by a teacher at Mills College; in neighbor states as well it serves, being the last word in clarity and illustration. Then there are the bird guides. Was that a Gambel quail that crossed the road?

To read the country while you run is possible even from a streamliner. With business in New York and home in California, I have done almost as much commuting, some years, as the salaried slave of Manhattan who maintains his golf-clubs, fig-tree, wife, and lawnmower east of Norwalk. I have come to know the stewards on both *Super-Chiefs* till I remember their children's ages and sexes; I know the old squaw who sits in the sun at Albuquerque and probably sold wampum to my G.A.R. granddaddy when he went out to California in 1902. The Parmalee transfer man in Chicago no longer speaks to me, because he has learned that I never give him any business. I have come to know the run from the Coast to New York almost as well as the engineers; better, perhaps, for I still really see it. Going east, what I notice is trees. The farther east you go, the more various and subtly beautiful they become. Californian trees are mostly evergreen, and thereby without seasonal drama. Kansas cottonwoods, Missouri burr oaks, Illinois elms, Indiana maples, Ohio white oaks, and Hudson river forests of ash and linden and beech and walnut, maple and oak, witch-hazel and birch — they are torch processions of color in fall; they are delicately budded in spring, bare with a hard male strength in winter, sweet with a flickering shade in summer.

But coming west — and everyone comes west if he can, no matter what he says, for the current of our American blood sets that way — it is the birds I watch. And just as the people who take you on bird walks around Central Park know that there is going to be a grackle flock, at the right season, in a certain grove, and a starling mob under the cornices of a given building, so now I feel as confident on my coast-to-coast bird rambles. Crows will rise as the smoke of the west-bound train rolls along the fields, just beyond Miller, Indiana. There will be herring gulls on the Mississippi at Quincy and, in season, flocks of mourning doves along all the telegraph wires and cattle fences of western Kansas and eastern Colorado.

As the train pulls out of Trinidad, look out of the left-

hand side of the car and you will see your first magpie. He
will shoot out of a riverbank osier and fly upstream in the
same direction as the train, showing his unmistakable tail,
as long as the rest of the bird, handsome white wing-
patches winking and shutting as he flaps. Ten telegraph
poles beyond, a second magpie races the train. And so on
all the way to Wagon Mound, New Mexico. If no ravens
soar at Lamy, I shall eat crow. Mallards and buffleheads
in migration on the sloughs and sluggish streams, thereafter. Marsh hawks quartering right beside the train, on
the Arizona border. A red-tailed waiting-on, in the same
grand style that falcons use, outside Flagstaff. Around the
station at Barstow, California, Brewer's blackbirds (like
eastern grackles but much more refined). Gambel's sparrows and roadrunners in the Cajon pass, and, just north of
San Bernardino, the windy, whistled rapture of western
meadowlarks, heard as you pass the open door between
cars, on the way to breakfast. And a mockingbird in Pasadena palms, audible as soon as the clatter of the train has
died, making the same style of grand opera love you heard
when you put your foot on the high step here, starting east.
Mockingbirds in the garden are like a stack of Caruso
records on an automatic gramaphone — incomparably
gorgeous, ultimately suffocating.

At home in Santa Barbara (in a garden restfully without
palms), the wren-tit bubbles forth his song in the sunny
fog; from the pines the canyon wren lets down the Sierran
cascade of his wild rapture. Bush-tits, tactfully silent,
ridiculously small, hang upside down to tug red berries in
the hardest possible way.

Of all the bird sights I saw on my last train journey

westward, none moved me so much as the ducks on the desert. Well, semi-desert, anyway, but awash then with the spring rains and the thaws and the sandy rivers braided with brief silver strands, the range lands cupping grassy lakes that would not be there when the north-going *Anatidae* no longer needed them. I never see the wild ducks scattering spray as they get up off the water, without thinking of their love of freedom which we, like paternal despots, have corrupted out of them. I never see a mallard in spring, without being glad that it is not autumn. And no guns pop — as Keats puts it so beautifully. Wild and beautiful and free, these birds (descended to us out of an ancient and watery world, before the evolution and the era of the singing birds) go gamely back and forth from the Tropic to the Circle, transcontinentally commuting twice a year, hunting waterways, hunting rice beds and eel grass, deserving the security which their armed enemies have denied them.

To cross America like that, and then to recross it within ten days' time, is for me to experience nostalgia double the whole breadth. I long for the places I have left behind, so many hundreds of miles behind that who knows when I will see them again? Yet as I rush west, eagerness runs ahead of the wheels. People who don't want to look beyond their picket fences or 'dobe wall are safe from the wish for otherwheres — like my colored houseman down in Carolina who would not go west with me because, he said, 'I don't want to get any farther from red clay than I can walk back.'

When Mencken was our Doctor Johnson, we used to groan that America is a standardized country, without

local costumes, customs, dialects, or folk songs. People
went abroad in those days, to Paris or Vienna, to discover
how to live — I was living then in the south of France myself. And it was a reproach to us that we are not varie-
gated like the piebald map and the mosaic cultures of
Europe. Now, abroad in the Northwest, I was seeing the
license plates of every state in the union. We are discovering, I thought, that as a people with a common language
and government, a single army, navy, flag, and oath of
allegiance, we are rich also in peaceful differences.

And in our tradition of getting up, pushing out, going to
see for ourselves, we are piling the baggage and the children
into the family car and setting forth to explore our many
climates, many natural provinces, Appalachian and
prairie, Great Basin and North Woods. No passports, no
boundaries! But even as New Hampshire asters differ
from Catalina poppies, so do the white wooden churches of
Massachusetts from the old yellow missions of California.
As the religious utterance of the hermit thrush in Adiron-
dack dusks differs from the careless ecstasy of a canyon
wren, so does the wry wit and the reticence of a Connecti-
cut farmer stand in contrast to the slow grin and easy welcome of the Wyoming rancher.

Eastern birds and eastern trees and wildflowers go well
beyond the Mississippi and stop somewhere in mid-Ne-
braska. I think of them most often in May, the month of
fog along my part of California's coast. I take time out,
then, at my desk, to look into my study fire and suffer
pleasantly for trout lilies and wild rhodora and shadbush,
for the chewink naming himself from thin-leaved under-
brush and the white-throat letting down his notes where

rain steps lightly through the woods. Already on my veranda the wistaria bloom has withered then; it began flowering in February. Already, before the Pacific hills have turned the tawny color they will be for nine months more, I long for spring again — but the eastern spring so hard to wait for as it comes up, week by week, out of the South.

The odd thing is that though spring comes out of the tropics, it is never found there; those are lands of perpetual summer. It is born, so far as I could observe in Florida, somewhere around the Kissimmee prairies; slowly it burns its green way into Georgia, where the jessamine on its vine opens in the woods just when the cardinal is beginning to call 'Pretty, pretty, pretty!' It lights, I remember, the cypress woods around Charleston with sudden spider lilies, and touches alive the tops of the bald cypresses themselves. Then the red-bud trees begin to bloom upon the hills of Tennessee, and where the Civil War armies toiled back and forth, slaying and bleeding, the negro children of Virginia pick bird's-foot violets. Then the spice-bush blooms in the Alleghenies; there are bluets around Stonybrook in Jersey, I remember, called also 'innocence' and 'Quaker ladies.' And then, some morning in York state, opens the flower of wild ginger, half-buried in warm loam under its leaves, inviting to its pollination what insect no one yet has learned. Azaleas burst from their bud scales airily; the bonneted hosts of bloodroot claim possession of the underwoods. Time now for harbinger-of-spring; time for white violets out of reach around the edge of marshes. The leaves will be rushing out overhead on all the paths I used to walk. Jade bloom is cast over the ponds

there, and the birds are at their nesting, those birds I do
not hear where I live now. The California jay has never
learned that whistle by which the eastern bluejay can
make a truant of me any summer day.

There may be places elsewhere that the birdsong of a
spring morning rings out louder, from more varied voices
than the wild matins at Kennicott's Grove in Illinois.
But I know of none. Not on my south Pacific coast, where
all the birdsong that there is comes from a few species.
Not in mountains or the dark North Woods which are too
somber for such rapture; not in Florida, I think, nor in
Europe for all its nightingales. First of all avian music I
would put the chorus of northeastern birds (ornitholo-
gically, of course, Illinois is scarcely distinguishable from
New England). Its leading talent lies in the finch tribe
with its field sparrows, song sparrows, white-throats and
cardinals and grosbeaks. The orioles support this, with
their kin the bobolinks and meadowlarks, and the thrashers and catbirds too; for soloist you have the thrush.

I can hear every voice as I name them, remembering
how as a boy I used to wake to them, in that prairie grove
where I was visitor. I remember the depth of the dew at
night, and the spattering of stars in a wide arc of silent
sky, and how from the guest house where I slept I could
see on the ceiling of the girl's room over the way the wavering shadow of her head and arms, where by candlelight
she brushed out her brown curls. When daylight came, at
five or four, I heard the doves at talk in the pines outside
her window. Why does anyone call them mourning doves?
That sound is all contentment with the day and world.

There was a wealth about the Grove in those days, that

lay deep in the farm loam, in the heavy heads of lilac and
the foam of bridalwreath banking the big cottage; it fell,
careless and light upon the wind, with the apple petals
dropping into black furrows that swept to the foot of the
orchard. It was in the golden dust of chaff around the
barn, that huge old barn heaped to its rafters with fer-
menting timothy and wild swamp grass. Had there been
secrets between us, that was the place for them — up in
the dim loft where the swallows nested twittering, and
flashed out again into sunlight. Below in the stalls
stamped the saddle mounts, and the draft horses champed
and blew out their nostrils. Always around the barn there
was a wheeling of pigeons, a coming and going with pails;
the milk and cream seemed to flow into the kitchens like a
brook. The ducks were on the march to the corn bin,
shaking short tails and talking of taking potluck; there
was always a peeping of chicks, and news of calves or
lambs or young turkeys come, always a nesting and suck-
ling and a great carrying of worms and grubs and seeds.
It was as if the whole world were created fair only so that
it might be fertile, and knew no reason but good law.

From my sixteenth year I was made welcome at the
Grove, a country kingdom in a bubble of its own. Those
first impressions are as keen and sweet as spring itself.
Day long the frogs chanted from the sloughs filled with
wild flag and cowslips; the redwings gurgled and hovered
over the bulrushes. Little jeweled warblers drove through
the leafing boughs in bewildering gusts, so many kinds it
then seemed impossible to me ever to tell two apart. Beyond the gardens, beyond the fields, rose always the wall
of the woods; in the depth of them shone tangled lawns,

secret dewy bog spots where the shooting-stars hung trembling and flaring on their stalks. To such inner shrines of wilderness one attained by fighting through a barbed forest of hawthorns, through crabapple and plum frothy with bloom. Those woods and hidden swamps and fragments of virgin prairie were a unique remainder of the temperate aboriginal America that has vanished.

There I first found my way to northern Nature, with a boy and girl who knew it better than I. Not understanding what I saw, I glimpsed the big ecological picture in that one square mile of land. I was to labor years in sketching its outline, not even now complete. For I was to come back here in many a summer, and at last when the boughs were stripped of their leaves, when the skies were cold and I felt older than I was. But, like a winter constellation, such a disposition of destiny lay in those days well below the summery horizon.

All the time that I was learning, in my young days, how to remember the Middle West, the South, the eastern seaboard, I was hungering for the West I had not seen. Always Americans have turned west, body and soul. They love the national tradition of unbreathed air, and they welcome a solitude that is not lonely but free. You do not breathe that freedom until the West begins, and it begins where the wheat lands end, and the cattle country rolls away and away toward the far mirage of snow-capped peaks. You can still gallop there for miles with never a bound to your free coursing. You can shout a song, and wake neither echoes nor neighbors.

You can say you're west when you hear the last of the eastern meadowlark's wistful whistle, and the first of the western meadowlark's glad jingled song, rapture in every note, hope forever undefeated. You're out west when, six thousand feet up and yet never a mountain in sight, you see the clouds like troops of white sheep, so low they look, as if you could flick them if you had a long whip and stood in your stirrups. You're west when the wind says so, whining around the corners of the windshield, or howling in a gale behind the observation car of the streamliner as the tumbleweeds roll after it without rest, even in death.

Utah is west in its own bare, brave way. A hard, bright hollow of the West's great palm, it is walled in between the Rockies and the Sierras so that its thin rivers find no way to the sea, but must die in sand or salt. Utah people are western, but Mormon western. They came here with the Word, with their seed; they came deliberately to this shut in land, this sleepy desert hollow, in order to pull the hole in after them. With the stubborn suspicion of a persecuted people, they shut the gates of the mountains fast; they locked themselves in, body and wives and spirit, sowed their grain and built their tabernacles and their towns all right angles and righteous-looking gables, and kept their elaborate genealogical and historical records. The parallel with ancient Judaism is striking, from their sense of isolated superiority, to the geography of the lands they inhabit; it is small wonder that the rest of America fell under the name of Gentiles, outsiders, whose ideas they no more cared to admit than their soldiers.

But Utah Territory is the state of Utah now; our wind, the big breath of America with a tolerant laugh on it, blows open the shut doors of creed. Pride in their 'come-outer' history made the Mormons I talked to seem quintessentially Americans. In Salt Lake City, where I called for mail, a big, jovial, rich-voiced man shouldered up past the clerk behind the General Delivery window and asked me if I was being treated right by the city. 'Because if you aren't, just come to me; I'm the Postmaster.' The door out there not only stands wide open; they ask you in.

Mail from home, since we had left the children behind, focused my chronic homesickness for somewhere else. That breathless night in the tall desert city while I lay on hot sheets, only just hidden by the thin walls of a motor court from the restless many crossing the pavement outside, I hungered achingly over an American home. For the tree-tops over a low roof in no danger, and the untroubled voices of children beyond the garden wall, for the bright sky with nothing in it bigger than a buzzard, and the sea below us, silvered over with a thin cool fog even on a midsummer morning, where only the giant kelp stir under the surface.

Because, of course, I had bought a paper, here in this the first big city on our route. I can take my newspaper, usually once a day, and down it, I hope, like a man. But I hope too that I can leave it alone. In the first week of September, 1939, when I had occasion to go by train from California to New York, I carefully neglected to buy a paper to share the seat with me. All the way across the continent, I was shut up alone in a compartment for three days and nights with nothing to look at, except all of America.

What I saw was the desert, where the plants struggle so bravely for, and somehow find, a living, where the hawks quarter desolation for jackrabbits. And I saw the Rockies, which are older than the memory of the most long ago of wars. And the Great Plains where the first windbreaks cast the blessing of shade. Then came the windmills, then the big barns, then the silos of Kansas, the pleasant farmhouses, the first apple trees, the first hardwoods on the river banks, in the last fullness of a summer's leafing. Could this be, could it ever have been, 'the dust bowl'? There had been terrible days then, terrible scenes, death to cattle, ruin for men, immigration, the end of the world — for Kansas. Here, in the gathering dusk, it lay at peace, fertile, rich, and undespairing. The end of the world, I thought, as a newsboy at a brief stop went calling his headlines along the platform. But a million times the world like this had come to autumn, the planet leaning into the arms of the longer nights, turning the warm cheek of harvest to the languor of Indian summer noons. And it

would happen again, I realized, a billion times, peace on
the farms and plenty in the bins.

Nothing so hides the view as the daily paper when you
get behind it. It swallows the whole world down and
chews it into pulp. Once it almost swallowed me.

I was not twenty yet. My parents both were journalists, and proud of it, as I am proud of them. I knew 'the
paper' — Chicago's big morning sheet — as the friend that
stood behind us, a composite employer worthy of my
mother's loyalty, my father's gratitude; had it not sent
him on a year's vacation with pay when his elegant thin
figure grew so much too light you thought the next cold
wind would blow it down? So it was natural enough that
I should accept a further goodness, when it offered me a
job, my first.

I was nineteen then, in a world grown suddenly grim
with war. I had been found literally too much of a light-
weight for any branch of military service. I had willing-
ness, a sense of literature, an excess of gentlemanly feelings, and no convictions in a rather hollow young heart.
Thus flimsily equipped I set forth every evening to go on
the night shift. I took the Elevated, at the hour when the
sky was a smoky lemon color over the cooling roof tops;
on its exalted rails the train of crowded cars went racketing
with a kind of mundane music. People came piling on,
went pushing out at every stop, and once again the dust
and the first fresh breeze of evening from the lake would
catch us all up in flight together. All across the city on
each side of the tracks the lights were just then coming on
behind every window, and the shades were not yet drawn.

So I could look at my kind, the humankind I did not

know. These were the people — the people who were not getting hanged, murdered, arrested, scandal-smeared. Neither were they building love-nests, starting 'bug' fires or burgling, still less jumping off skyscrapers, bridges, and the deep end. They were just at supper, most of them, in families, men, women, and children in small united groups under a common lamp, happy to be together, school and office and drudgery behind them. This was the heart of human life that I was looking at, and there was nothing black in it at all.

But every evening I was sent out from the city room to go and get 'the story.' That meant news. The bigger the news, the blacker the print. It was May in the lake city; even the slum pavements shone in the last light. I criss-crossed the sprawling web of streets, climbed up and down unending, various flights of stairs, to knock forever on doors where I was not wanted. Divorce, rape, murder were behind them — news, in short. So were men and women, dazed and pitiful, on whom a stranger could in decency but close the door gently after him again.

The city editor was patient but ironic. 'Nothing there?' He tossed over papers and found one, a tip phoned in from the police court on a boy bandit shot and killed. 'Go see the family. Get the story.'

Now when I went out the dark was purple; a glint of silver light was on the river whose two contrary branches run like artery and vein into the throbbing heart that is the Loop. From the El car, half-empty now, I watched the passing halos that the street lights made in cottonwoods and willows; there the mayflies were dancing and dying. The boy's father had not even known he had a gun; the

man kept wiping his hand across his lips, as though to
brush from them any words about his son that were not
the real truth about him, as he knew it.

But that was not news. As I went back across the city
sinking deeper into night, a bitterness like bile was in my
vitals. Only Jesus Christ, I thought, had any right to
interview that man tonight. As for the story, maybe
Dostoievsky could have got it all.

Back in the city room the lights were brighter, the
staccato of the telegraphs was faster; the nightly action
was driving toward the big push. At eight o'clock the
bigwigs begin to come down, on a morning sheet; from
eight to twelve every room in the big building, down to the
basement where the presses run, swells with the pressure of
importance; after midnight the paper will be put to bed.

And none of that importance could I feel. I knew it
beat in my father's pulses; even after he retired, he still
dreamed — so he abruptly told me once — that he was
back there in the city room. I did not want to disappoint
him. I sat down at my typewriter and, summoning what
pride I could in craft, hacked out some lines to be read
indifferently next day and forgotten even as the page was
turned.

My shift did not end till two; it might be four in the
morning before I got home. The stars then were clearer,
for the lights were few and dim with coming dawn; in its
freshness I could smell the lilacs that I could not yet see.
From the east, from over the great cool lake, some mercy,
newly sent once more, in spite of all our sorry yesterdays,
was coming now to spread in radiance and freshness over
all the city. In the waning dark I felt the offer of its puri-

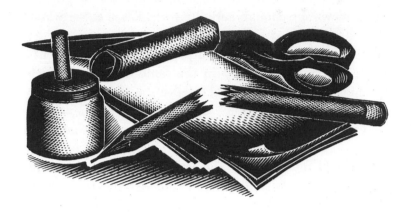

fication. I felt the grime upon me, felt our common sin against each other, suffered a weary, sickened ache over the poor bedeviled multitudes that slept still, as I came home from one more night's bad work.

At the end of a fortnight I fired myself for willful incompetence.

War, of course, is news. It is exactly what news is — event abnormal, monstrous, contrary to the current of biological happening. A vast web vibrates to its reporting,

by air, over the wires, on newspulp, or in a few magazines
with a view long enough actually to embrace seven whole
days. The weaving and the maintenance of this web are
marvelous; the men at the outposts, the correspondents
who must think accurately in the same breath on which
they speak, are many-jeweled intellects as brilliant as they
are bold. I thank them for the terrible news they serve
me; I admire them; I could never, as I proved that fortnight, be one of them.

Yet I call myself, none the less, a reporter. I do not
bring you news. It is all old, old stuff — what is going on
in the field I cover. Nature is just living, and it is good to
live, to be alive, good enough for any chipmunk or gentian.
It is even good to die, since death is a natural part of life,

a merciful necessity in a world which would only starve and
crowd and smother itself if there were no natural mortal
end to every existence, no return of the borrowed capital
of living matter to the great clearing-house of the mold.
It is right to die, in the woods and fields, and good to live;
in every wildflower there is symmetry and balance, in

every scampering quadruped the tingling adventure of hour-to-hour existence — felt intensely, thought about never. The birds in the leaves, the snake under the stone, the spider zigzagging down her orb web, bound though they are to the same struggle to which we are captive, do not, like us, ask questions about it. Yet they answer our unhappiest and deepest question. The cottontail dashing from the weasel in great, heart-bursting bounds of terror, the turtle sunning himself on a log, the robin turned to let the sunset burn on his red breast while he whistles vespers, all these affirm that life is worth the living. For them their world is a harsh one, despite the peace that we find in it. The cornered shrew cannot escape the owl's talons; the kinglet dangles on the thorn while the shrike tears it; the woods are not peaceful to those who battle behind the leaves. Yet it is for life that they are fighting; it is to keep the precious gift of it that every creature struggles to the last breath in him. They do not need to think, to know how worth the having it is. Or to know that life is hard. Dumbly and fiercely our unhuman fellows proclaim by their devotion to it, by their instinctive, sometimes passionate obedience to its laws, that life is also good.

These are the facts that I go out to get. This to me is the story.

6

SAGEBRUSH

COMING out of the Promised Land of
the Mormons into Wyoming is like stepping out of a house
into the open. For threshold are the winding canyons of
the Wasatch Mountains, clad in maples and cottonwoods,
box-elder and scrub oak that in the fall, they say, fire the
slopes with warpath color. Up and up you climb, to a zone
of grass and pine, up and over the top and suddenly, like
an escaping bird, you are launched out upon Wyoming.
You are free. This, old Shoshone country, old buffalo
country, old and modern cattle country, is more spacious
than even the Mojave, for the mountains are pushed far
back to the rim of things. The eye is filled only by the
endless roll and dip of sagebrush-covered plain tilted up to
where the frontier vanished. The sky looks not the same

as in Utah where the red cliffs seemed to stain it a deeper
blue. This high arc is the azure of wild flax flowers. This
air, stinging pure, and strong with the whiff of sagebrush,
is liberty itself. It is the West at last, in all the greatness
that was legend to me long before I saw it.

An intimation of that far-off and virile grandeur came
to me on the wind, in my childhood autumns; it arrived,
rolling and dusty, as tumbleweed. I knew this plant to be
out of the flora of remote prairies in some state of a different color, and so I saw that these could not resemble my
home prairie which stretched, smooth and marshy, right
up to the back door of our straggling suburb by Lake Michigan. Prairie as I knew it meant misty distances, and a
sweet south wind that brought thaw and the sound of
church bells from the Bohemian settlements beyond the
groves. It meant these island groves of willow and cottonwood, and the piping of frogs from too far to walk, and
shooting-stars that came to flower in the tardy springtime
of this mild flat wilderness. But tumbleweed, that rolled
in, galloping and cruel as a ball of vegetable barbed wire,
must come out of some flora strange as that of Turkestan.
It arrived seasonally and always from the same direction.
It rode the west winds, the first autumn gusts before the
gales that would send the Great Lakes shipping, battered
and ice-coated, into port. And though it raced and
bounded like an animal, it always arrived dead. For these
plants do not break free until life is gone from them, save
for the shining seeds that are shaken out at every bounce.
So they piled up in great windrows, and were thickets at
the sundown side of the tall board fence behind the school,
where the eighth-grade girls and boys would promise to

meet each other as soon as the early dusk came down.

Only once I found a living tumbleweed on the lake shore, the triumph of some sprouted seed. I thought it beautiful, as I bore it into the house, bigger than my head and chest, its rank verdure shot through with angry purple. The candle flames in my mother's green-gray eyes shot up when she saw it. She laughed at the ignorant admiration of this east-born child of hers; out west, she said, they paid you bounties on the tumbleweed, and fined you if you let it grow. The cattlemen and ranchers hated it. Then the livid ball of thorns in my hands felt like something that could return hate. I believed her when she told me that tumbleweed was the ill will of the Sioux, shot east at the palefaces.

My mother had lived in the West during the last Indian war in history; she had gone, as a reporter, into the prison tent of Sitting Bull, old Tatanka Yotanka himself, conqueror of General Custer. She was born what she called 'Middle Michigan,' and in her latter years she drew this origin snugly round her with a laugh that mocked her own elderly cosiness. But in her youth, of which I was a late last child, there was about her the greatness of the West. It threaded her voice still, as she sat telling me, the firelight giving a glint to her eyes and the opal ring on her hand and the toe of her slipper so small for her vigorous step. Acoma. The Alamo. Cody, and Cripple Creek. Gila and 'Cibola' and Virginia City. Names like old trumpets that you can still pick up to blow two ghostly notes upon them. Glory names, that hurt my heart.

For in and out her stories ran the thread of personal history. Before ever I was born it happened and was over.

My parents' fighting prime had been spent in the West.
My father, at peak strength and brilliance then, was managing editor of the biggest sheet between the Missouri and
the Rockies. My mother, working with him, had built up
the first woman's page in all that country, had lived that
page through a mail heavy with the hardships of the ranch
women. Often she answered those letters by personal visits. She would go, on her own, three hundred miles to
straighten out a tangled life, find a strayed husband, extricate an overworked girl, kidnap, once, a child covered with
welts. Those were the days when she sold everything she
wrote, and what she wrote of then was bounded by a fierce,
dusty, lonely horizon. Her stories challenged the all-
powerful railroads till they threatened suit; the Populist
Party reprinted *Jim Lancey's Waterloo* in stacks of thousands, to distribute it as a fiery banner.

Mother's voice held pride and bitterness as she told the
story of the squeeze of the 'roads,' of the banks' fury
against the Populists. And how my father, going out himself to investigate the sufferings of the people, found deserted farms, the houses standing open, the farm machin-
ery — unpaid for, doubtless — rusting in the bleak fields.
In one open door he faced a gray wolf.

But my young parents could not fight the pack alone.
The railroads and the banks that had squeezed the farmers
to submission, to emigration, squeezed also the owner of
my father's paper. Wages stopped. The paper had not
paid for nine months; the banks took my father's home.
And one night he came home shaken in a deathly chill. He
survived, but his health was crushed. The young days, the
bold days when the fight had a zest in it like the tang of

sagebrush, were over. They took the back track then, to safety for their children.

The green candles lowered their light again. 'Burn it,' my mother said, and I put the tumbleweed into the fire; it snapped and sizzled and fought back.

That autumn, I remember, we boys saw a strange dog skulking through the vacant lots. He was a dog and not a dog; he was wild and fierce, and his unkempt tawny flanks were hollow with hunger. But he was also frightened and confused, with a whipped-looking tail, an outsider who knew it and would not come in. We chased him with shouts and sticks, afraid of him without being sure why. As we pelted after him across our yard my father came to the door, and cried out. 'That's a prairie wolf!'

Here was the untamed — fair game to us. Knowing our fences and alleys better than he, we drove the coyote toward the old barn where Alderman Jones used to keep the respectable glory of coaching horses. We cornered him there and locked him in, and we peered in at him, chattering and pointing, while he stared back at us with a hatred and a hunger born of wider spaces than we knew. In the morning when we went to look, there was no wolf. He had torn up a loose board, tunneled through the flimsy sand on which our houses were all built, and got free again.

The West came once more into my young world, and once more made the Nature of it seem soft as it was sweet; once more it struck at our tepid atmosphere with a violence that was challenge and threat. I was standing on our front porch, in the September dusk, listening to the torrent of sudden wind in the trees. It wrenched the leaves off and bore them not down to earth, but aloft; they seemed to go

straight up into the darkening sky, never to return. The
air, I saw then, was full of twigs and branches. Three mill
men were running along the street; they were bent almost
double and were jabbering in a Slavic tongue. One
shouted, asking to crawl under our porch. I looked over
my shoulder at what they feared. It was coming out of the
west; it boiled and tumbled and rolled toward us with a
glaring yellow eye like a coyote's furious stare. I heard its
great hollow roar and the whistling scream of its attack,
and then my mother dragged me into the house. Behind
us sounded the tortured wrenching of fences going down,
a roof coming off, and the crash of the great willow by the
kitchen door. The rain broke as we reached the cellar; it
beat like stones upon the little windows, and in the gloom
I lay against my collie bitch, and heard my mother say
'tornado' in that fire-threaded voice she used for what
came out of the West.

I was reminded yesterday in Salt Lake City of one such
terrible sending that has come again and again out of the
western sky. In that hard season when the Mormon settlers here were looking to their first crop to save them from
starvation, it came upon them in a black cloud. In a hur-
ricane the horde of insects descended then on the fields of

precious grain and began ravenously to devour all. And just as one more chapter of Exodus was writing itself over an American soil, lo! from Great Salt Lake the avenging angels came. And the gulls fell upon the locusts, grasshoppers, and crickets, and smote them, head and thorax, and the Chosen People were saved.

I am mightily pleased by the monument to a sea gull which they have raised in their city. But with less faith in miracles I am still uneasy about locusts. They are a typically western violence, a biological overgrowth bred deep in the continental interior, in semi-desertic foci remote of access. Thence in their time, at the summons of an urge partly climatic, partly swelling mysteriously within the race, they will arise and disperse in long-faced, short-horned, strong-winged multitudes, writing disaster in the sky. No communal swarm are they, with mutual helpful purposes, like bees and men, but an anarchic mob, each ravening appetite out for itself. Nor is this a true migration; there is no single goal, no return but of a few stragglers, no sure end to the gigantic excursion except death. And that comes only in its time; man with all his armaments cannot withstand the devouring march. Gasoline blowtorches may blast holes through small agonized groups in the dark cloud. Airplanes may drop poisoned dust. But only when Nature says to the locust, 'Thou shalt go,' will the insects depart in blind obedience as they came.

What it is that originally prompts them to mass revolution lies deeply buried in a complex of conditioning factors. Climate is one; the course of a locust outbreak extends over several years in ever widening circles, and a sequence of intensely hot summers, dry autumns, mild winters, and

wet springs favors successively the vernal hatching of the
eggs, the development of the young 'hoppers' or wingless
phase in summer, the terrible flights of the full-grown
adults in autumn, and the safe overwintering of the eggs
laid late in the season.

For like all insects these move through a rhythmic life
cycle. The eggs are sown in the ground, like dragon's
teeth. Some internal crowding, some piling up within the
species, of an impulse to grow, to burst out and to wander,
causes these eggs to bring forth locusts multitudinous in
number, monstrous in size. These are the locusts of plague.
They are the same species that may keep semi-harmlessly
to their restricted place in the biota year after year. But
now they are enormous, they are legion. Hormones must
prompt this monstrous growth and multiplication. And
appetite, a will to live become senseless and hideous, sends
them forth upon the land.

In this first, juvenile phase they are wingless but as
armor-plated as the larger adult form; so they hop and
jump, tumble and scuttle through the corn and wheat, the
barley and the rye. In the span of a few weeks their wings
have sprouted; these harden, and when they are ready for
flight the full-grown locusts rise, in millions upon millions,
into a sky they darken. They may mount fourteen, fifteen
thousand feet for their big 'hops,' to roar over the land and
settle like doom where their erratic, insensate, and almost
drunken fancy dictates.

Not without warning come the locust plagues. They
gather momentum not simply at their source, the places
where they permanently breed (which for the Rocky
Mountain locusts lie between Great Salt Lake and the

Big Horns of Wyoming), but in a wide circle around these perennial infections, in the periphery called the temporary breeding grounds. ˮBeyond this lies the area that knows them as a visitation. The Great Plains states, the wheat and corn belt, distracted in 1929 with debt, drought, and a ruined market, experienced them as a final calamity. In Nebraska and South Dakota four million, eight hundred thousand acres were laid waste as if by a foreign invader, and the United States Army was helpless before it. Cars on the roads, at the height of the horror, skidded in the slush of locusts, were brought to a stop by locust blizzards and stalled in locust drifts. Nothing devised could halt the onslaught; with that inhuman, ungodly sideways motion of their jaws the insects chewed and chewed through the growing granaries, until they ate themselves out of board. They laid their eggs upon soil that would not nurture their progeny. Birds devoured them; diseases, themselves epidemic, seized them. Their own ravenous impulses died within them. The recall was as implacable as the attack. Again the wheat dimples in the wind, again the corn is heavy in the ear. Even the country that bred this total warfare lay innocent and clean before me when I came to it.

But the locusts await, no doubt, their hideous resurrection. They are not forgotten; their dire coming in the seventies is part of the history of our westward struggle. Out of their hot interior valleys, as from a factory that never rested, they came looming over the pioneers' horizon; they swept as far east as central Iowa, and into Missouri. The Governor of that state faced helplessly a people ruined and overwrought. Farms were devoured to the barren

earth; the country banks were going down; the towns all
felt depression sucking at them like a rip tide. The
preachers took the opportunity to thunder at the Mis-
sourians that this was the Lord's judgment wreaked on a
worldly people. The farmers growled; they rallied, and
demanded of the Governor that the pulpits be put to a
more useful purpose. Decree a day of prayer and fasting,
they argued, and the Lord'll rid us of the pest He sent.

The Governor devoutly promised them their day of sup-
plication, of deliverance, and hied him to consult the state
entomologist. You will recognize him. He is Riley, the
tall youngster absorbed in yucca moths. By all means, he
told the Governor, appoint a day to exorcise the locusts.
Say, June third. And on that day, banned by book and
bell, those hordes of Satan did indeed begin to quit Missouri. As Riley, deeply versed in their life cycle, knew they
inevitably must.

He had audacity and flourish, had Riley, traits seldom
found in the great men of science. There was artist in him;
his gift for drawing, mated with a genius for observation,
had carried him, without benefit of university training, to
this state post, at twenty-five. It was the day of side
whiskers and frock coats and a contemptuous regard of
entomology as mildly mad bug-chasing with a net. 'The
Professor' was the affectionately scornful name that Riley
won. Even the genuine professors of his science looked on
him with suspicion, for entomologists up to his time, like
Scudder, collected moths and butterflies and beautifully
mounted them. They addressed each other in learned soci-
eties and wrote incomprehensible monographs on this or
that of academic interest. To gardeners and farmers,

thick-skulls with earth beneath their nails, they left any actual struggle against the hosts of cutworm, army worm, buffalo bug, Hessian fly, cotton moth, and potato beetle.

Meanwhile out of Missouri for nine years came flowing Riley's annual reports. They were written in language that farmer and gardener could understand, printed in type that could be read without store spectacles, and illustrated with Riley's own drawings which showed the pesky enemies as they look when you find them eating up your crops.

So Riley brought the entomologist out of the useless mandarin caste to be the hunger-fighter that he is today. He dragged his science out of the universities, out of the glass cabinet and the museum, put it under state and federal control, and made it work for its living. And at that work he set America in the lead it has never lost.

His neat success with the locusts enabled Riley to go before Congress and get an appropriation set aside for a Commission of Entomology to handle such pest problems in the future; on Capitol Hill he sniffed the gunpowder of politics with the savor of a born warrior. Back at his Missouri post he attacked the problem of the Phylloxera insect which was ruining the French wine grapes; seven billion, two hundred million francs had been lost to it in the provinces which furnish the great cellars. This nasty little midge had come into the Bordeaux vineyards originally upon some American wild-grape stock, and Riley, applying a principle then new to scientific philosophy, advised the French to graft their delicate stock upon now Phylloxera-resistant strains of American grapes. For putting new blood in their withering vineyards the French government decorated Riley.

So, confident and individualist, he took in 1878 the post
of Entomologist to the then young and feeble Department
of Agriculture, while remaining also head of the Entomology Commission he had created. He had married well; in
Washington he set himself up in a handsome style, unpre-
cedented in his humble Department. And under the mansard roof of the old red-brick Agriculture building, where it
blazed in humid heat among its unspeakable canna beds,
he was his own authority.

Science was young then, in the Government, and Riley
worked for it like a politician. It was not in him to work
for other men. But going himself to 'the Hill' for money
and influence, he brought about his downfall. Ousted
from the Department, he continued as head commissioner
on entomology from the privacy of his home, a sort of
Sherlock Holmes laughing at Scotland Yard. He knew his
turn would come again, and with the election of Garfield
he was indeed returned to power in the Department. No
civil service ruled it then; firing and hiring as he pleased,
Charles Riley went to work with restless energy to build
up the army of the insect-fighters. He disregarded his
superiors, kept up grapevine communication with congressional friends, put his finger in every pie, and so got
his way through energy, political intrigue, and sheer personal charm — he was a tall fellow with long wavy hair, a
lush mustache, a graceful and romantic bearing.

Out in California was trouble; the citrus scale had crept
into the orange groves. Among American scientists not
yet world-minded, Riley was of a stature to look beyond
the seacoasts. And his head danced with the insect fauna
of the entire world. Determining the scale to be an acci-

dental import from Australia, he moved his own private heaven and earth and succeeded in getting a commission sent to Australia to find the natural enemy of the scale. This now familiar principle of biological control was a new concept, viewed then with skepticism even in California. But from the day that the Australian ladybird beetle was liberated in the citrus groves around Pasadena, the scale was doomed.

In Washington the fickle winds of politics blew cold on Riley none the less; Harrison succeeded Cleveland; the entomologist now found himself isolated. Distracted with angers and intrigues, he could not concentrate on his work. He could not sleep, he thought, except in the barber's chair, and he used to hire it from the barber just to doze in. Cleveland came back, and Sterling Morton was appointed Agriculture's Secretary; the winds now were southerly and favorable. Riley in high feather prepared to captivate his chief; he gave for him a reception in his handsome home on Washington Heights. A red carpet led up the walk; windows blazed; within, society, diplomacy, and intellect glittered among the guests, and flunkeys ran about with punch. But the new Secretary shook his head; this fellow Riley was extravagant; let a man less forward have the coveted Assistant's place. In a huff Riley resigned. At home he prosecuted brilliant and unofficial research, and in the Government the wheels of progress ground. Secretary Morton, smelling out intrigue, induced the President to bring all chiefs of scientific bureaus under the Civil Service. The day of free-hand genius, the day of the titans was over. Worn out and in failing health, Riley fell from his bicycle to an ignominious death.

Long ago the Bureau of Entomology outgrew the red-brick walls that cradled it. Like an insect of repeated moults, it has cast off more than one casing too small for it. Now there are great white buildings to house government science; they are cool when you step in from the hot streets. And whatever question you come to ask, you will find some minor official individually equipped to answer just that in particular. The great wheels run with a smooth and mighty complication of little cogs. I know, for I was one of those cogs once. The least of them, but complete with civil-service appointment, office desk, and title by which to sign my letters. I was twenty-three, and 'D. C. Peattie, Assistant Plant Introducer.'

'I suppose,' my father said to Mother in that voice of his so dry you heard no humor, 'you will be looking soon for them to make him Secretary.'

Mother drew tight her thread. 'Well, he's a little young still,' she answered, with what small doubt seemed reasonable to her.

And here I was, on no assignment more official than my own impulse, free, in the midst of the sage. Even old Fort Bridger was now out of sight, and I had walked away from my car in the road, to feel how wide the world was. Here I

heard a new sound, not lonely though there was no other,
not monotonous although it has no end. This is the wind
going softly, tirelessly through the sage. And the sage, all
of a level height and content each bush in its station, lets
the wind go through its fingers. Nothing is regretted in
the passing, nothing sighed for as the pines sigh; there is
no rustle or rumor here as in the aspens. For the sage is a
plant that does not sway or fight in the wind, that never
raises its voice. It is untroubled, even as the land there is
unpeopled, and all it remembers to say when the wind goes
over is 'Shoshone! Shoshone!'

This gray-green plant that grows unbroken to the sky-
line, a dry and quiet sea, is key to the ecology of our high
northwestern desert, as creosote bush is master key in the
Southwest. Sage and creosote bush are mutually exclusive. They are king each in a region where the other cannot set root. Dominant in places so dry that little else
will grow there, they succeed where they do, not because
they love drought, but because each is without competitor
in its serene endurance of aridity. The creosote bush,
more of a shrub than sage, almost a little tree at its tallest,
extends its undisputed sway far south into the west Mexican deserts but cannot push its northern claims beyond
southwestern Utah, southern Colorado. For sagebrush
persists in a region where snow lies long in winter, and
creosote bush cannot endure the snow. So that sagebrush
is the desert dominant from British Columbia all the way
to lower Nevada, lower Utah, northern New Mexico. It is
that tang upon the air to which American senses leap at a
first breath, in recognition of a racial heritage worthless in
coin and precious beyond explaining to a foreigner.

I have heard a European say to me, of my country, 'You have no history.' To him the sage would look as naked. I might embellish it by speaking of its key position, showing how the ecology of plants is significant not for its own sake alone but because it determines the ranges of the fauna dependent thereon, the mammals, birds, reptiles, insects, even the native *Homo*. Thus in the complex of the sage I could point out to him the Shoshones, a people not preferring to endure the hard conditions of life any more than does the sagebrush, but there because they were unable to compete with their fierce neighbors, the Sioux.

But this of course is not history or legend; it is simply Nature. And the European's Nature is beloved to him largely for its wealth of association, for the nymph in the lake, the magic in the juice of heart's-ease. In the Old World, before ever natural science began to make its way out of the Schoolmen's lecture halls toward the woods and fields, every animal and plant and snowy peak was known and named and understood from many angles. So that no one can say who first heard a nightingale and found a name for it, or picked a white narcissus and wound a story around it. Poets and peasants, herbalists and historians have so clothed every natural bit of Europe that there is no unwrapping any of it.

Here in America a Nature nameless, save for the half-lost syllables of red men, waited in grand completeness for the coming of the discoverers. So you can say — and feel a tingle saying it — of almost every range that it was first sighted by the Verenderyes, by Pike, by Frémont. That this tall spruce was named by David Douglas, this berry earliest described by Meriwether Lewis. Science itself becomes the rich association. For me there is an overnote in the careless delight of the western meadowlark's singing, when I remember that it was John James Audubon — on the afternoon of Monday the twenty-second of May, 1843, near Cedar Island, South Dakota — who first noted it was not the wistful eastern meadowlark he was hearing, but that the bird he had not yet held in his hand was a new species.

I would not give up this verve of discovery, this sense of new greatness that runs through New World Nature, for all the hangman's legends that stain old Europe's mandrake, not even for the poems that make a skylark sing better than it does, to an American when at last he hears it.

There is no legend which could more adorn the sagebrush than does the name of the first white man ever to behold it. The year was 1541, and at the spring; the man was Don Francisco Vasquez de Coronado. There among his hollow-eyed knights in armor, mounted on the first horses ever to stamp our sod, he sits in his saddle and sees the Colorado sagebrush go rolling out and up toward the distant Rockies. To come upon him there is to me quite as much a marvel as were the prairie dogs and bison to him, and to his chronicler who knew not even any names to call them by. The sage he speaks of as 'like our Spanish marjoram.'

For these adventurers deep into a continent all new, unnamed, unmapped, great with an unbreathed greatness, had only the old associations to bring to it, only the old earthy, glittering dream of gold to lead them. It had marched them out of Compostelo, two hundred and sixty Spanish gentlemen in polished armor, with sixty footmen

carrying crossbows and harquebusses, with priests chanting, cheers ringing, banners flying, to seek the Seven Cities
of Cibola. Ahead lay the American wilderness, vast, indifferent. It had only to wait. It had more than Indian
arrows in its quiver; it had sunstroke and blizzard, poisonous rivers and wastes without water, mountains without
passes, plains without landmark, chasms without bridges.
It had, at last, after bitter months for Coronado and his
decimated army, the cities of Cibola. And these were but
Acoma, Laguna, Pecos — dusty pueblos with never a
glint in a brick of them. With nothing to yield but parched
corn, jerked meat, water, things seized on as more precious
than rubies or ingots.

In one of the Seven Cities was a Plains Indian's slave,
called by the Spaniards 'the Turk' — some crafty Kansa
or Pawnee, one suspects. He lit the dream again; he told
Coronado that the land of gold lay far away in his own
country, and was called Quivira. So once more these
knights of Spain have come pricking across wilderness in

haste to come up with the foot of the rainbow. Instead they rein in among the endless sagebrush.

Where, demanded Coronado, lay Quivira? Eastward, the Turk said, and northward, just a little farther. The army turns, and rides on eastward, high at first in hopes. For spring was on the prairies of Kansas, and the wildflowers bowed beneath the proud Arabian hoofs. The strong grass, writes the chronicler, Castañeda, rose up as soon as the troop had passed, so that you could never find your way back. And in the air was that marvelous smell that is only America — the tang of high adventure. On and on, until — perhaps near what is Wichita today — the leader sent the main contingent back and, with thirty picked horsemen only, and the Turk, kept in chains against the likelihood of desertion, turned north in a last desperate cast of the die.

At that moment, perhaps only four hundred miles away, across the breadth of Arkansas in the dark cypress country, Hernando de Soto is crossing the Mississippi. Rival explorers but fellow countrymen, both men are now thoroughly lost. Each proud in his gleaming armor, they are like two suns rushing through the loneliest spaces of the sky, which for a moment are approaching, near as astronomers reckon distance, but still just too far to give light to each other. Their errant parabolas swerve apart; they miss one another; the American wilderness swallows them both. De Soto goes down the river, to his death. Coronado spurs northward to legendary Quivira.

Probably somewhere near Lincoln, Nebraska (at a guess), Coronado faced the fact of utter failure. He forced from the Turk confession that he had deliberately led the

expedition away to lose it in the wilderness, to separate
the commander from the army and permit the Indians to
crush each party in detail. Coronado did what any general might do with a false guide; he had him garrotted on
the spot. But only bitterness was in the mouth of the con-
quistador as he retraced his course. Autumn turned the
prairies purple and gold, in the last splendors of its bold
composites. The winter drained the color from the plain,
leaving it dead-looking as an old lion hide. The grass, sear
and brittle, no longer sprang up behind the horses' hoofs;
it left a trail now, marking clearly the retreat from failure.
Traveling by another route, the main army had got caught
in the first blizzards, in a howling Texas norther. The
Mexican Indian allies had their feet frozen; the Spaniards
had to mount them, and walk, floundering through the
drifts in their cold and heavy armor.

Returning, Coronado found his garrisons massacred,
and all Cibola flaming with well-earned hatred against the
Spaniards. So with the coming of spring he set the rem-
nant of his host upon the road to Mexico, leaving only a
few friars to struggle for the souls of the savages. But the
Indians had had enough of Christians; the blood of the
monks was spilled. Coronado himself resigned the gov-
ernorship of New Galicia, and retired to his estates and
the white arms of Beatrice de Estrada, his high-born wife.

All that to him was wilderness, was Cibola and unat-
tained Quivira, is no more — the loneliness, the savagery,
and the distance. Symphonies in Philadelphia, wars in
Europe and Cathay are washed into the ranch house
kitchen by the radio; the movies bring Arabian Nights'
Entertainment to 'Tiguex' and 'Cicuyé,' Albuquerque

and Trinidad. The distance has been obliterated by the ranch jalopy; on the deserts about Yuma, where Alarcon left his letter for Coronado in the wild hope it might some day be found, the airline beacons weave across the night sky, beckoning on the mail planes. Nothing is unchanged, not even the mountains, which show scratches on their flanks where later men hunt gold. Only the wind is the same, that historian and prophet of the West, which whispers what it has to tell. If anything in this young empty country could remember so far back, it would be the wind. And it would remember a man who leveled his lance at golden Quivira on the eastern horizon, and charged — only to find it the American sun, getting up in glory on a prairie day.

7

A HOUSE

THAT WAS HOME

OUT here in the West, somewhere in Colorado, my grandfather was following his own young dream of gold when the Pony Express brought news of Lincoln's election. So, he knew, the battle was joined, and he too turned his back on the visionary lode. As soon as he could hasten home, he married his Amanda Maria, and marched off to the war to the tune of 'The Girl I Left Behind Me.'

He was a graybeard when they carried him to the old soldiers' cemetery in Pasadena, but the high sense of romance and adventure in him had been buried long years

before. The Civil War broke his health, and five daughters
piled on responsibility. But underneath, some of that
romantic ambition survived, and it came out in his building schemes, in a passion for pillars and porticoes, sweeping drives and many-stabled barns, broad fireplaces and
stairways and acres. Perhaps what he saw in the war, of
the old South, enlarged these visions. But none of them
ever came off; he had not the means to carry them out
except on a scale so economical that the attempted
grandeur turned out to be nothing but pretentious. He
built at least one 'folly' which he was never able to complete beyond the façade. And he founded a home.

Out in the dunes south of Chicago's limits, as they were
in the fifties, some man of wealth had chosen for himself a
lonely site amid grand old oaks that rustled with a fresh
wind off the lake. There he built himself what, in those
times and that place, was a mansion, where he kept coaching horses and delighted to drive in solitude along the hard
lake shore. He died in his prime; for some time the house
had been standing empty and neglected when my grandfather bought it cheaply and, one spring evening about the
year 1877, brought his wife and five daughters, my mother
the eldest of them, here to live. You had to drive out from
Grand Crossing on the mere trace of a road, two ruts across
the prairie through flowering sloughs and over deep dune
sand, to reach the lonely 'old Ferris house.' May is a
treacherous month along the coasts of Lake Michigan, and
it will sometimes let the winter back in a furious last attack. There was no heat in the big empty house that night
when the storm broke, no stove; the beds were not up; the
family slept on mattresses upon the drafty floor. All night

the wind screamed around the cupola; the house echoed like a hollow conch to the roar of the lake. With the waves sounding as though they were piling over the dunes, you could not tell, awake in the dark, whether it was wind or water that shook this empty new home to its foundations.

But in the morning the clouds parted; the marvelous winy air which follows a Great Lakes storm washed through oak boughs that seemed overnight to have burst their buds and flung out catkin and tiny leaf. It smelled of wild-grape bloom, and the crab too was in tart blossom. The flickers were calling from tree to tree — 'Wicky, wicky, wicky!' — and down at the lake shore where the eldest, the sixteen-year-old sister, raced and laughed, the gulls were tossed, the sandpipers skittered, and the wild rye and marram grass in the wind described circles on the sand with their swirling blades. The lake itself (my mother told me) was a rolling sapphire crested with the long white tops of even waves that piled up on the beaches.

For forty years that house remained the core of our family life. My mother was married from it; Grandfather planted a poplar sapling before the door that day, and when I came to consciousness it had lifted its talking leaves above the roof. The old lifeboat that had been washed up in a storm and dragged to the lawn to be filled with earth and flowers, was still there, as my grandfather had left it. A straggling and somewhat commonplace suburb was growing up, a few blocks deep, between the dunes and the prairies, but the dunes still lifted their bright sandy swells, the prairie stretched away to the west. From the cupola I could on clear days see an immense distance. South were the steel mills, the settlement

of the Poles, and their churches. North, the Loop rose up
in the pride of buildings as much as twenty stories high.
Eastward, sometimes, Michigan showed its green coasts.
West you looked beyond the school and across old Jim
Bushnell's farm, over the prairie all the way to the low blue
morainal hills beyond. And saw the gap in them, called
the Sag, through which Marquette and La Salle had
pushed their canoes.

There was a fifth direction from the cupola, and it was
down. Down through the tall old house, by ladder first,
down into the attic under its snuff-brown mansard smelling of the slow crumbling of wood with powder-post and
death-watch beetles in it. The trunks shoved back into
the dark corners were plastered with West Indian and
European labels; there was never a fancy-dress party
announced but that all the children round about were
outfitted from those big dome-topped trunks, with bright
silk tatters that made a matador, a gypsy, a maharani.
There leaned the totem pole my mother brought back from
Alaska when the Northern Pacific sent her there to write a
guide book. There had come to rest the obsolete reservoir
Grandfather put in before they built the pumping station;
a Baptist deacon stole it once and presented it to Grandfather's own church, and to the Lord, for a font. Gram-
pa's Civil War canteen hung on a nail there, and a spider
lived in it. His blue kepi was also there, with a bullet
hole through the crown; when Mother struck the dust out
of it one day, there rose to her the sharp smell of gunpowder from the Wilderness.

And books — even into the attic oozed the books in our
house. The juveniles with which my sister and brothers

were done had been piled there, with *St. Nicholas* for years back, *Chatterbox*, a most immoral set of trots for three years of high-school Latin, Japanese fairy tales on cloth, and a family-doctor book displaying all of a lady in her birthday suit with windows in it opening into the most astonishing complexities which were explained in marginal balloons wherever arrows were shot into this smiling martyr. But I never could study her as thoroughly as the interests of science would dictate, because the attic was lit only by horizontal slits of windows that ran along the floor; through them I saw the green tops of the oaks, where the jays screamed 'Vacation! Vacation!'

Down again, by a breakneck flight of stairs, to the long hall of the bedroom floor, in winter carpeted, in summer cool with Indian matting. There was no chamber that, in the course of family evolution, you had not slept in, been punished in, had sore throats in, and Christmas toys, and young desires. At some time or other every room had been the guest room, and it was a brief era when there was no stranger within the gates. Some stayed for years; many who came and went had about them that tingle of the West (it was on their return from it that my parents had bought this house from Grandfather). At Christmas, and for the autumn 'big games,' the college mates of elder brothers left a small boy no place to sleep but on the library sofa, where dreams were the finer for the flicker of firelight through them.

The stairs down from the bedroom floor were wide and easy, and crossed by a mezzanine with a niche where someone else but Mother might have put a statue; she left it empty for a child with a book. I saw my sister come down those stairs slowly, all in white. When she went up again she changed her clothes, and ran down the stairs laughing with a man who, I saw, was ravishing her away from me. I wept so that I forgot to throw my rice. But when they were gone I dashed out and hurled it furiously after them into the dark snow.

The front drawing-room, with its slim fluted columns, its little marble mantelpiece and gilded triple mirror above, had just that faintly formal graciousness with which my mother made welcome a distinguished visitor. But beyond it, behind it lay the heart of the house — the library, walled with books halfway to its beams that were driftwood from some old wreck. There my father, in a leather chair turned with its back to the room, his slender feet on the lowest shelf, sat reading, the book held close to his eyes, a pencil for marking it between his fingers. This was the room warmest with family life; here was the widest hearth. The mantelpiece was made of a great beam my mother had found upon the shore one windy day long ago. My second brother, late on a Christmas Eve, painted above it the stencil he had been secretly working on, while I sat by in the soft light and watched. The house was still as fallen snow; upstairs they slept; the clock ticked on toward Christmas morning. When the work was done, the Gothic letters across the red brick chimney ran, 'O YE FIRE AND HEAT, PRAISE YE THE LORD.'

In warmth thus blessed, the house opened its doors. The one from the library led to the dining room, where the Sunday morning meal was served in the style one might call Late High Breakfast. Guests from all over the city and farther knew those meals, and those who live have not forgotten them, I think; my parents both talked just as well before their morning coffee as any of the best of talkers after wine.

Back of the dining room, of course, lay the kitchen, with thirty years of culinary tradition. And so on, down into the basement, where the coal came in as a glittering black avalanche whitened with snow. That was where we let Red-Nosed Bill sleep, since he had no other place to go and his family mustn't ever find out how low he'd fallen, because they were very nice people in Michigan, and the more he drank the nicer he got himself. There were sawhorses down there; they made fine ponies for a winter circus — admission one penny, but don't look at the equestriennes when they do somersaults because the starched frills on their panties show. In their barrel the Michigan apples, brought over every year by lake boat, breathed cidery sweetness in the dark.

If environment could make a writer of a youngster, I should have been producing my first publications at a tender age. This was a house where writing was the business of the day, and of the night too. The peck of my mother's typewriter sounded from her sunny room from early until late; in the evening my father went down to his work on the paper. He came home on the owl train; on Friday nights he always had a long black satchel full of books for Mother to review. Other late commuters were gnawed by curiosity. At last one put the inquiry: What was it that he carried every Friday in that bag? Father, keeping one elegantly trousered leg over the other, rolled a cigarette. 'My burglar tools,' he answered with grave courtesy.

For twenty years my mother, in the highest tradition of criticism, reviewed books. They poured into the house every week; they filled the many-nooked library to the number of five thousand; they marched in cases up the stairs and crowded into every bedroom. Not that Mother gave place to anything that did not earn it. Worthless books she burned, and taught me to; she would no more have passed them on than she would have made charity out of decayed canned goods.

It was my father who was the bibliophile, who bought books for their choiceness, because they were curious items, had beautiful bindings, were delicate duodecimos (he ever tended that way, not toward folios), or because they bore odd imprints. He had books in languages he could not read, and books he read in but seemed careful never to finish. Habitually he gave at a time from ten minutes to an hour to a book, slipping it back then and tak-

ing out another. He was a man who never in his life
smoked a cigarette to the butt, and he smoked all day; he
told jokes constantly, and they were seldom more than
two sentences long. Sipping, tasting, compressing, varying, he knew his classics; many a page I found turned
down, many a paragraph marked. Those books of his I
have are filled with annotations in the margin, for he had
the old copy-reader's habit of correcting errors, automatically; misspelled names, inverted dates, were irresistible to his thick soft pencil.

My mother read even more copiously, insatiable all her
days for story. She brought to books both an ardor for the
romance of life and an unfailing broad morality; in her
view, art was responsible, as the one witness from whom
nothing was concealed. She took art lightly otherwise,
made household word of it; the cook might treacherously
leave us in a huff, and Mother would remark, '"Let the
galled jade wince. *Our* withers are unwrung."' And my
father, from behind his Amiel, briefly agreed that '"more
was lost on Mohács field!"'

Form in our household, free as it was, demanded that
you make a joke of irritations. Conversation had rights of
sanctity; no one telling a good story was suffered to be
interrupted, and any silence that grew heavy for others
was considered either a sign of illness or a piece of sheer
shirking. But a member of the family reading was not
lightly to be disturbed. Books had their place in the middle of things; I remember my mother's getting up from
the table to go and get Villon, when he appeared to be both
apt and unrecognized, to read aloud his scandalous and
deathless measures over the supper teacups. It was long

past my bedtime on the night when my father discovered I had never heard *The Ancient Mariner*; he promptly found it and, sitting on the edge of my bed, read it all to me. Then there was that snowy Sunday morning when he took me to the couch before the fire and opened a book that began '"Tom!" No answer. "Tom!"'

So it was natural enough that, at the beginning of things, I wrote. All my paper then was gloriously blank before me; no manner was too grand. Poetry, of course, was best if it was done tragical; the earliest lines of my own to stick with me now, begin, 'After all is sorrow, sorrow — tears today, no hope tomorrow!' At ten I came upon a Roman legend that struck me as offering material for a magnificent tragedy. I wrote out my play in a large bad hand. My family was ready to listen, not with any deaf indulgence but bringing me the compliment of serious consideration. I read aloud the title, and brought down the house. Amid the peals of laughter, my father went to the Shakespeare shelf and took down a volume that, I saw, was titled like my own work. *Coriolanus.*

To fall absurdly because I flew so high was not a thing that dashed me, or I would not have sprawled so many times as I grew older. In high school, inky grandiloquence still was coming easily. One final June day I won a scholarship to the university in English literature, owing to a facile familiarity with the Lake Poets and the Brontës; it was the worst-spelled paper, said the judges, that they had ever seen. But I signed for no English courses that fall, or ever. 'Themes' I knew to be the opposite of what editors want, and mine was a house where publication was considered the initial criterion of worth. To my parents, the door that led most directly to the profession that was theirs — and to be mine, they had always believed — was journalism. So, at nineteen, I took that job as cub reporter. In a fortnight that career was over.

Now I was far from the happy ignorance that rewrote Shakespeare. It was not a happy thing to know how little I had to say. Increasingly I knew it; I lapsed into that silence so unnatural and unwelcome among us, and became the despair of a family where convictions were considered synonymous with morality. But looking in my heart, I found nothing there but some tremulous adolescent emotions which I saw it would be better to outgrow. It was all too easy to spend ardor on the great performances of other men. I had been happy among their muses, their tragedies and comedies, pictures, architecture, and music. But I had no such mistress of my own. Without, I now was hungry, empty, gone astray. What it was I wanted, and where to look for it, I had no notion.

From that book-filled house the approach to Nature was only through a love of beauty, a pleasure in wonder, an interest in the curious and historical. These paths did not lead far. My sister early taught me to repeat by heart *The Cloud* and *The Daffodils* and *Ode to Autumn*; a born medieval in her exquisite devotion, she would never have thought to worship as I do. My mother told me about Aristotle because she adored all greatness, and about Darwin because she loved his challenge to revealed authority. From my father I had heard something of Linnaeus, and how he named all the flowers in the then known world, and in Latin at that. Father himself had a mind to analyze and catalogue, and a tremendous respect for foreign languages, of which he could speak none. He was always buying books on Italian, French, or Spanish, books whereby you taught yourself. Wistfully he would try them out, only to give up in sudden fatigue and put them in his children's hands, with a dry remark that it was for us he'd got them anyway. If he had not been born into a world too narrow, if he had not had to work too hard for other masters, I think my father could have found great satisfactions in science. Instead, he toiled to let his sons find them, the eldest as an engineer, the next as a geologist and geographer. Myself, I was at twenty still a restless mental mugwump.

And now the old home came to an end. My eldest brother had long ago left it for one of his own; my second brother was off for the war, my sister had gone the longest of all journeys. So when his paper sent my father to New York as correspondent, the house was emptied and closed.

Months after we had left it, I went to say good-bye. My parents then were managing to fit their spacious life into three rooms on Ninth Street in New York; I had stayed behind to finish out the college year that followed my attempt at newspaper work. That quarter I was taking Coulter's course in systematic botany. Coulter had been a pupil of Asa Gray himself, and the book I had under my arm, when I went out to look our old home over for the last time, was Gray's *Manual*. May was ending, as were my student days — so I supposed, for in a fortnight I was going east to join my parents and hunt for a job of some sort in New York.

The house had been standing empty and shut up all

winter; it was colder inside, much colder than the gentle
day without. The moving men had taken out every stick,
and brooms had swept clean after them; even the hearths
were brushed bare to the old fire bricks. Only squares
where pictures had been remained on the walls. Between
its dainty fluted pillars the front drawing room looked
cleaned and swept for guests who would never come, nor
would the triple gilded mirror or the Virginia settle ever be
moved back. The lilac bush, in flower, still tapped and slid
creaking on the pane where I had watched for my father
coming down the street. In the library the driftwood
beams looked down; the floors gleamed softly, naked of
rugs. But nothing was so utterly absent as the books.
The shelves, the open shelves, had been built into the
house; they were still there, like the shelves in a store that
has been sold up. And I could have put my hand out and
touched the spot where *Manon Lescaut* had stood, and *The
Amber Witch*, *The Third Circle*, all of Balzac, the rows of
The Yellow Book. Over the cold hearth the Gothic letters
spoke: 'O YE FIRE AND HEAT, PRAISE YE THE LORD.'

I went around, trying doors and windows, for it was my
responsibility to see that the house stood secure. I was
the last of the family to quit it.

Behind me the door shut fast. I went out into the rambling wide yard, over the uncut spring grass beneath the
tall oaks that I had always known. But I did not know
them; it came to me, with Gray's *Manual* in my hand, that
I had never known them at all. Two had been cut down,
and the others were marked for felling, for most of this
tract had been bought already and houses were to be
crowded upon it. The city was shouldering its ugliness

close. This sweet May day was outgrown. An era was over when there was plenty of time, and money enough, and you could still put off making up your mind. The world was at war, and I was twenty; and my father was working too hard in New York. Time for me to get to work, then. No time left to learn.

Except the oaks. I wanted to salute them, once, by name before I left them. Standing beneath their old green boughs, I opened my book and with a forefinger went tracing through the keys and their descriptions. These trees, whose burning garnet autumn foliage, whose fringed and top-shaped acorn cups I had known so long, whose yellow inner bark of twigs my teeth had discovered early, now were proved to me by these evidences to be black oaks. *Quercus velutina.* They became fixed for me, like stars. Let the axe take them. They were in their place. And like a firmament slowly broke over me the grandeur of a system where every oak puts down its roots eternal and unshakable, yes, and every transient flower. Like stars, I saw, each plant, perhaps each animal, had not only its place but its relation with all others, its measurable distances from them, as if, in evolution's slow tremendous course, all exerted pulls of varying strength upon the others. Species and genus and family, class and subkingdom and kingdom glittered, still dimly, in that infinity. This, with the breath of lilac in my nostrils, the watchman's rattle of a flicker calling after me, was Nature. I closed the book, and walked away from the old address that I would never give again. I had no other, but I had at least a new sense of direction overhead, astronomically sure, and spreading over all the living earth.

8

WYOMING

IN THE EOCENE

THAT glimpse of the abiding order in all living, which came to me as the old order of my own life changed, was but the first flicker of an uncertain compass needle. Not yet had I felt the irresistible drag toward the pole. I was keeping secret still my quickening toward Nature, which was wistful because so ignorant. As my eastbound train went clackety-clacking over the Sandusky marshes, I craned at the marsh flowers. They were tall and brilliant in their Junetime pride, but they smeared into a blur when I tried to make out what they might be.

Birds I did not know got up off the water and went
wheeling, dangling waders' legs, on cambered wings to
settle on a farther shore. The train smoke blew across
them; and I would not have known them if I had had a
longer look.

Twenty-odd years lie between that train journey toward uncertain future, and my trips to New York now,
when a glimpse of familiar wings along the way is a rest
from plans for business to be done. Twenty years is no
time at all when the business is study of science. What I
have learned is just enough to find my way farther. That
is all any man can ever know, if his subject is Nature. He
can grow peacefully gray acquiring all extant knowledge
— perhaps adding a mite more — about even so small a
province as that of the sedges, the viviparous fish, or
methods of insect pollination. And if you make America
your field, all that you may have learned in twenty years
is but an invitation to limitless discovery.

In that second score of my allotted years, with my
country for my book, I read, as a naturalist, the pages
from the prairies and the north woods; I knew the Appalachian South, and the Tidewater South, and Florida
down to the 'glades. The Potomac from Harper's Ferry
to Chesapeake Bay became familiar ground, and in my
college years I took much of New England on foot, from
Blue Hills to White Mountains, from the Berkshires to
the coast of Maine. Coming West at last, I had in three
years made myself at home in California, an empire in
itself with a range from Sierra to desert, and had devoured
the Southwest too, five hundred miles of it a day sometimes, in gluttony for its great spaces. One quarter of the

continent alone lay on my map uncolored, as *terra incognita* — the ultimate stronghold of what wilderness is left us, the great Northwest, realm of the sage and the spruce. And now I was entering into it.

Travel in the West, once the momentum of it gets in your veins, becomes a cumulative habit. It is a stimulant of which you need more every day. And every night you fall asleep exalted and exhausted, promising to stay here where you dropped, for a week or so, to dwell in stillness on the grandeurs you have beheld.

But every morning there is the river of the road still running past the door, a river that falls into all seas, and runs uphill over mountains. And there are the mountains themselves, the snowy ranges of adventure, and what it is that lies beyond them you must go and see. The morning air, the first deep breath of it, sluices away the dregs of fatigue. The inexhaustible freshness of this country is your own again, and nothing shall hold you now.

I lay this freshness to the absence of distracting foregrounds. In the East one travels, usually, to get from A to B, say, Albany to Boston; there is a shortest possible way and one is apt to take it. But on a trip from Albany to Boston over the Mohawk Trail, you would see easily a thousand times as many objects as on a run of the same distance in the West. And at first this is very pleasant, with lovable towns every few miles, and orchards bent with bearing, lilacs by the farmyard gates, churches that look externally so cozy with their Maker. Every moment something distracts the attention and, for those who must have it distracted, this, and not our one day's buzzard-

like glide across three Wyoming counties, each the size
of the state of Rhode Island, is the perfect journey. For
one day, at least. But about the third day, in crowded
country, you have reached satiation. Out West, by then,
you have just got started.

For myself, I know that to be distracted is to be unable
to think — thoughts, at least, of any length, breadth or
depth. And that the racing wheels beneath me, the unbroken road ahead, and the wind rising to a high unwaver-
ing whistle at the corner of the glass, let out my thoughts
like birds from a cote. They may fly far and far, and
bring back at least the twigs, the promise of a country
beyond the sea of sage, a country unexplored, green-
forested, snow-capped, like the Wind River Mountains
toward whose base we rushed all morning without coming
up with them.

It strikes me that there is something scarcely moral
about clipping off in a five-hour flight a journey that
would have taken Captain Bonneville five days to make,
when he plunged into the Rocky Mountain wilderness
here in 1832, not to be heard from again by his government
for three years. We were going twenty times as fast as
the Sieur de Verenderye when, in 1743, toiling across the
plains from the Mandan villages of Dakota, he saw —
first of all white men — the 'Shining Mountains,' the
Wind River Range. Here Stuart led the Astorians back
from the tragedy of Oregon in 1812. We shot across his
trail light as the shadow of a hawk. But, like Vega that
grows in a lifetime no nearer visibly to our approaching
earth, the Shining Mountains gleamed as inaccessibly wild
as ever. Up there, ten thousand feet and more above the

sea, lie a million acres set apart to be wilderness forever,
free of roads, buildings, or any camps, calmly repelling
all but the boldest foot-traveler by their canyon depths,
their glacial heights where the sound of the vast ice fields
at their geologically patient labor is as the cracking and
crunching of monstrous bones.

But here below a man feels power-drunk with space and
speed, with the flying sage, the slowly swinging peaks, the
naked arch of the sky, the wind and sun. At noon I
swerved the car to a stop, where the road crossed a river.
One of those lost-looking western rivers that are fed only
by remote snows and are destined to creep across a plain
where, you would say, Nature does not wish a river to
flow. So fast does the dry air evaporate it, the parched
dust drink it up.

There was a spare fertility here, and we found flowers,
lupine and Indian paintbrush and wild roses, when we
tramped down with the picnic basket into a pasture thick
with arrowgrass that I hadn't seen in twenty years, not
since I botanized the dunes and lagoons of the Calumet
country a thousand miles away. Out from under the
bridge shot a flock of little triangular spirits that took the
air with wheedling and complaint. What are you doing
here, swallows, friend swallows? In this lonely place on
the plains, in the sage, by this lost little stream so far from
the cliffs you love? But the rough-wings only cried out
against us because we had found them out in their solitude.

After we had eaten, I went off loitering down along the
stream. Its waters thrust on slowly through a wavering
forest of weed submersed and drowned, but happy to be so.
I recognized the crinkled foliage of pondweed, the finely

dissected leafage of water-crowfoot which collapses when
you lift it from the stream, and the lime-crusted branches
of milfoil, which does not. There was an elegant mare's-
tail, fit for an ornamental aquarium, and much waterweed,
an *Elodea* with pellucid leaves.

And how came you here, waterweeds, in this stream
which is one of the twice ten thousand rivulets that gather
out of seven states, draining a basin greater than the empire of Charlemagne, until together they carve the chasm
of the Grand Canyon and so at last reach the Gulf of
California? (A long way, that, a thousand miles, from
high Wyoming.) Part of the great circumpolar flora that
stretches all around Eurasia and North America, they were
as much at home here as where, I suddenly recalled, they
wavered once beneath my gaze, in the amber waters of a
stream that flows through the French town of Maintenon.

One goes there, of course, to see the comfortable old
château of Madame de Maintenon, that fat, compara-
tively virtuous mistress of the *Grand Monarque*. Having
paid my visit to that untenanted shell of glories past, I
stood, in a mild rain, upon the little bridge in the town,
watching the loach investigate the gleaming charms of a
new tin can on the bottom, where the rain drops dimpled
the surface water. This was one of those orderly European
streams taught to move between walls, with water gates
coming down to it, and footbridges spanning it. It would
flow on like this, dutifully, into the Eure, and the Eure
into the Seine, and the Seine to the sea, not far away — a
hundred miles at the most; it would never dwindle or dry,
and seldom flood. Its gentle course was doubtless rich
with history; upon the walls of the château were names

of great lords who had fought at Agincourt and Crécy, fought the Saracens and the English, the Germans and the Spaniards. A church bell began to toll. It is a sound that I love; it calls and calls me, but to something I do not want. It seemed to be tolling out all the dead men and women of the town for centuries agone. To be mourning already for the children in their peaked caps pattering over the bridge, the boys who die in war, the girls who get their sons. One of those girls was watching me through the small panes of the pastry shop over the bridge, her white face framed among Napoleons and cream puffs; it was an invitation, clearly, to come in out of the rain, away from staring at nothing but the waterweeds, to the sweet stuffy intimacy of the *patisserie* ...

I looked up from the *Elodea*, around me at Sublette County, Wyoming. Where all the old cattle wars and Indian wars were not a tick of Maintenon's clocks. Where church bell cannot sound to church bell; oceans of silence without echo surround any steeple here. There is room here for a thousand years to come and bring what they may. There is, it seems, no past at all to venerate.

And yet it was here, where even the swallows look far from home, where there is sometimes not one human in fifty square miles, that the history of the living world rose to a great and decisive climax, perhaps the most significant since the coming of life to earth.

To see Wyoming as it was then, you would have to lower the Wind River rampart from its thirteen thousand feet to young hills. You would have to sink the whole of the Great Plains several thousand feet, and put a lake to the south of this stream, and a few smoking volcanoes about,

and imagine that the eastern sea was no further off than
a long bay up into southern Illinois.

That would give you Wyoming of the Eocene, which
began fifty-five million years ago and was the opening of
geologic modernity. There are many deposits of the
Eocene on earth, but none tell quite the fateful story of
the Wyoming rocks. For then and here great things were
afoot. Four-footed things, with warm blood, milk in their
breasts or young in their wombs. The Middle Ages of life
were over; the armored saurians were gone with the last
of the Cretaceous; the sands of Utah have drifted over
them. Now to replace them came the placental mammals,
the modern animals, and they took the stage with unex-
plained suddenness. From western America they started
out upon their conquest, which has culminated in the
lordliest placental of them all.

Before them, making possible their rise, had come the
flowering plants, emerging in the Cretaceous period just
previous, taking first root in the folds of the Appalachians.
With this new flora there came into the world sweet foliage,
good pasturage, soft browse. By the Eocene these plants
were free to march, rooting and seeding their way (they
had twenty million Eocene years to do it in) across Illinois
and Nebraska and the Dakotas, to the foot of the Wind
River hills. And at that time and in this place, the new
thing called grass sod was perhaps first dented by the foot
and munched in the broad herbivore teeth of Hyracotherium, he of the Green River fossils, a creature still only
eight inches high. Fifty-five million years later his
descendants, the horses stolen from Coronado, were back
in Wyoming, forked by the galloping Sioux to hunt the

buffalo. For North America lost its primeval horses, just as it did its camels and elephants and tigers, in the last glacial period. But not until it had given them to the lands whence the conquistadors brought them here.

Wyoming has been lifted up, since then, five thousand, six thousand feet, and its mountains have buckled into ramparts eight thousand feet more. Till the snows were gathered on their heads, and the rivers were split and spilled and sent rolling away to different destinies — some to the Gulf of Mexico, some to the Gulf of California, and some to the North Pacific. The whole state has been lifted closer to the sky; its air, once heavy and damp and warm, has been dried and cleansed and set into boisterous circulation; its skies have been peeled of clouds, its soil parched. The sage has come, a modern plant if ever there was one, a shrubby composite pollinated by wind and thus well fit for the wind-swept plains that it inhabits. The rough-winged swallows, moderns too, have found it out; every year they journey all the way from Guatemala to nest in it. As it is rich with a great past, so Wyoming is full of the future. It has only begun to live.

This is to think by biological time, of course; but whatever the clocks say, that is what we all live and die by. It is the most accurate, as it is the most inexorable. 'All in good time,' we say, and we mean by that some grand inevitable course of happening in which event is foreordained only by those events which went before.

The worst time I know is the empty tick-tocking of a giant pendulum, neon-lighted at night, which swings from the staring clock face over the door of a certain mortician's establishment in Los Angeles. No wonder the crowd hurries past it. It is not so much the reminder of my own steadily approaching demise that horrifies me, as that the measure of time should be a hasty counting out of what is left. Of time, at least, there is no end. And those who talk now of the end of man as an imminent possibility are thinking by the mortician's clock, not biologically.

In moments of despair like the world's today, of despair at ourselves as a race, the grand hope of evolution looks a cheat. The emergence of the placental mammals in Wyoming of the Eocene appears from this distance to have been a magnificent event, and, taking ourselves for the end product of that trend, the result of fifty million years of struggle is a disappointing child. Here we, the genus *Homo*, have had — so far as science can discover — about a million years in which to put distance between ourselves and the chimpanzee. And when we go down to the zoo and peer at the poor wrinkled old gaffer in jail, he embarrasses us because he is so human.

But a million years is nothing, to the wind in the sage, or to the mysterious urge toward change inherent in all protoplasm. There is little Hyracotherium tittuping on his four-toed feet across the Eocene horizon of the Wind River country; ten million years later he has become the three-toed Mesohippus of the Oligocene that followed. Not for twenty million more years is produced Hipparion, swift as an antelope on his long legs and his one-toed foot that we call a hoof. And still that department of destiny which concerns itself with horses required some thirty-four million years to roll on while modern Equus was preparing, till you could lay your bet on Sea Biscuit at the Santa Anita track.

So genus gave way to genus in a long line of bigger and faster horses. So species yields to species. No matter how good an organism is, it changes, or it yields, to something better adapted. Do we hear, in slower tempo, the pendulum of doom in this? How long may any one species of placental mammal expect, in the nature of things, to live?

Referring to the record of the rocks, we can roughly say that the mean maximum might be something like ten million years — which gives *Homo sapiens* at least another nine million of life expectancy. Unless, of course, something suddenly goes against the species.

And at the moment the most powerful living enemy seems to be going against *Homo* — himself. His increased efficiency in the mechanism of suicide looks fatal. But all the wars there have ever been only prove that the ultimate conqueror over mass murder is life. Even what we call total war today is not killing more than a small fraction of the soldiers engaged and the civilians exposed; the proportion does not seem to be as high as in the days when Tamerlane slew every inhabitant of the cities he sacked. The most appalling casualties of battle are obliterated in one generation. Race suicide does not to the biologist appear a likely danger — unless it turns into Thurber's war between the sexes, and his wild-eyed women get the worst of it. For whereas the loss of women would be biologically fatal, even an annual reduction in the male population of many animals is viewed by Nature as a reasonable way of cutting down on non-essentials. And if the human race exerted itself far enough in destruction to apply that method, polygamy would simply come out in the open and balance the budget.

This jovial and amoral view of the present horror is
not merely flippant; it is Nature's own. And Nature also
gives warning that races do become extinct. It is worth
while, then, to see what mustn't happen to our human
race.

First of all, its young must not be wiped out by other
organisms, as the giant reptiles may have been destroyed
by the new mammals, some primitive little egg-sucker,
perhaps, wiping out the race of dinosaurs still unborn. A
human baby is a terrifyingly destructible object. But no
other animal in the world takes better care of its children
than man; no other brings such a large proportion of them
to maturity.

Secondly, there must not be in the species a collapse of
the reproductive mechanism, any mysterious failure of
the will to continue, like that which appeared in the vanishing heath hen and, despite conservation's every effort,
finally extinguished it. Females especially must remain
abundantly fertile; the seed must set; the egg must be
viable. Sterility, stillbirth, abortion are fatal if they become predominant. Alarmists point to the high incidence
of these ills among 'overcivilized' women. But they are
not exclusive to our society; a large proportion of birds'
eggs, for instance, are destined never to hatch. Some
sterility is, if not normal, at least common even in healthy
races. And in our own, where the use of hormones is daily
better understood and surgical adjustment becomes constantly more practiced, it is probable that the technique
of medicine will shortly make it possible to render practically every human fertile.

Third of these presumable apocalyptic dangers is epidemic, some contagion against which no individual of the race has any immunity. In just this way the American chestnut, king of the forest thirty years ago, has been wiped out before our eyes by a fungous disease from China.

Over and over has epidemic disease of one kind or another attacked the race of man, and none has ever conquered. On the contrary, man has overcome many of the worst, and every day his technique for this form of combat is perfected. One century of modern medicine has so swiftly raised our life expectancy that we have birth control as a symptom of our new well-being. This also is a source of worry to many people. But a low death rate goes with a low birth rate; high birth rate equals high death rate; church and state are powerless before these equations.

The remaining likely danger to a species is that a closely related one will arise beside it, competing for exactly the

same food and habitat and winning the ground by greater
strength and adaptive powers. So the Norway brown
rat has driven out the black rat of the days of Hamelin
town. But no rival appears on our horizon. Man is the
sole extant species of *Homo*.

And man, after a million years, is as new and undeveloped an experiment as ever were those first placentals
in the Eocene. They carried life far forward in that un-
heard of thing, the womb; what man has introduced into
the history of life is intelligence, and novel as it is, groping,
imperfect, undeveloped, it is potentially capable of possibilities inconceivable today. All our failures, our sins
against each other, of which selfishness comes first and
war is a symptom, are due to the rudimentary newness
of this thing called intelligence. It is five hundred million
years or so behind instinct in its utility; the termites
settled their social organization ages ago, and now wage
war only against ants, never among themselves.

That it is dangerous is true; so is blind instinct dangerous, which sends the lemmings into the sea. Granted that
intelligence is an experiment. But look back at evolution
to see what has become of all the major experiments that
Nature has ever tried, and you will discover that nothing
that was good has ever been permanently lost. The eye
and its sight, for instance, once invented, have become
better and more firmly fixed. The hand, the care of the
young, the green leaf, the seed, have all grown more effec-
tive. What has failed has been sloth, stupidity, dependence upon armored plates and mere ferocity. The rigid,
the self-limiting order goes down. Intelligence pushes
up, with the current, the mighty, the irresistible current of

evolution, which branches like a river, like a tree. Final product there is none, not even man. He too must change, and by the one fiat which has held since time's beginning, he must grow. Nine million years would seem an ample era for any species to grow toward improvement. And after that, after *sapiens*, perhaps, some species as far beyond him as he is far from *neanderthalensis*, some newer species not merely intelligent but wise, may walk the earth, deserving of his place on it in the ancient sunlight.

9

YOUNG MAN

NOT OF MANHATTAN

I F EVER I lived to the hurrying metronome
of mortality, it was when I was twenty in New York City.
At no time in my life did I know more nervous stimula-
tion; nowhere else was I ever so miserable. I suppose I
ought to have been happy. Raw as I was, I got a job in a
publishing house by asking for it — for the reason, no
doubt, that the president of the company had been, upon
a time, one of the countless young men for whom my
parents had found jobs. This job of mine paid fifteen
dollars a week, in theory, but three dollars were removed
from the envelope to buy me the compulsory security of

a Liberty Bond; the president was making a patriotic
showing from his employees that last year of the war.

The work was interesting and pleasant. I can thank it
for such knowledge as I possess of the way that books are
read, judged, refused, accepted, proof-read, publicized,
and sold. I observed the firm's authors being handled, in
person and by letter, and was presently detailed to do a
little handling myself. So now I recognize the technique
when I am treated to it.

My associates were kind, and many were cultivated.
Some have dropped out of the picture, others have come
forward in it to greater prominence. I meet them occa-
sionally around the different shops in New York, for the
personnel of publishing is ever being stirred with the
Great Horn Spoon. But when I go back to the outfit
where I worked nobody remembers poor old Rip. Twenty
years ago in New York is as far back as the Eocene.

But then it was an aching present. For one thing, to be
in love there was a torture of loneliness. It seemed the
fault of the entire city that she did not come, did not
write, did not say, when she wrote, what I wanted to hear.
She had escaped me; she had emerged from the chrysalis
of pink taffeta and, more mature though younger than I,
moved now beyond my reach in the world that belongs to
men. And because I knew myself for a boy, I hated myself for it. There are still streets in New York on which,
when I walk them today, I meet this old despair. I see
myself stalking there like an unhappy green heron, hunting for some feeding ground, some cheap restaurant where
the noon meal might for once have savor.

It makes an old joke now, shared between us. But once

it was a curse upon the stones of Gotham. They rang for me with nothing but defeat, mine and that of all the unwitting multitude around me. All day and all night I heard that mortal beat, the sound of footsteps, the tread of a city of fourteen million soles, pellmell down the subway ramps, up the elevated stairs, into Grand Central and out, marking time in the theatre lobbies, stampeding in the ferry exits. Forever — when you came to listen — they tapped, pounded, shuffled, limped, lagged, faltered, pelted. The smallest hours of morning were still loud with the leaderless army.

Of this I too was one. In the wilderness of Manhattan I had lost my glimmer of direction. Every day I grew more politely difficult for my family to live with. Every evening the barrel organ on our corner of West Ninth tinkled the *Addio al passato*. The humanoid eyes of the monkey, I thought — looking down into them, into the little upheld cap — were kinder than any you see on Fifth. And emotion rose up in me like dark arterial blood in the throat of a man wounded in the chest, choking, startling when it comes to light, incredible as belonging to one's self.

Yet in a city of seven million, all hiding their wounds from one another, I would grimly have agreed that I was one of the fortunate. If the job had come easily, so did a variety of pleasures. I was that useful supernumerary, the 'odd,' the 'extra' young man. I went much to the theatre, often with my mother, who fed her heart there; she was detesting New York as a place where people prefer to starve to death rather than get to know their neighbors — a woman sculptor had done just that, two doors from us. My father loved its every street; now in the last vigor of his life he was commander-in-chief of the New York offices of his paper, and in wartime at that; the clack of the telegraph was in his ear, on his private wire he could get you Washington and Boston, Chicago, London, and Paris in two minutes, and at the center of this web he was snug as a spider. He enjoyed dining friends at the Brevoort or the Lafayette, and I was usually of the party. On other nights I resolutely danced to the strains of *Dear Old Pal of Mine* with 'nice, wholesome girls' trotted out to me. Others, as healthy but not so nice, were offered by generous young males who wanted me to feel at home in New York City.

But I had no such desire, though I explored it nook and cranny, seeing all the parts I never see now. They were the sights possible for a young man who had Sundays and a few Saturday afternoons to spend, and what was left over from necessities of twelve weekly dollars. I knew the fish in the Aquarium well, and the Battery, and the calm of St. Paul's and Trinity. I went abroad, to the limit of my means; my knowledge then of Staten Island was enviable, and I had some acquaintance with the Palisades and Tarrytown. Toward far-off Montauk I cast wistful eyes, but the fare lacked me, the time was not vouchsafed. Once on Labor Day the dispensations of Providence got me as far as Tilly Foster.

Wherever I went, even in the metropolitan district, I took my Gray's *Manual* with me. Humboldt his Brazil, Banks his Australia, Hooker his India. And for me the flora of Hackensack and Tottenville and Far Rockaway.

It took me time to learn it, green as I was. I might sit down, with my manual and my pocket lens, in a midge-haunted lot somewhere in the suburbs, to identify a small crucifer, and only after a long hour would I discover that what I had got hold of was a stray from somebody's radish bed. I had no vasculum in which to carry home specimens in a fine state of freshness. I had never even heard of a plant press, and couldn't have afforded one anyway. Instead I spent a dime on a notebook, and in it I drew up from the living plant my own description of every detail, often adding a sketch which might be bad enough; but there is no way to observe like trying to draw what you see.

So I began to know another citizenry, the plant population of Greater New York. It is perhaps the most exotic in the country. For just as the metropolis is the first catch-all of the immigrant races of the world, some of whom never leave the sight of its towers, so there is a waif flora of immigrant plants as firmly rooted around their port of entry. They have been established here since the days of the old ballast dumps from the sailing ships. They have come in holds bringing cargoes from all over the globe; they stowed away in the bales and bundles, perhaps on the very shoes, of incoming foreigners, as burs in wool, as seeds in the soil sometimes so reverently transported from the old country to the new.

They are cosmopolites, these plants, tramps to whom all ports are alike and every city is home. Many appear to have no native land, or none that will claim them. No written flora anywhere in the world admits as indigenous that lusty weed, a chenopod, called Good King Henry. Or fat-hen, city goosefoot, low amaranth. They reached us from Europe, but in western European manuals they are assigned to eastern Europe, which in turn passes them to the Caucasus. And in the Caucasus they refer these wanderers across the Caspian, for an origin, to the country whence the Huns and Turks came upon Europe. Not that for certain these plants first issued from there, but it has long been popular with botanists to fix this as the source of mysterious roving plant tribes, just because so little is known about the land of the Oxus and Samarkand.

And what little we do know about our waif weeds in Turkestan shows them clinging close to the heels of man. Just so the crisp-leaved amaranth has stuck to the streets of Manhattan and Brooklyn. Like a chorus girl, it regards Jersey City as the Far West, though it plays sometimes to Albany.

Had they not been aggressive, had they not been able to outwit man's efforts to destroy them through these

many centuries, such city weeds would never have been
able to keep their foothold around the wharves and new-
made land, along the highways and up the alleys. Some
have a lusty alien beauty of their own — king-devil and
orange hawkweed and cotton thistle — all harsh and
fierce as they are. I came to understand this, to pluck a
stalk of stramonium, its white trumpet-shaped flowers
exhaling a warning of their poison, with zest because it
had come here out of the tropics. To snap, with gritted
teeth and pleasure, the prickly stem of a blue-devil arrived from the hard-pressed flora of central Europe.

Not that I did not long, amid the stone and steel and
asphalt, for bluebells and a thrush. Even Chicago, sprawling over its prairies, had let a little of Nature into its
borders. But there was the minimum of natural life here
on Manhattan, an island on which millions crowded together and many were yet as lonely as on the Dry Tortu-
gas. Like a maroon escaping, one day early in the summer
of my coming I got away to Staten Island; there, toiling
through a swamp, I pushed abruptly into a clearing bright
with flowers I had never seen before. The woods were
encroaching upon it; the brambles claimed it; a solitary
chimney told the story of a house here once, and an
abandoned garden. It was a garden, I began to discover,
planted to flowers once popular but long since relegated
as Victorian in style. For by my manual I named them
all, that long, sweet-scented, drowsy afternoon as the sun
slipped west. Day-lily, prince's feather, dame's rocket
breathing an odor like a violet sachet. Hyssop, and
spearmint, gill-over-the-ground, and apple-of-Peru. Moth
mulleins and lamb's lettuce, dusty miller rioting from its

once prim bed, and cypress spurge weeping on a grave mound all but sunk to earth's level, under the shade of a tree-of-heaven. Of such, survivors of old gardens, and wandering escapes, is formed another plant society which clings to the footprints of man, and is regarded with hostility by the native American woods.

I came back that evening on a churning ferry with people who were hurrying in to New York to dinner, the theatre, the night shift. We passed the opposing boat bringing the day shift home. Everybody was reading the newspaper; coming or going, all were absorbed in the doings of the city as reported that day, in the events of the world — and those were stirring times. Alone, I did not read; I had no part. I was sad at the thought of my idleness; I thought myself asleep. Was I not storing up for myself an early but lasting failure?

The near-by salt marshes were rusty with sunset light, and filling up with the might and sorrow of the ocean rising in its tide. The crooked creeks, bordered with black mud where long-legged wader birds went mincing, were gutters of blood reflecting the sky. Across the bay the towers of Manhattan were lighting up their violet points; they prickled and trembled in the murky conflagration of the sky. Each building's pattern was a constellation, the whole a galaxy.

Thus, from afar. But once within the city, I knew, I would find it nothing that it seemed across the water in the twilight. Like the interior of a star, it was all a seething storm of light and motion.

Now, said I to myself, there are young fellows all over the country would give their bottom groat to be in my

shoes, coming into New York of a Saturday night. To
have a foothold, even shallow as mine, on those fabulous
cliffs, a place to make in the mightiest and tallest city in
the long history of the world. And I could not wake to
any of it; nor did the evening listen.

Looking back, I recognize how much, for all my week-
ends of self-teaching, I missed of the scant biota of New
York City. I supposed then that any excursion into ornithology would require not only a little knowledge of the
subject — of which I had none — but some greener field
than Manhattan. Among the birds I remain an amateur
today, and rejoice in that status; since botany became a
profession for me, I have the greater sense of holiday in
birding. When I go forth with my binoculars around the
Pacific coastal city where I live, I have a chance of
spotting any of some four hundred species, waders and
swimmers, singers and predators. Yet whenever I travel
east, I am still glad to meet again the pigeons strutting
on the sill of my Forty-Third Street hotel.

With his marvelous adaptability, his intelligence, the
fascination of his Mendelian strains — bred, interbred,
and bred out again to the normal — the pigeon is far
more significant than would be the sensational incident

of a skylark loosed in a penthouse potted tree. For, after all, skylarks have been tried — they were introduced around Flatbush, only to perish in a few years — and found wanting. Wanting, that is, in power to survive.

The ability to endure constant association with human beings is the first prerequisite of those birds that do not merely pass through the metropolis in migration, but make it a home. They must be able to face a jumble of man-made peaks and canyons, a glare of lights by night, many speeding, all blinding, and a powerful upward draft from high buildings, which even the airplanes feel. They must be content to find insect fare very nearly nil, grain supply scarcely better, and nesting sites — if a tree, a shrub, or a tuft of grass be required — rare or totally lacking; the modern great city offers not even telegraph lines to perch on. Traffic is a constant danger; so are hungry prowling cats and rats, and if a bird enjoys any success in the city at all, he is likely to meet the definite hostility of municipal authorities who are prepared to blast him out of town with a fire hose, poison his food, or shoot or trap him.

The advantages offered him by the city are few but real. They include warmth and shelter in winter, opportunities for scavenging around refuse piles, and an absence of competition from other species.

For there are not many birds fit by their natures to consort with us in our human rookeries. It takes some previous experience of mankind to succeed in this, and food habits related to our own, not confined in a finikin way to a few forest insects or the nectar of flowers. It takes a high prolificacy in the species to cover the accident

rate inevitable in living where humans order things only
for their own convenience. And most of all, it requires
some human qualities in the birds themselves. They must
be social, able to endure and enjoy crowding, to act as a
flock, to pool common interests and make concerted attack upon local problems. They need much intelligence
and probably more of a vocabulary, more power to com-
municate, than we find in the solitary singer in the wood.

Thus it is not surprising that most of our regular resi-
dent city birds are European species. For the conditions
of life in Europe have been at work for centuries selecting
out for survival the creatures that get along with man.
Although they must be clever, adaptable, sturdily able
to hold their own, they must not carry any thieving or
aggressive mischief so far that man will be goaded into
destroying them. If they cannot be good like the pigeons,
they must be able to gauge the limits of man's patience to
a nicety, like the English sparrows, and just escape his
most awful wrath.

Our one native metropolitan among the birds is the
most welcome of them — the common harbor or herring
gull, a cosmopolite of ports the world around. As a scavenger of city and ocean refuse he is invaluable, and therefore
in most civilized communities protected by law. To be
useful to man is a good guarantee of survival, but the gull
has another in being also useless dead. His flesh is nau-
seous and inedible. He is not worth the killing.

And since pot-shooting is not permitted on Forty-Third
Street, my pigeons are free to come and get crumbs from
my breakfast roll every morning that I am in New York.
This gentle and uxorious citizen is the rock dove of

Europe, who was established here in early times by the first colonists. A less endearing immigrant, but one just as thoroughly Americanized, is the sparrow that we rather unjustly call English. It was deliberately introduced at Brooklyn in 1851 and 1852; intended to eat up a harmful insect pest, it soon earned a reputation as the prime and classic example of a pest itself. War has been waged on the English sparrow, with guns and poisoned grain and traps, but these are ineffective against his cheerful fecundity. Or rather, his wife's industrious matronhood; the female is often seen carrying straws for a nest even in February, and as many as four broods are crowded into the year's cycle.

Nevertheless, this populous progress has been somewhat checked. First, the coming of the automobile and the consequent disappearance of the horse from our streets changed the course of sparrow history, since this gutter-snipe thrives best around horses. Next, a challenger was introduced by the same biologically innocent would-be benefactor who helped establish the sparrow. And the general verdict is that we have about got rid of a cat by importing a tiger.

The man who opened the cage of English sparrows in Brooklyn in the middle of the last century was one Eugene Schiefellin, who seems not to have found the native American avifauna good enough for him. For in the course of the next forty years he tried to acclimatize skylarks, nightingales, chaffinches, bullfinches, and, I think, European robins, thrushes, and blackbirds. These poor bewildered aristocrats from abroad all refused to thrive. Then fifty years ago Schiefellin released four score starlings on unsuspecting Central Park.

Perhaps the first of their nests in town was that discovered under the eaves of the American Museum of Natural History. With tender pride their Assisi used to come and beam upon the nestlings. Doubtless he stayed the naughty street boy's slingshot, quite unaware that starlings are themselves the hoarse-voiced street boys among birds, whose gangs, gathering strength and numbers, were to defy and outwit the police of many a city.

The first six years of their infiltration the starlings spent consolidating their hold on Gotham. By 1908 they had reached Poughkeepsie and Philadelphia. In 1916 they had passed Boston and, to the south, were entering Washington. Well over the Appalachians in 1925, they found the Middle Western farms and cities to their liking, and today are pioneering Texas and Kansas, with stragglers reported in Colorado. No one knows if Rockies and deserts can hold them back.

They have their friends, and points for which they are admired. A certain braggadocio, not unintelligent, distinguishes the starling. In spring and summer his black attire shows the gleam of metallic green and blue highlights. His tail is rather stumpy; on the ground he walks zigzag, toeing out with a Charlie Chaplin gait, half shuffle, half strut; the heavy yellow bill is constantly stabbing the ground. Aloft, the flocks keep together in a marvelous flight formation, all turning, wheeling, soaring, sinking, or alighting at once, with a fervor of single purpose.

In winter the plumage changes; a white speckling appears, which wears off toward spring but gives the bird a travel-spotted, raggedy-man dinginess. Then the streets and squares where the starlings congregate look and sound like a hobo college; there is a gabbling and wheedling and clucking, an uproar of chatter in various call notes which drives distracted the sleeper roused by it at gray dawn. But if they shorten the nights by their racketing, and drop filth over the streets and the most dignified of public monuments in the city, starlings invade even more impudently the country where native birds lived equably until their coming.

Their food habits are more beneficial than harmful; cut worms, wire worms, grubs, caterpillars, and above all the hated weevils, go down starling gullets by the ton every year. But by outmanoeuvring native species, the starling substitutes his one assertive kind for twenty lovelier. Even as a useful eater of insects, he competes with the happy meadowlark. As a devourer of wild fruits, he cuts into the supply of many songsters, especially thrushes. Nesting as they do in hollows, starlings are rivals for such sites with economically valuable and beloved species like our woodpeckers and bluebirds Their methods of conquest here are clever and efficient; they leave the woodpecker in peace till he has excavated all the holes needed by the local starling flock. Then it moves in, ousting the woodpecker, to breed and multiply. Around nesting boxes put up by humans to catch a song, the starling is a bloody fighter, driving out bluebirds, martins, and wrens, unless the holes are made too small for the invader.

There is no hope of exterminating the starling. He has his American citizenship papers now. Vainly have the police and fire departments of our cities fought the flocks; rockets have been shot into their night roosts, fire hoses have blasted them from the boughs; clappers and bells, blank shots and bird shot, fumes and sticks have been tried in vain. Heroic efforts may dislodge the birds for a while, but they return soon, or settle in some other place where they are no more welcome. And meantime their numbers wax. Poison is ineffectual. The only successful method has been trapping. Hundreds may be caught in a single night and killed. But this is done over the protests of their friends, who would extend them the benefits of liberty. Quaint and intelligent, starlings are companion for the city man with whom no wood thrush will stay to sing. The farmer gets more good from their raid on his insect pests than harm from their theft of his cherries.

If there lies in the starling's history one certainty, it is that there is danger in meddling with the balance of Nature. Once these were aliens, still struggling to get a toehold in the American environment. Their dispersal began only as daily flights from a city roost for the night, to a feeding ground in the truck gardens outside. Later, some came to spend the summers in the country, returning, as tramps will, to flophouses in town for the winter. Finally these birds adopted the country freely, and latest experiments in bird-banding show that at last *Sturnus vulgaris* is beginning an annual migration, north as far as Canada in summer, south as far as the Gulf coast in winter.

Nature needs to be let alone. Free to her own devices, she cleans her own house, knows no wastage, makes no biological mistakes. She solves for herself the problem which men are still finding insoluble — that of a balanced economy.

What alone has forever upset it is this man-child of hers himself, this *Homo sapiens*, in particular the white man, the builder and the destroyer.

When the first European settlers landed on America's coast, something came down to the shore to meet them. It marched proudly; until then it had been invincible. The newcomers called it the wilderness, and they took it to be their foe. They had come with the gun and the plow, with horses and cattle, with ambition and magnificent dreams. They entered an Eden such as the world will never see again, the last unspoiled wilderness of the temperate zone, teeming and complete with a life of its own.

The species man had long had his place in this life, a part of it, keeping the age-old balance. The red man never dammed a stream, never drained a swamp, never exterminated an animal. What ground he cleared for his primitive agriculture was negligible. On the prairies he lit fires sometimes to round up the game, but the only lasting result was to keep the Appalachian hardwood forest wall pushed back to the east, preventing it from encroaching upon the prairie, the great meadow, the American steppe-land on which the bison herds depended for their lives. In no way did the Indian break the charmed circle of the wildlife community.

One can but dimly picture today that great biota, the

prodigal abundance with which this continent was originally stocked. It beggared even the expletives of the
pioneers. What they say of the passenger pigeons sounds
like the tall tales of tall woodsmen, save that the accounts
agree. Flying at a mile a minute, hour after hour, the
jewel-breasted doves would darken the sky sometimes for
days together. Audubon calculated that more than one
billion of them passed over Kentucky in a four-day flight.
By his estimate, each pigeon consumed a pint of beech
mast a day. To feed such a flock the beech forest of the
Middle West, rooted upon primeval, rich and black deep
loams, must have produced over a billion bushels of nuts.
They stretched, those forests, unbroken in green majesty
across an empty empire larger than any European country
save Russia. Over the sea of tree-tops the roar of the
pigeons' wings was such as to drown the crack of rifles,
and the crying of the birds was one great voice, the voice
of a continent.

On the prairies thundered the wild cattle of that continent, the bison, whose footsteps made the earth tremble.
When the mating bulls began to bellow in the fall, the
sound from the great throats was heard for miles around.
Though these creatures were reckoned by the millions,
there was pasturage for them all, and room enough for a
long annual migration.

In veracious recordings we have glimpses of deer, elk,
antelope and bear, raccoon and fox, water fowl and
salmon, whose profusion at the time of the white man's
coming made this virgin land the richest in wildlife he had
known within the memory of his race. But when the white
chips flew out of the first tree he assaulted, the ring of steel

on living timber was the sound of doom for an immemorial order. It rang in another era, the one we recognize as our own.

The first task was to clear a space around the coastal settlements; to leave the Indians no lurking place; to push back the toppling green wave of the forest; to give the dreamer's mind room to think. Then the pioneers planted the seeds of civilization. Our ancestors, unlike the Spanish in the New World, did not bring civilization to the natives; we got rid of the natives and kept civilization for ourselves.

There is no achievement of which Americans are prouder than their conquest over the wilderness. Indeed, why not? They gave their lives to it; they died fighting Nature; they shortened their span of years with the toil of felling the hostile forest, breaking the prairie sod, pulling out rocks, grubbing up stumps, draining away the marsh.

It was from a hard first necessity that our young nation destroyed the balance of American Nature. It was not possible for us to live as the Indians lived, simply as a part of the wild fauna. But we have wasted, we have robbed and slaughtered and made wanton ruin of our wealth. History convicts us of setting fire to our forests, the last great stand of hardwoods in the world, because that was easier than cutting them down. Much of our incomparable system of lakes, brooks, mighty rivers, we turned into sewers where no fish but the worthless German carp will live. Our marshes, cradle of a million water fowl, we drained for crop land that we did not need.

We fattened our hogs on the gleaming bodies of the passenger pigeons, not being able to think what else to do with the birds we shot for the fun of killing something. The bison, pressed ever farther to the great wall of the Rockies, we slew also for sport, cutting out only the tongues to feed an epicure hunger, leaving the giant carcasses to rot all over the plain.

Once they are gone, the trees and the grasslands and the clean bright water, the screaming wild fowl, the beaver and antelope, we can only remember them with longing. We are not God; we cannot make America over again, as it was in the beginning.

But we can come to what is left of our heritage with a patriot's reverence. As I was coming now, after the long flight over Wyoming sagebrush, to the somber majesty of Rocky Mountain needle forests. To long slopes penciled with Englemann spruces straight and tall as the masts of vessels that have suddenly come alive again and put out branches. To the cool and dancing flora of the North once more, after years in the sun-bitten, relentless splendor of southern California's semi-tropics. As the car swept through the Hoback Pass it came crowding to the road's edge, that blithe populace of harebell and daisy, larkspur and yarrow, clover red and white, and the frail-faced wild geranium. The brooks came tumbling after us, glittering and laughing at every fall over the stones. Late gold as the sunlight slanted through the high valleys, the air was fresh with pine boughs, and dew still at the roots of the grass, and spring not yet departed though summer had just come.

Here the moose and elk and mule deer browse, and the marten hunts the pine squirrel. Grosbeaks and crossbills nest here, liking the northern air as I liked it washing

sweet through my lungs after desert dust; in quiet canyons the solitaire might be singing. This was an unspent
piece of the great original treasure. It lay locked away
here — in its broad basin the 'hole' that Captain Sublette called after his fellow trapper Jackson — by the
mountain barriers all around it. Before us, beyond the
summits of the highest forest, rose in snowy grandeur its
guardians, the three abrupt and massive peaks called by
the *voyageurs* the mighty breasts, the Grand Tetons.

10

A CABIN

ON FISH CREEK

NEVER had any man a more kingly sense
of home than I in this cabin where I had slept a single
night — but how deeply! All that I most required was
here, and nothing else. There was a room, one big room,
giving me length to pace in, space for thoughts to grow
longer. There was a roof, beamed with the boles of what
had been tall trees once; there were walls, log walls, snug
and unornamented by more than their own forest pride.
I had two beds at one end of my room, and my wife lay
happy on hers; at the other end was a stove with wood
burning in it and a kettle boiling on it. The table was

broad enough for my typewriter and the full rank of my books, and when I sat down at it I looked through a window at pine trees and wildflowers and a brook where trout leaped. This brook, which ran right past my door, filled my house endlessly with its low, sociable music. The birds outside put in a melody here and there for variation. And for a glimpse of something higher than the fullest earthly contentment, I had but to open my door, step over my threshold, and tipping my head I would see what I love better than any sight except beloved faces — a peak that lifts in everlasting snowy purity into the blue summer sky. The grandest of the three Grand Tetons, seen intimately between two pine boughs, as you keep beauty secret in a locket.

Now here was I snugly at the heart of the life I love best. It had taken twenty years for that sorry young man astray in New York City to get here. I thought about him, as I walked up and down in my pipesmoke, the sound of brook water going along with me. The old discontent sharpened my peace, gave it the edge a good poem has, and I could recollect the very moment that he started off this way. He asked directions of a policeman on Madison Avenue. Asked him the way to what was his destiny, and the officer said to take the local from Grand Central Station.

The Bronx Botanical Garden is attached, more or less, to the Zoo, and there are few who are not diverted from it by the charms of a giraffe or blue-bottomed mandrill. For those who wander in, as I did on that day, the garden is a prospect pleasant but not exciting. It all resembled Nature as a flower show resembles a garden. I investigated the greenhouses; the high glass roof sheltered tropical ornaments in a steamy atmosphere not unlike my aunt's conservatory off her old back parlor; nursemaids and children and a few old men with canes loitered on the walks. I wandered out again. Presently I found some beds set out, not formally for a floral effect, but planted in families. This was strictly botanical; my attention pointed like a bird dog. I was not meant for a horticulturalist. Over the trees there glimmered at me the roof of a high bald building, and I walked toward it, certain as the dog on a scent.

In the botanical museum I spent some time over the public displays, the series of labeled specimens in swinging frames, of plant fibres and essential oils, the charts and photographs. But it was something gamier I was after. When at the bottom of a top flight of stairs my way was barred by a chain with a pendant sign, I knew that I had found it. The sign said NO ADMITTANCE.

There was a guard at hand, and he was watching me. Point blank I asked him for permission to ascend those stairs. For answer he asked whom I wished to see, and I said, 'Anybody.' Therefore he demanded who I might be and, suspect, I replied that I was nobody.

This ended it, of course. But not for me. All that I knew was that those Olympians in seventh heaven up above were my friends, and that it was my business they were conducting, without me.

The guard stepped off to lend benevolent advice to some more orderly visitor than I, and because Nobody was admitted up there, Nobody jumped over the chain in one long-legged scissors-vault.

The librarian, as I entered, looked up with welcome

behind her eyeglasses. I had got past the bureaucrats, it seemed; I was entering the democracy of science. Out of his office came Doctor Barnhart, the historian of botany, probably the best-informed man in the western hemisphere on even the most obscure botanists. The obscurer the better, evidently, for me he welcomed with incredible kindness and affability.

I had not learned, in those days, that all scientists welcome one another, and that you begin to be a scientist from the moment you wish to be one. I had not then found out that, so far from keeping to themselves their knowledge, men of science eagerly desire to share it. I did not know that the advanced are not supercilious to beginners, for the fine and humble reason that they know themselves, even the highest, as beginners all.

Did I wish to see the herbarium? suggested Doctor Barnhart.

At first it looked to me like a vast loft, lighted from above, filled with rows and rows of tall narrow cases arranged like houses on streets. There were avenues and cross streets, and a main artery with a park of tables running down the center. And every house door, I discovered, bore the name of its occupants — Orchid family and Canna family, Ginger family and Arrowroot family; behind their Latin I knew them. I saw how all were arranged in the same order as the families in my now well-worn *Manual* of Asa Gray — the order of their evolution from the first and simplest flowers to the modern splendor of orchids and composites.

And I, still overwhelmed by the 4885 species in Gray's range (which is from Virginia to Newfoundland and west

to Kansas and North Dakota), was here confronted by
dozens, scores, hundreds of families I had never heard of,
tropical groups from Demerara and Cayenne, Antigua,
Yucatan, Tobago, Maracaibo, and the Keys. Here in this
gigantic repository were the plants of Paraguay and the
plants of Baffinland, and the flora of any point between.
Nearly a million specimens were housed here, Doctor
Barnhart remarked, and he opened a case and showed me
how they were stored — dried, pressed, fixed to a stiff white
sheet measuring eleven and a half by fourteen and a half
inches, which is a size standard all over the world, so that
specimens, when exchanged, will fit into cases at Kew,
Tokyo, or Cape Town. And every one was ticketed with
a label bearing its identity, the time and place of collection, and the name of the collector.

Unlike an amateur collection, which is a personal possession oftenest emphasizing the rare and lovely, this great
one belonged to nobody in particular. Yes, even to me. I
or anyone else could come here to study it; and any number of plants would be sent to the ends of the earth for
study by others. Here plants gathered by the hand of Asa
Gray himself, or Sir Joseph Dalton Hooker, were merged
in with the humblest beginner's specimens. The purchase
price of a rarity was exactly the same as of a common
thing — ten cents a sheet. For specimens are judged on
their merits as materials for the advancement of knowledge. And that knowledge is forever widening, describing
several thousand new species a year, working out the
course of evolution, discovering new economic plants and
new uses for old ones, completing the provincial floras of
state after state and country after country.

Among the cases we encountered a young man, gentle and deliberate, by the name of Pennell. I was also introduced to Doctor Small, authority on southern floras, and to Doctor Britton, here the chief. I listened to these men and marveled, never having encountered science before outside the classroom. These men were not teachers preparing others to teach; the way in which they talked of travel and research took my breath away. If you became interested in a tropical island whose flora was unknown, you simply went there; business first, you know. If a plant you required to see grew on top of a far-off mountain, you climbed that peak. They seemed to assume that I had just come back from somewhere fascinating, and when I told them it was Staten Island they did not smile. They asked me to sign in the book of visiting botanists. Because, when I wrote my name there, I did not feel like a forger, I knew that I had begun to identify my weedy self.

Rain was now meditatively falling upon our cabin roof. I saw it dimple the running waters of the trout stream, and smelled a fresher perfume from the forest flowers beyond my open window. Within, the blent smokes of wood and tobacco were a goodly tinge on the air, and there was another, lovely and faint, which I perhaps imagined because the source of it spread quiet beauty from the table between the two beds. My wife, I saw, had fallen asleep. I paused there, and buried my face in the great bouquet.

This had been pressed upon Louise by a country girl we met below the pass that leads out over the western side of the 'hole,' into Idaho. Up there the girl had picked her flowers; they quite filled her two arms, and when my wife cried out at seeing them, the pleased, shy daughter of Wyoming tore her armful apart and gave us half.

They were a native columbine, most of them creamy white, a few pale cloudy blue. Every giant flower was poised upon its stem airily as a winged insect, lifting its spurred petals in a two-inch spread. Your *Aquilegia* fancier will point out proudly blooms like that in his eastern garden bed; these were wild, with all the delicate exciting appeal that flies from what is planted by our hands. Strangers to me, they wore the fleeting beauty of the newly discovered. It is a charm that anything in Nature wears, once at least, for every man.

For even the most famous of naturalists must necessarily have begun in complete and bottomless ignorance. And while the common fund of scientific knowledge grows every day, with every added mite, there rises in each generation a new rank of discoverers to whom the world is fresh all over again. I am sometimes asked whether 'all the birds haven't been discovered?' Even when they are, all over the world, the individual ornithologist has no reason to take up table tennis instead of his chosen science. A bird that is new to me is just as new — for all I care — as if no one had ever seen it before. Over and over I have known the zest of following wings through briar, through mire, peering with my glasses, trying to memorize call notes as I went, tingling upon the verge of great ornithological discovery — of a bird described by Linnaeus almost two hundred years ago.

Plotting the rate of publication of new species as a curve, I find that it rises as a rapid parabola in the Linnaean era and reaches a peak in the days of Alexander Wilson. But even in Audubon's time the sport of species-making in the eastern United States was falling off; with only one new species in forty years — a warbler — the curve has flattened so low that it must soon sink to zero. Yet long after you and I are gone, boys with their first bird glasses will be discovering lark buntings and marbled godwits.

The amateur spirit, which is that of doing a thing for the love of it, does not in science differ from the credo of the professional. Darwin, Fabre, Gilbert White, all had amateur rating; they did not earn their living as naturalists. Those who hold down other jobs, whether in the office or the nursery and kitchen, keep their appointments with Nature like a lover. They have been writing to me now for many years, and most of the letters, the best of them, have come from people who wanted to know how to learn.

Some are young and hunting vocations and avocations; some are older and have at last the time to do what they want. Most challenging of all have been those who were in the full swing of life. They heard the beguiling whistles of the birds; they glimpsed from the commuter's train window the fields filling up with wildflowers; they saw the wheeling of the unknown constellations over their suburban roofs. And they saw that human life is short; the years rush down the stream and do not return; and all about is a greater life, zestful, enchanting, and deeply significant. They ask to know; they bring their minds, like thirsty cups, inquiring for the fountain.

It springs for everyone, and it is found in all places. On the flat tarred gravel roofs of the city, unknown to the sleepers below, nest the nighthawks by the thousand. To the puddles in an excavation for an office building may come the knots and sanderlings that inland people travel far to see. The whole mystery of life is in the luminous inky cloud of frogs' eggs in a ditch, and the riddle of instinct is there for anyone to read in the pavement ants.

Nature at home is just as filled with beauty and wonder as the places where bronze-limbed girls wear red flowers over their ears. I was once, while working for the Government, told off to entertain a visiting English naturalist. I asked him what he wanted most to see, and he said, 'A rattlesnake, a poison-ivy bush, a milkweed flower, and an opossum.' Exploration begins at the back fence, and the limits of the field are the ends of the world.

But in a world so wide and so new, a naturalist, if he would seriously learn, must stake out for himself some province to define and master. It was upon one of my frequent visits to the Bronx Botanical Garden that I discovered, twenty years ago, how much earlier I had all unconsciously laid claim to one such province as my own.

The day was late in winter; I was turning over the sheets in the herbarium; the specimen I lifted next from out its neat manila folder looked back at me familiarly. I had seen this plant before, long, long ago with the eyes of love and only a child's understanding. Now I saw it, in the first glimmerings of my comprehension of the great plant system, as science sees it. And I knew before I looked at the label what would be written on the spot where the place of collection is entered. For though there are many kinds of trillium in the world, there is no other place where this kind springs.

Therefore the label bore the name of the mountain where I had heard the thrush when I was eight, and watched dawn and sunset from the rocks. The word was like a secret between myself and Nature. Deeply it had lain buried with that other life closed years ago, which now opened suddenly beyond this flower. There the white fall plunged and the mountain-tops rolled misty blue away, and all at once I could remember how this trillium smelled, a dark honey perfume. I lifted the specimen closer; the flower rose serene out of its three great rhombic leaves, solitary and symmetrical; under my hand lens it spoke to me in the tongue I was beginning to understand.

I took my specimen in to Doctor Barnhart. I said — most casually remarking it — the place name which was passport to me. Doctor Barnhart reached for his atlas, and turned to the page that mapped the Carolinas. Historian of botany that he is, he began to trace out the routes of the collectors who had gone that way. First went old John Bartram, Philadelphia Quaker, Botanist to George Third. But he had passed a hundred miles to the north, collecting seeds for his garden. Alexander Garden, Charleston physician, correspondent of Linnaeus, dapper godfather of gardenia his namesake, had gone north in 1755 with Governor Glen when the treaty with the Cherokees was made at the foot of 'the Saluda Mountains.'

But he had missed my country by forty miles to the southwest. My mountains must have been sighted, a smoky
penciled line upon the west, by André Michaux, emerging
from the wilderness with new plants commanded by
his king for Marly and Marie Antoinette's Versailles.

Somebody, Doctor Barnhart remarked, closing the atlas,
ought to get down in that country again. He might find
Michaux's mysterious magnolia. Or even his shortia, the
flower once lost for a century.

Twilight comes early in December; it comes swiftly under dark trees, and when torrential rains are falling it is a
wall of blackness advancing among high peaks, overtaking
the traveler at one step. The traveler, that pouring December eighth of 1788, was André Michaux, coming north
from Charleston to gather flowers in their seed, to dig
roots and take cuttings at the time of year when they are
dormant and can best endure transplanting. He was late
this year, as he struck the Cherokee country, delayed by
fever caught on the coast; the drenching winter rains, that
seem never to stop, had caught him as he toiled up the
long yellow rivers toward their source in the Nantahallas.
The rocky streams were overcharged with run-off; they
roared above the roaring of the rain, and filled the steep

ravines with the sound of their warring. Ahead, the Indian guides loped like mountain lions, never looking back to see if the poor Frenchman were keeping them in sight, or had lost his way upon the bear trail that was all the road into this wilderness.

A long way this, from Versailles upon its plain, where he was born, where his new-found magnolias and azaleas and rhododendrons will go to bloom exotically down the stately *allées* of the palace. And a longer still to Madagascar, where in a few years the great plantsman will die. A long way even from Charleston it was in those days, and he was treading where never before had the white man set foot, or science penetrated, when suddenly in the dusk he saw a wavering row of unfamiliar green, little rosettes of long-stemmed leaves all dancing in the pelting rain, under the overhanging laurel. He knew — how does a plantsman know these things before he can be sure of them? — in a glance that he had something new. New not only to him but, he guessed intuitively, to the world. Your born plantsman has a seventh sense for the very look and stance and feel of a plant that is somehow, in a small but a discrete way, different from anything else that grows. And the real gardener knows, even from the look of a leaf on a winter's day, when he has new value in his fingers. So Michaux paused there, in a place that had no name, to gather a root and a leaf and one little seed pod of a flower that also had no name. He was alone, adventuring, young; he thought he had all his life before him, and did not guess how soon it would be over. He had no idea that the leaf and pod he gathered would send many expeditions out in vain to discover the flowering plant. And that for

three hundred miles around they would search for this
spot where he paused in the rain.

Yet he took some care for the clues he left behind him.
He wrote out that night, in an Indian hut where eight per-
sons and six big dogs huddled around the light and warmth
of a fire, *Directions for finding this shrub:*

> The head of the Keowee is the junction of two consider-
> able torrents which flow from cascades from the high moun-
> tains. The junction is made in a little plain which was
> formerly a city or village of the Cherokees. In descending
> to the junction of the two torrents, having the river at the
> left and the high mountains which look to the north on the
> right, one finds at about 30 to 50 paces from the confluence
> a little path formed by the Indian hunters. Continuing in
> this direction one arrives at last at the mountains where one
> finds this shrub which covers the soil along with the *Epigaea
> repens.* [Trailing arbutus.]

At this point the diarist breaks off, probably on account
of the discomforts of his surroundings. He had tried to
camp under the trees, but the rain had frozen in the blan-
kets. Now he stifled and shivered alternately in the red
men's hut, the smoke of which escaped through a hole in
the roof. An Indian offered him his bed of bearskin, but
at last, distracted by the dogs who howled continually for
their place by the fire, Michaux arose in the early morning,
the rain having ceased, and went back to his camp on the
Keowee, where he picked a great quantity of the scalloped
leaf. 'I did not find it,' he says significantly, 'on any other
mountain. The savages of the place told me that the
leaves have a nice taste when chewed and give forth a
pleasant odor when pinched. This I demonstrated
effectually for myself.'

Plant and diary should certainly have elucidated each other. But the diary, in French, found its way into the archives of the Philosophical Society of Philadelphia, there to be forgotten, and the herbarium specimen went to Paris, where, since it had no flowers, it could not be identified; so it was shelved among the conundrums which scientists have given up. And there it lay until Asa Gray came to Paris in 1839. He was making the rounds of all the European museums, to see every American plant they held, before writing his compendious flora of North America.

Now here was one American plant which he not only did not know, but could not even guess at. The label said merely '*les hautes montagnes de Carolinie*' — a designation as large as Belgium or the Tyrol. The leaf, you might say, was much like that of galax; the seed pod could remind one of some *Pyrola* or shinleaf. But as it couldn't be both, so also it was neither. Now a seed pod, with its chambers and coats, is a ripened ovary, and an ovary is the heart and soul of every flower. So Doctor Gray sat down and drew up from the seed pod an imaginary description of the flower, predicting that when it was found it would be a solitary bell-shaped blossom with five stamens opposite the sepals, and an ovary of three united carpels terminating in a single long style.

Then, returning to America, he set out to look for it. He failed. Again he tried and again; never a scientific expedition turned south that Gray did not beg them to find shortia, as he had named his hypothesis for good old Doctor Short the Kentucky botanist. But the Mount Mitchell Range was combed in vain, and Grandfather

Mountain, Roan Mountain, the Great Smokies. Still no
shortia. The odd thing was that other kinds of shortia
were being discovered in the mountains of Japan and in the
Himalayas. For it belongs to that strange group of flowers
that are found in eastern North America and eastern Asia,
whose floras so much resemble each other. But not in
Europe, and not in the Far West.

At last Professor Sargent of the Arnold Arboretum dug
out Michaux's old diary. He set forth, confident of his
quest, and on the ninth of December, ninety-nine years
and one day after Michaux had found it, he picked on the
banks of Bear Pasture Creek, in the one region in the

world where it grew, *Shortia galacifolia.* Grown to flowering, it fulfilled Asa Gray's predictions to a dot — a neat piece of accuracy comparable to the magnificent prediction of the orbit of Neptune from the perturbations of Uranus.

These fragments joining through a hundred years are in the great tradition of science. I felt its glory, and that I was following it, when I started south not after shortia alone but for my remembered trillium and any and all good things that might fall to me as a collector. For now I had a vasculum to sling across my shoulder, and two plant presses, each a double lattice of stout ashwood with straps to bind it. I had stocked up, too, on the specimen driers that go in a plant press — extra thick blotting paper, cut like herbaria sheets to the same standard size, of a highly bibulous stock. One of my two suitcases was crammed with nothing but these. At Biltmore I changed trains; and when, arrived in Tryon, I threw up the suitcase lid to get my driers out, I found instead a stranger's clothes tenderly wrapping a revolver and two quarts of snake-bite whiskey. My dismay must have been slight compared to that of the Southern gentleman who reached for his liquor and found the thirstiest blotting paper that the Cambridge Botanical Supply Company could offer.

Margaret Morley lent me driers. She was leaving the field forever, and she gave me her microscope, all her scientific library, and her blessing. She it was who told me where to find the walking fern, and the seven kinds of trillium. (Even the Carolina wrens whistled 'Trillium, trillium, trillium!' all day beside the brooks.) And where I should look for the seven wild gingers hiding their flowers close to earth under their leaves, and sweet pinesaps, and shortia itself. After tramping sixty miles, sleeping on the ground by my campfire or in the cabins of mountaineers, my fingers, too, touched it at last. There on Horsepasture Creek, in the Blue Ridge near Toxaway, I gathered a few plants to colonize nearer home.

In that wild place, the loam-bound roots in my two hands, I felt at the center of things. I had simply walked off that map which shows New York City as the axis of America. No one had detained me; my parents, who asked nothing better of their children than some sound conviction, had seemed relieved when I announced that I was quitting. Only years later did I learn that they suspected those mixed fevers and languors which New York gave me to be what is called the malady of poets. The truth of it was that I was quite healthily beginning at last to go about my business.

I climbed Mount Mitchell to breathe its balsams and spruces. I learned the six pines and the two hemlocks of my province, and mastered one by one the azaleas, the early pink, the kind with leaves fragrant in drying, the flame azalea, the late white one. And the trilliums and the laurels and the magnolias. There was no saxifrage I had not scaled a cliff to pick.

Not that it was this detail that mattered, any of it, nor even the sum of all the details (which a decade later came out as a two-hundred-page publication, describing the more than a thousand species of flowering plants here native). The gain which counted, made in that summer when I came of age, lay behind and beyond mere systematics. It does not matter what class of organisms — plants, birds, insects, or strange sea plunder — first stirs the understanding to a grasp at the structure and function of living things, and their relationships, at evolution and geographic distribution and ecology. The principles will carry over to any other group. They leave an impress on the mind, which cannot be erased. Graved deep enough, these given laws are tablets of a faith.

This I know now; then I was simply happy, alone with Nature every day and all day long. No one knew in what glen or on what ridge I wandered; no one was there to watch me as I changed identity, tramping and climbing and sleeping noons or nights whenever I fell weary. Confusion and uncertainty ran out of the soles of my boots. Conviction slowly came.

The new vision added dimension to a world that had been flat. Everything in it now had atmosphere behind; far-off ranges came at a stride miles nearer in this clearer air. I saw newly; I knew at last what it was that I wanted to know. I understood how I wanted to think. I found that for me the natural world, seen with the eyes of science, was — and is — reality.

I did not know much, but what I had learned I had to believe. As art (which had been the preoccupation of my youth) *feels* its way intuitively toward reality, through emotion and sympathy, so science *knows* its way, step by hard-won step. And Nature was what I wanted thus to know; it came to me with the exaltation of a conversion.

Not all at once; it came slowly, as the full-blown southern summer waned and I went north, to tramp New Hampshire's Presidential Range above timberline for its arctic-alpine flora. It came decisively at last in Agassiz Museum, in Cambridge, where I was only a visitor to see the glass flowers.

There was a rime of frost on the bramble canes, and the air smelled once more of going-back-to-school. And that is what I did. All at once I had so much to learn, that Harvard, even three years of it, looked like just the beginning it was.

Now, in the cabin on Fish Creek, Wyoming, I had what most I lacked as I sprinted, that first autumn, through the Cambridge streets. The elm leaves then were falling, the practice whistle blowing from the football field across the Charles; Boston with its theatres, restaurants, bookstores was only five minutes off by subway though most of it remote by pocketbook. Now I have seen all the plays — they give old plots with new names these days — and heard the operas I used to hunger for. I long ago attended my last class; I got the coveted job and gave it up for a bold risk. I have her arms now, and the arms of our children around me. I have a car, and here were all the Rockies to visit in it. Here on the table stood my dissecting microscope; my choice of books lay spread beside it; and the room with those great white columbines in the dark corner shone as a chamber does with a bride in it. The rain had ceased; the brook ran still murmuring. My drowsy wife opened her eyes and smiled. If ever any man has riches, I have, and know it. And I know too, as I began to guess at twenty-one, that the last of these with which I would ever part is the one that nothing in heaven or on earth could take away from me. Call it my faith. My belief in the Nature of things.

11

MY TOWN

IN THOSE years at Harvard I attended some
three thousand lectures, recitations, or laboratory demon-
strations, and I remember scarcely one on which I did not
hang eagerly and fascinated. Course after course, I swung
up the ladder. After the thronged and haunted pavements
of New York, I rejoiced in the cheerful monasticism of this
life. There was little of the college boy in me now; and
those Georgian rooms at the top of Stoughton were shared
by others of scientific bent, all of them honor students,
spendthrift of brilliant talk, careful of money, restless with
athletic energy, dowered with extraneous talents. Otto
the chemist played Chopin while the slower rest of us finished at our books. Bunny, exhausted by his physics,
would take over the piano to relax in Bach, till the gilded

youths on the floor below hammered for peace. The lamp-lit pool of that evening study was all the swim I wanted to be in. Little tempted me to cut a class, but once or twice I forgot lectures for days, to write poetry. The Dean called me up for it. To these fellows in a jovial Order, I was thus something of a joke they were fond of, and I accepted this contentedly.

But by the middle of my last year I was eager to be done with this study I had craved. I hungered for some fresher air, blow it hot or cold. For the more nearly a university meets the ideal of the academic, the closer its atmosphere becomes to the regulated temperature of a mental nursery. Abruptly I didn't want to learn from others any more, not even from the wisest. Being no greater a scholar than I am, I was a sponge saturated with the life cycles of the fungous diseases of wheat, and the moult successions of the dragon-fly. I wanted life to press me a little drier, so that I could absorb something better than lecture notes. I wanted money that I had earned myself.

So it was that in my last Christmas holidays I went down to Washington on the rumor of a civil service job. Norman and Bunny and Alfred and Otto compelled me to buy a new suit, and surrounded my departure with worry and counsel. Not that one of them had ever applied for work. All would be going on with more preparation; one would pass after graduation into medical school, later an internship, finally and far off, practice. Another would stay on for post-graduate studies in botany; sticking close to his teachers, he would almost automatically become in time a teacher himself. A third had his plans to go to Germany for four more years of study; his destiny would be a college research laboratory. Me they looked after, when I set off with my suitcase for South Station, as if I were a child who had sincerely decided to go out and kill a bear — in a wood where there really are bears.

To walk into the Office of Foreign Seed and Plant Introduction, that day after Christmas years ago, was for me to take a deep breath and grow up. Here was no odor of chalk dust, no camphorous smell of the herbarium, or laboratory reek. Back in the classroom of beloved old Professor Robinson the icons were portraits of the 'German fathers,' fine old herbalist-botanists like Brunfels, Fuchs, Bauhin, Dillenius. But on these other walls the pictures were scenes of a wide new world, of tropical crops and plant explorers in far borderlands. Out of that world came the urbane and genial gentleman who greeted me. Trained in Strasburger's laboratory at Bonn, at the Universities of Berlin and Breslau, and the Hanbury Gardens of 'La Mortola' near Ventimiglia, he had begun, in the year when I was born, those famous plant hunts that took him through the East Indies, the West Indies, West Africa, New Guinea, China, Ceylon, the Persian Gulf, Egypt, Australia, and South America. It was a green young sprout that David Fairchild now collected. My duties as 'Assistant Plant Introducer' were to begin as soon as I obtained my degree.

In mid-June, with my fellows, I received it. On that Class Day the lovely old room at the top of Stoughton, the corner room that had been Oliver Wendell Holmes's, was lit with the flowers and silverware of a spread, the girls and mothers of our pride. In the deep window seat my parents sat, looking dearer to me than I had ever had the eyes to see them, and older. Strangely, I saw, they had shifted out of a ruling orbit, and shone quietly as satellites. As anxious to please as to be pleased, like the other parents, they scanned the laughing girls. Mine was there, in a big black hat and coral ruffles — with another man than I.

That night and that night only in all the year do the fountains of Harvard play. The sound of their rushing fills all the old close; it washes away the confetti and the laughter of this last day and bears them with the finished years down the dark spillways to the sea. Under the glowing lanterns in the dusky boughs of the Yard we wandered, while the young male voices soared from the steps of Widener. Never had illusion sadder loveliness than on that night.

Next day, in empty Stoughton, I finished packing my trunk, and boxed my books and my microscope. The hammer blows rang through the old building, and the Yard policeman came up, perhaps out of idleness, to see what I was doing. I said good-bye to him, and to the shell that had held the soft student years, and took the train for a man's life.

A maid's first man is psychologically indelible. Or so they say, who are supposed to know about these things.

But I say that a young man's first town, the city where he goes free on his own, is his town forever.

There, beyond the watchful protection and privilege of family, he is but one among the many, and so at last supremely himself. There he tests his strength, and makes his first important failures. The foolish things he said and did may well be remembered against him where earliest he threw himself on life. His escapades live after him; the good that he did not so much do as intend, is not recalled, for it was a part of the anonymity in which he walked, all but invisible.

But slight as then his presence was, long after he is gone he will still haunt the streets of that town, with his ambitions and his discontents. The resilient strength of his new majority will have been left there. Success may attend him later on and somewhere else; if he could, he would take it back, through the years, and clap it in the hands of that incredulous younger man, who needed it more.

My town is Washington.

It is indelible in my blood. How I loved it I have never told, and could not; it is a secret incommunicable as a first troubled affair of the heart, and like that, remembered with a twinge. For I was banished; I shall never go back there to live. I seldom visit that city now, and am not made happier when I do. For the happiness I had there once was the kind that cannot be lived over again.

Of all cities Washington is the one where I have had the longest thoughts. Even the streets are the most pensive that I ever walked, those slanting avenues named fatefully, like battleships, for the stars in the flag. The elms and lindens and ginkgo trees make of them green tunnels in the summer that comes so early and stays past its time.

Wherever I have been since I left Washington, whatever I might see from my window, I have known what the season was bringing to my town. Watching a cruel April wind lash the steely trees of Illinois, I knew that primroses from Mount Vernon were fresh in the hands of some white-headed, grinning negro on a street corner where I used to pause. In France I heard the nightingale, as every May came round, and so I could be sure the chewink was calling up the morning, just over the river in Virginia, with his humble splutter and trill. Now when the spring that California calls winter comes back at the end of the year and the parched hills turn green again, I do not always see what I am looking at. I may be remembering a Georgetown November twilight, the lamps on the arc of the Key bridge disappearing into mist on the opposite shore, the Catholic bells clanging above the roofs, the rag-tag children yodeling from yard to yard.

Astronomers and navigators reckon by Greenwich time. But time to me is read from the slow swing of the shadow of the Washington Monument, which is the American idea done in stone, and the tallest gnomon that ever sundial had. At sunrise the shadow stretches west along the Mall, pointing to the white temple which enshrines two quotations from the greatest of all our prose writers, that flank his figure carven in giant thought. As morning advances, the shadow creeps east by north. It points out the Red Cross building, then the White House, then the Treasury. By noon it is running up Fourteenth, toward sunny F, where the clerks and stenographers are swarming around the fountain lunches like bees at fallen pears. Under its inexorable finger they hasten to place their racing bets, snatch a purchase of stockings, rummage at the open bookstalls, and scurry back at the clang of the One bell. By then the shadow has moved on. At three perhaps it will lie cross-town, in the direction of Ford's Theatre; at sunset it has lengthened out and out, pointing command at Congress under the dome on the hill.

That dome you can see shining at you from deep in the marshes of Anacostia, down where the frogs croak and the beetles crawl upon the tropic-looking pickerel weeds; it looms up whitely above the misty blue-green of the alluvial woods, less than two miles away and looking half of that. This capital of the world's greatest nation is a small ark of urbanity afloat in the opalescent heat haze of Tidewater and Piedmont South. Down any of its raying outer avenues, there is a glimpse of country shining, like a bright face looking in the window. In the southern and western part of the city, it is Virginia that you see at the end of the street; east and north, there is green Maryland for a prospect. Even from the town's wide heart, the distance is not far to the lotus beds at Quantico. To ancient oaks of the old dueling grounds at Bladensburg. To cricket song at Falls Church, mayflies along the canal that George Washington surveyed, fireflies of Chevy Chase, pawpaws and may-apples along the steep wooded hills beyond the bridge built by Jefferson Davis.

South and North meet here, and forgive. This was head-quarters to McClellan and Hooker and Grant, but Lee's old home shines upon it from the heights of Arlington. In the older, the central and southeastern parts of town, be-tween rows of brick buildings looking like the one where

Lincoln died, and that other where Mrs. Surratt allowed in
stealthy visitors, the troops used to bivouac. Those
streets knew the tramp of reinforcements ever arriving
from the North, always pouring south, under amateur
generals who led them to the defeats at Bull Run and
Fredericksburg, the Wilderness and Chancellorsville. Defeats borne with a courage and integrity seldom men-
tioned, defeats that tallied at last to victory.

So that I never could pass the Old Soldiers' Home without thinking how Lincoln rode his horse out to it from the
White House alone in the hot moonlight, that July night
of 1864 when Early and his Confederate cavalry were
sweeping down the Seventh Street pike upon the almost
undefended city. Whenever I walked the little street that
divides the White House from the gloomy old State, War,
and Navy Building, I was following the tall shadow in the
stovepipe hat and the shawl over bent shoulders, that so
often late at night went over to ask Stanton and Halleck
for news from Antietam, Shiloh Landing, and a little town
called Gettysburg.

Now the trains, many every hour, go puffing across the
Potomac. They are bound for Manassas, for Fredericksburg and Richmond; they go north to Frederick and
Harper's Ferry, and down the Shenandoah. I used to see
them from my office window, pulling out for Dixie. They
looked like shuttles weaving the garment of the nation
whole again, knitting the North my ancestors fought for
with the South I loved.

No one could have been much more obscure, in that city
of prestige and public figures, than I was. I had a big desk
among other desks in one of the old red-brick government
buildings along the Mall. I got used to finding cockroaches
in the drawers when I pulled them out, and to the rats that
came out at night to eat the backs off the books for the glue
in them. I ceased to notice the grinding thrum, the sudsy
stink that came in the open window from the building
opposite, where they washed paper money grown too
filthy for circulation.

For the job I had was one that Linnaeus himself might
have envied. It consisted in identifying, as they came into
the office, the pressed specimens which corresponded to the
living plants that the agricultural explorers were sending
back. They might arrive from Ecuador or Nicaragua, from
Siam and Turkestan, Kenya and the Sudan, the Canaries
and remote Yunnan. Manchurian steppe and Brazilian
jungle contributed their quota, from any one of a hundred
families strange to me, of twice ten thousand exotic species.
Bewildered, I plodded; a correct identification might be a
matter of ten minutes, ten hours, even ten days. But for
my search I had at hand the greatest botanical library, the
greatest of herbaria, in the western hemisphere. Further to
enlighten me, there were experts in every field, whom I
might seek out in offices scattered all over the city.

For scientifically Washington is the cerebellum of the
nation. No other capital in the world maintains such a
vast corps of trained scientists. Knowledge, highly spe-
cialized, is here to be had for the asking, at the Bureaus of
Standards, of Mines, of Fisheries, of Entomology, of
Weather, at the Naval Observatory, the Surgeon General's

Office, the Forest Service and the Park Service, the Biological Survey, the Coast and Geodetic Survey, the National
Museum and the Smithsonian. Beside these various
official bureaus — and those among us who criticize their
government may well ask themselves what private enter-
prises can compare with the disinterested administration
of these services — there are centered in Washington independent groups of inquiry, like the Carnegie Institute and
the National Research Council. So that a man setting out
on any path of science in the capital discovers how it
broadens out, becomes a highway with cross avenues of
approach, a very city of thought populous with a confra-
ternity of ideas.

It follows that in Washington I found men of my kind.
Among New York's seven millions the naturalist is a rare
bird; I dare say you could catch most of the local specimens
by dragging a net over the American Museum and Audubon House. In Boston the species seemed to me a little
commoner, much rarer in Chicago. In Washington there is
a dense congregation of them, a whole gabbling rookery of
birds of a feather.

In that young bachelor year I went much abroad with
fellow naturalists. When a worker in the Department had
business that took him into the field, he would call up his
confrères to say that the botanical garden of Buitenzorg in
Java had sent in a request for a medicinal plant that grew
only in the Powdermill bogs of Maryland — and did they
want to come along? It would instantly develop that the
listener had a particular and official reason for collecting
rare beetles of these magnolia bogs. Or that an important
bird record from that Maryland county needed verifica-

tion. Or a series of land snail specimens were required from that very spot.

That's how I got to Licking Banks, where the kingfishers and swallows have nests in the sides of the clay cliff, where the burrowing bees make their home and are parasitized by those curious meloids, the blister beetles, which ambush the bees in flowers and, attaching themselves to the nectar-seeker, are transported to the subterranean nests. And I went to see the bobolinks and ducks settle in fall upon the wild rice of the Eastern Branch, and in spring down into Tidewater Virginia for exquisite little prothonotary warblers at Dyke. Thus too I saw the Patuxent valley, where they are still finding fossils antecedent to the modern flowering plants, those born after the long age of the ferns and cycads. And Plummer's Island, the property of a biological club which maintains on it a special museum devoted to nothing but the biota of that tiny gem in the Potomac.

From these men and in these places I saw how the working scientist puts in practice that faith I had attained, in one growing and indivisible Nature. I began to learn how a local fauna and flora are dealt with by trained naturalists, so as to give all finds a meaning and a correlation. I watched these associates turn up problems and attack them, quartering them and subdividing them, treating them ecologically, seasonally, making a whole out of the close scrutiny of many parts. Myself, I was only a tagger along, mostly silent, happily ignored. What I was seeing was field demonstration of theory I had learned in the classroom. What I felt quiver here was the web of life, dew-hung and brilliant with concepts fresh to me.

A world known previously through single experience or
between the covers of books now tingled with communicating complications. Intellectually, it stretched limitless.
Geographically, it loomed enormous as I looked ahead.
For I knew what possibilities were intended for me when I
was taken into the Office of Foreign Seed and Plant Introduction. Incredulous, I saw them glitter beyond my present daily work.

Beside my duties as a systematic botanist, I was detailed to handle the distribution of the living plants in
which our office dealt. They came in from the ends of the
earth, cradled and cherished. They were sent to be grown
at one of the experiment stations, such of the stock, at
least, as survived the journey. Finally, after years perhaps, they were ready for distribution to private collabora-
tors. If in the course of time they proved their worth —
and how thoroughly now is proved the worth of durum
wheat and avocados, Mongolian elms and Japanese per-
simmons and tung oil trees! — they worked their way into
commercial horticulture, where our office need encourage
them no longer, but could turn to the new, hard problem.

It was for me to try to make a mite support a clamorous
demand. Our plants were given away free, but this was no
Congressional Seed Distribution. After years of work, we
might have only a hundred cuttings to dispense, with thousands asking for them. From every state a forest of hands
was held out for the little we had. These people hungered
for our green shoots as the childless for sons. An ultimate
purpose of our office was to serve them.

The aces, the knights, the sometimes temperamental
stars of this service were the plant explorers. Theirs was a

job of hazard and skill, performed on a bank clerk's salary. They had to be not only trained botanists, but expert horticulturalists, which is a combination not frequent. They had to be linguists and diplomatists, and prepared for hardship and crisis. They had to be young, without hostages to fortune. 'A man with a wife and children doesn't cross a rotted rope bridge over roaring rapids,' said Fairchild warningly to me, 'even if that is the only way to get over.'

I knew that the explorer closest to me in the service had at the beginning of his training given a promise not to marry for ten years. I knew what was expected of me. And that in return I might expect to see some day Andean peaks, or the plains of Gobi. High and fabulous as Kinchinjunga loomed the future toward which I was traveling.

But I shall not see Kinchinjunga now. For near the end of my first year of service, I married.

Now indeed I was learning to know the web of life. I was braided into it.

He who travels alone may travel fastest, but not so far, I think, into living. And it is notable on our journeys, like this present motor trip through the deserts and Rocky Mountain ranges of the Northwest, that while I am at the

wheel, it is she who reads the signposts and points out my
way. So it has always been, with us. I was not turning
aside but straight into my highroad, on that May morning
that was our wedding day.

For happy omen, it was the birthday of Linnaeus, when
all good botanists celebrate by an excursion to the fields for
the gathering, in his memory, of the fairest flowers. Her
hands were filled with white ones; the birds were loud outside the open windows of the empty small stone church on
Gallatin Street, for the day was still fresh at half-past nine
in the morning. But how can any hour be too early for a
man's wedding?

For our brief wedding journey I emptied my small account at the bank, and seriously had the paying teller
transmute this dross into gold pieces. The office granted us
just five days of leave. Five May days, cloudless as if the
little town where we found ourselves had no more tears to
weep. There once courage stormed heights so great that
perhaps no American need ever be so brave again; the
grief of that battle is half-buried there, like the cannon
balls imbedded in the pillars of one of the quiet churches.
Here, I remembered, my grandfather had lain for weeks
with wounds got in the Wilderness. For me all was healed;
and there was nothing in those skies now but swallows,
barn swallows morning and evening and all day, sweeping
the zenith clear, sociably remembering old nests and
steeples, encouraging each other with small words.

Then we were back in Washington, establishing a home
as impromptu as our sudden wedding. For her too this
was a city without ties, a free privacy. At the office I would
think of her walking the summer streets with her market

basket, the streamers of her hat down her back, and say to myself that no one knows her, no one will find her; I have her hidden.

Every fortnight I gave her my four yellow bills, and she put them away in the treatise on ferns. Every evening after supper I would dictate to her my first book, while I washed the dishes for her. She sat at the kitchen table, her fingers flying on the keys, lifted only for an instant to push the dark curls back from her forehead, in the hot summer night. As I talked it loosely, she set it to rights as she put it down. It was like old times, when we had set in type our early writing, alone together up under the gable roof of the high school. It was like the future, all the years of our collaboration to come.

Hotter and hotter the summer grew. The blaze of bright air was like suspended breath; the leaves hung heavy, ready to tremble. In our happiness we were aware that we were waiting. The torrid spell rolled the city in an opal haze of heat. One night the haunting cries of the newsboys came up from the streets. In San Francisco the President was dead. Next day our office was dismissed, the flags lowered. We went out of the city for three days. When we came back the heat was broken, and somehow we were sure. And presently we knew. We were not alone any more.

So of course we had to plan on something cheaper than these rooms, something out of a city that would be no less hot next summer. She went forth daily to look for this. Whether it is to be for years or for only a night on the road, she is infallible in knowing our home when she sees it. This next home was the smallest house I have ever seen.

It grew on the side of a pine-covered hill, like a toadstool pushing up through the earth. The pine wood was a small one, and thin; beyond it lay suburban baldness. But within it were odors of leaf mold and our chimney smoke; the sunset died just over the crest of the hill, and sometimes a troop of cavalry, black against the glow, rode by from Fort Myers with knightly hoofbeats.

The Christmas tree we set in the window was small; no other kind would fit into our toadstool. When the last bright ball was hung and the lights set glowing, we ran outside to see it through the window. You must remember, in such a life as ours, sometimes to step outside it to look at how the lights shine.

May came again. My book was not yet finished, but her task was done. She had seen the night through, around the clock, and I too. There was a lightening in the skies, over beyond the Eastern Branch, beyond Bladensburg and the Powdermill bogs. There was a first shaky rapture of robin song on the hospital lawn. She had wished for a son first, and I for a daughter, and yet I wanted her to have her wish. In the end, it seemed, she always gave me mine.

12

THE LONG GOOD-BYE

THAT life is doubly fortunate in which a man finds himself single in his two main convictions, love and religion. On a bright morning in Montana I could see with happy clarity how straight the road ran behind me and ahead. We were walking, my wife and I, in swinging gait beside a rocky brook walled in by spruces; the valley was a narrow one, here just wide enough for brook and road together. Its walls were steep; night still lay upon the westward-facing slope in a long cool shadow, and there the dew was undisturbed upon the sage; from the slope that faced the morning issued the smell of sun-burned pine. Cleaner air no one has ever breathed, or trod more honest earth. My companion was the only woman I have ever wanted,

and I have talked in poor parables if I have not been plain
about the fact that Nature, in its most timeless sense, is
my religion.

This long trough in the Rockies, pungent with sage and
spruce, was the Gallatin Valley. As I looked back, on that
crystal morning, I saw it, for all the turnings we had taken,
as a continuation of Gallatin Street where we began. We
were stepping along now with the fresh and even stride that
makes fatigue look farther off than the most distant crest.
But the pace has not always been this.

Now once again I halted and she was patient with me. I
did not know for sure what I would find when I strayed off
the road; I was looking for something I had never seen.
Here the trees were tall enough for it, the moss deep
enough. Say if you like that I had caught its faint scent
without recognition, but when I parted the undergrowth
beneath the conifers I saw it at once — the delicate trailing
vine with small round leaves and tiny nodding pink bells
hung in pairs from a single stalk. Twin-flower, favorite of
the jovial great master of Uppsala whose anniversary is
ours — *Linnaea borealis*, his flower of the north.

Not all the signs along the way are, if you read them
right, as pleasing. The day before, in Yellowstone, I saw
the awful truth let out — that we are all dancing on the
pretty surface of an old-style inferno. Those fumaroles and
solfataras and bubbling mud baths at which we tourists
enjoyably gaped are enough to frighten the God-fearing.
A geyser is all hell spitting at heaven. It isn't the spittle
that counts, but the contempt behind it. Even the rainbow
in Old Faithful is merely accidental beauty. That jet
springs from nether regions that seethe with forces as

indifferent as are the violent stars, to the lightly rooted
life upon our queasy planet.

But life undaunted marches right to the mouth of the
pit. Around earth so quaky that signs warn away a footfall, I saw gentians burning blue. I saw the algae along the
steaming run-off, wavering their banners in sulphurous
seepage. For life fills this unfinished and imperfect sphere
to the dangerous limits. It brims to the top of the cup, and
wherever it occurs, in moiling waters or spectacular ero-
sion, it is the finest thing in any scene.

So that if life is what you believe in, life essential and
ultimately unknowable, you have evidences everywhere
that it must prevail. And it is to me a private cause for
alleluia any time that I newly discover it come to flower, as
now in the minute perfection of *Linnaea.*

The two pink bells, like a mirror reflection, trembling
nodded back to me from between my fingers. Over and
over, through the years, some slight thing in the natural
world has surprised me with this living look of my little
daughter.

Of all our children, hers was the babyhood I knew best.
I was so close to her then I almost caught a glimpse of the
world as she must have seen it, bright as dew with the in-

nocence on it. I could bathe and dress her; in the streets, when my wife and I both left the house, I carried her wrapped in a pink blanket, the tiny head bobbing over my shoulder, so exquisite that people turned and looked after her.

In those first weeks and months of her, we had one regular appointment, she and I; this was at two o'clock in the morning, the time for a necessary extra feeding. When the alarm clock woke me I would smother it; then in the dark I went to gather up the light warm burden and bring it to her mother, who was still sleeping the thirsty sleep of one who must repair the cost of a whole life. While the child nursed and my tired wife drowsed, I sat by the bed and kept watch of them for twenty dark and silent minutes. Altogether those minutes made a piece of life I shall not lose. It was summer then; I was not cold, but I had to fight for vigilance against the ache to sleep. I used to watch the stars, through the scanty pines whose boughs and needles broke up the constellations. There, beyond the sheltering blanket of our atmosphere, stretched coldness indeed, the icy black of outer space. And here was I, in the snuggest of Nature's many mansions; here were the three of us together in the night. Three, you know, is the number that will just enclose an area, just balance anything that can stand alone.

If we could go back in life, to the moments that we cherish, we would find them, no doubt, strangely thin. If I could return to those two o'clock vigils, I should have to leave behind me much of the best I have — my three sons, my job in life, that sends me every morning to my desk impatient for it as a horse to feel its master in the saddle. I wouldn't have about me that apple of my eye, my working library, nor my study with its fire and its long window looking on the pines and mountains, all at the heart of this spacious old nautilus of a house beside the Pacific. No, if I am given to illusions, they are not about the past but the future. It is my favorite tense. I hope I shall not be afraid to live in it to the end.

My mother loved to look ahead like that; they tell me she was full of bright new plans within an hour of her final breath. One thing she loved to plan was a new home, a new house; perhaps her zest for this was handed down from grandfather's grandiose dreams of building. Now she foresaw for us a larger home, which she and my father could share when they would. So they gave me the little money they had saved as my share of bequest, and in a countrified 'development' on the hills above Cherrydale, I bought a bungalow.

Yes, in my innocence I engaged myself for payments on a house that had not even settled yet, and was never built to live in but to sell. I accepted the assurance that land values would rise (though nothing rose there but the taxes). I agreed to terms whereby I was to go on paying the original interest even as I retired the principal. I swallowed sinker and pole.

But a fish cannot be eaten twice. They may threaten to scatter my bones, but I will not buy seven feet of earth to bury them in. How free I am, I know from the head-shakings of the bound, who menace me with a homeless old age. They remind me of the fable of the ant and the cricket. But an ant cannot dance and sing if she would; she is too busy repairing her dwelling so that she can die in it.

I can live where I please, and when I am ready to go, nobody has my foot in a trap. I could go back to Virginia and
tweak the nose of the County Collector. I could come and
live in Montana, and sometimes I think I'll do that. It's
a fine address. So is Arizona, Maine, Louisiana, and I
like the Indian place names in Washington State. You
may find such wild syllables on my letterhead one day.

But I only attained this unrepentant state of anarchy by
serving my term as a good suburbanite.

In Virginia, beyond Cherrydale, I sowed and mowed and
watered my lawn. I planted morning-glories and zinnias,
and worried over my crocuses. I went to meetings about
better sewers and water-main assessments. I shoveled the
snow a city block to the nearest neighbor's, and then because he did not carry on, I shoveled it another block to the
trolley line. I carried the ashes to the holes in the road and
filled them in. I fought the fires in the vacant lots.

My wife did the counterpart of my task, within the
house. It was filled with pretty things, wedding gifts,
things from our childhood homes, new things hardly won.
But what we most loved, in those years, was the sunset
above the winter tree-tops down the valley, and the smell
of the Appalachian earth when spring broke through it.
There were azaleas and mayflower in the hill behind the
house, and blueberries for Celia and me to pick while her
mother stirred the muffins. On summer evenings we set
our table on the grassy terrace, and in the dusk the tree
swallows skimmed above our heads, and underfoot the cat
played with the crickets. At the bottom of our hill was a
spring that came out of the roots of a great tulip tree; I
went down there for drinking water because I liked the

taste in it of the granite underpinnings of the far-off Blue Ridge. When autumn cleared the air we could see away and away to the west, to dark pines on sketchy ridges. But we could never quite see the mountains.

When I bought the house I had a job with the permanence of civil service behind it. Three months later my immediate superior was about to leave the Department for wider scope with a big tropical fruit company; this man was my explorer friend. He had stood by me at the altar; before he went he spoke his mind for my sake. There were no shining mountains in my prospect, and he told me so. I might move up, in years to come, to the desk beyond this one with the cockroaches in it, when its present owner, grown gray in the service, should die or retire. My friend knew what I wanted to do, and he said I could do it. As a last favor, he offered to sack me.

I let him. My wife, with no regrets or sign of fear, put the last little sheaf of yellow bills in the fern book.

I thought I could become a writer by writing what somebody required of me; I was sure I had to have a job. As though you learned to swim by standing on the shore and rowing one foot over the edge in the stream! So every day I started out with the commuters, job-hunting. I learned the soft pneumonic cold of Washington that winter, and how it can reach the heart as well as the lungs. I tried for work so hard I left myself, body or mind, no chance to get at writing. The thought of my debts made me jogtrot all the way toward the admonishing whistle of the morning trolley.

Spring came, that precocious, ardent, trustworthy spring that begins only south of the Potomac. There was a bird I noticed every morning on my way to the cars, tumbling out his joy from a persimmon tree on a vacant corner. A song-sparrow, he was. Bird, I thought, you must not talk to me like that. Life is the price of anthracite; reality is bills in the mail. I must hurry and not listen. I must not believe you.

The maples flowered, the soft red maples of my Carolina Blue Ridge. On the naked wood they budded scarlet; they burst out golden, pollen-laden, and set fruit, the first delicate keys like the wings of stone-flies. Trees, I thought, too long you have beguiled me. You have deceived me with your scarlet proclamations. Tend to your business and keep your sap up, and I will tend to mine. Though my sap is in my boots.

So I ran faster every morning. And still I had no job.

The song-sparrow shouted after me. I stopped, my bones dissolving with the sunshine; I looked up at a bright and gentle sky, and began to listen to him. Up on the tracks my trolley car went rattling by. The last bus spluttered down the highway to Rosslyn and the Key bridge. I turned and walked back home.

I sat down and wrote about the maples. Then I wrote about the song-sparrow — just a page about each. These I took in to a Washington newspaper office, and asked for and amazingly was granted a chance to do such pages, three a week, seeing the year around, like an almanac.

I wrote about frog's eggs on the first day of spring, down along the Potomac. About the whitethroat, the bird I did not know in childhood who sang on my mountain-top in the long rain. I wrote of the swallows over my roof-top,

and old springhouses on Virginia farms. Of tulip trees that
cast their big gold leaves and of stopping by a run to watch
the bubbles under the ice, and nibbling the bark of sweet
shrub. Of burrowing bees, and blind beetles, and milk
quartz. It was an everyday world that I had to write of,
lying just beyond the suburbs. I used ruefully to think,
when I sat down at my desk, of Hudson's pampas, his
Magellanic eagle owls, rheas and wood-hewers and crested
screamers; yes, and of Bates with his Amazonian butterflies and Wallace with his birds-of-paradise. I have been
fortunate in never having been obliged to live with ugliness, but neither have I ever adventurously known anti-
podean marvels to report upon. Mine has all been small
game.

Those short first pieces flittered into the light of print
and out again, transient as any newspaper work. They
deserved no more. But they were pages of life as I lived
it, fearfully, slogging the low woods with my worries, as I
loved it, hotly, walking the hills in the wind. Celia's hand
would be wrapped around my forefinger. She learned to
name whatever we found, and when she heard the black-
eyed Susan had a Latin name she regarded this as a high
joke, and always said *Rudbeckia hirta* for the fun of it.
Flowers she never tore or crumpled; she could be content
with one for half a day, touching its center gravely with
an affirming finger.

I was selling now to other papers, and to small magazines; my wife's writing earned too. What profits we were
making were unsound, because they depended on so few
and such uncertain markets. So that an editorial frown
could in those days make me literally tremble. I never

worked in tranquillity, and what I wrote was not much of it worth reading. But we were at least hard working and professional about it, though at my desk in the dining-room I had to listen to the cook frying and mumbling, and ordering more butter on the phone. Louise had no place to write but our bedroom, where she perched on the bed. Between us trotted Celia, like a copy boy, carrying exchanges of manuscript and bringing me toys to mend.

Then one day a Philadelphia 'slick' sent a check in three fat figures, and our seamy finances appeared to us turned right side out and glittering. On the strength of such golden prospects, we dared to have a son. We were wrong about the prospects, but never about Malcolm.

Outside the window by my desk, I can remember, there was a mountain laurel bush. I stared at it twice ten thousand times, searching a word, searching a dream. It was a young bush, I suppose; or the soil was thin. Anyway, it never came to flower. Every year we expected great things of it in May. But it did not bloom. Just once or twice the bush and I both thought — but, no.

The climate certainly was not favorable. One year Celia had pneumonia; her fever chart is a line that is still a red moat in my eye. The next year her mother had it, and five days after the ambulance took her to the hospital, it came back for me. And convalescence is a long grade. We were sick; we were financially bogged; we were hungry for sunshine, and for some land where art is native and deep-rooted.

Better artists than most who went overseas in the twenties have known that thirst and slaked it long — Tarkington, Lowell, Longfellow, Irving, Cooper, Motley, they went. Emerson went, with Thoreau scoffing at his back. Lanier was sick with longing for Germany and England, and died with it. Hudson, an American by birth, could not wait to get away from the pampas he loved so well in retrospect. Frank Chapman and John Burroughs have recorded their hunger for Europe's Nature. It was the European flora that I wanted so to see. How explain that a man may ask for foxglove and Canterbury bell, narcissus and hyacinth under old olives, scarlet anemones and saffron crocus, when all these are to be admired in home gardens, improved, enlarged, doubled, and hybridized? But such garden flowers are beautiful words torn from their context. I wanted the flora, intact, of the Mediterranean poets, the northern herbalists, Linnaeus himself. Until I knew it I felt, as a plantsman, uneducated, unfulfilled, and deprived of heritage.

So we prepared to go. My wife's patrimony was now added to her other stakes. The little house smiled at us with flowers in the vases, books on the table; we closed the door for the last time, leaving it to strangers, not knowing we would never see it so again. One child I carried, and one ran ahead. Now forward was the only way. Now the bush must flower, or be cut down.

The ship sailed at midnight. Our heads together at the porthole, she and I watched the dock swing backward like a closing door. Behind us in the hot little cabin the children slept. A spume of strangers' farewell cheers rose from the pier's end. Deck and dock flung back adieus. 'Enjoy yourself in Paris! Write me a postal card!'

The water widened; the audience crowd slid out of sight and hearing; we passed into darkness where only a few dim lights showed long wrinkled reflections on the oily Hudson. Suddenly my wife leaned out and called —

'Good-bye!'

Her young voice rang astonished, courageous. The side of a retreating warehouse gave it back. That echo is still in my ears.

I drew her away, into the light, to look at Celia sleeping in the gold and the brown of her curls. We could not know that she had just ten days to live. In his own warm sleep our boy made a little chuckling sound, reminding us that he was also there.

Montana is the third largest state in America. It has only some half a million inhabitants. That means that every child, woman, and man in the state has a quarter square mile to himself, which leaves room for thoughts to go seeking.

Montana is rich, in its own way. There must be a thousand great trees for every inhabitant, a million blades of grass; by actual statistics there is a horse for every one, there are two head of cattle for each human, and five sheep. No one can say what the proportion may be of man to the great wild beasts — deer and moose and elk and antelope, grizzlies, black bears, lynx, bob-cats and

cougars and timber wolves. But all Montana's proportions are large. It has more great plains and high prairie
than any other state in the union. As for mountains, the
name Montana means its mountains. Their bases are
rooted in the north. They begin, leisurely and confident,
at that life zone which southern mountains barely attain
when they aspire highest. Montana mountains start
there; they soar up into the arctic-alpine zone; on their
fingers, lifted as if to test the wind, they catch the flying
snows. And, come to poise there like northern birds ven-
turing south, grow little gleaming flowers of Greenland and
Ungava and Keewatin.

Colorado is high, having more peaks within its borders
than any other state. Wyoming is wide, with the breadth
of the plains between the Big Horns and the Grand Tetons.
California is handsome, with a splendor of success. It
takes all three adjectives to describe Montana.

Leaving the Gallatin Valley, we tested this greatness,
traveling over Montana's passes and through its long valley corridors, across the old buffalo plains of short grass
that breathed hot breath upon us, and up into the brandy
and ice of coniferous air. We thirsted in it, waterless, and
we plunged our hands into its snows.

And, up under the borderline, we came at last to Glacier
National Park.

The Grand Canyon is carven deep by the master hand;
it is the gulf of silence, widened in the desert; it is all time
inscribing the naked rock; it is the book of earth. But
Glacier belongs not to earth but to the sky. It is cameo to
the Canyon's intaglio, upthrust to the Canyon's profund-
ity. Not wind or water, but the great axe blade of ice cut
this out of aboriginal rock.

A mountain is as high as it looks. For all the ranges I have seen, I could always imagine something higher, a peak that would tower to the zenith. Not in the Alps or Colorado or California did I ever see mountains of that nightmare height I dreamed of and was afraid to see.

On a bright morning I drove in from the level of this world through the gates of the Park. The sunlight glanced on the flat sprays of larch and arbor vitae as we wound through the forest past the long still lake; the brooks were clear as glass, dimpled with the splash and bubble of trout. Up out of distance where they waited rose the bastions, gray stone seven thousand feet straight up to the impersonal threat of glaciers in the sun. As we approached them, they climbed into the sky, looming up higher, higher, touching, I thought, the place where the Pole Star hangs. They hung above me, the implacable fulfillment of a dream too bold.

Once under them, they spared us the sight of their greatness; the forests clothed it; the boles and the sweeping boughs marched past. The car, ascending, took a hawk's way presently, soaring in a spiral, up and up, till the giant conifers of the valley bottoms were a carpet of moss, till the ears rang, stoppered, till the trees shrank back from the past gales, leaned leeward, flattened like punished great cats, grew cretin, stopped. Up till the presence of the glaciers breathed cold upon us, and the sound of our passage rang against the immediate ice.

In the ultimate passes the air is so thin, so pure it catches at the heart like an exalting premonition. Here above timberline the brows of the mighty gray bastions bend near. There is no frown upon them, but they are stern. Between them, in the high-slung cradle that the glaciers have carved, bloom the arctic-alpine flowers of this chill and austere paradise.

I would no more attempt to keep an hour by pressing the flower of it for a keepsake than I would fancy that I had a crumb of life put away with a baby's shoe. I do collect for sure identification, and small specimens I am apt to slip into the manual that I may have in hand (in the Parks I carry a collector's permit). So between the leaves I ruffle here at my desk I now find the fragile mummy of a glacier lily that grew, a single flower nodding at the top of its stalk, with petals flaring backward and upward as though this were some six-pointed golden star still falling and just about to touch the mountain sod. In pages listing the *Silene* clan, lies a bit of dark rose-purple that was moss campion which, scorning the lowlands, consents to grow nowhere that snow does not lie seven months of the year; two months of clear ground suffice its small intense life. A white cousin, an arenaria, danced in the wind from a rosette of leaves no bigger than a mouse's ear; it is here. I shake the pages of the book; a chalice flower drops out, and one called white dryad, shivering dyrad of the north, for which even the New Hampshire peaks are too low; it likes the highest summits of Colorado, swings north across the Canadian Rockies to Alaska, completes the polar circuit through Siberia, and is found again alighted on the Alps. Here is a sprig of red heather, and a pussy-toes clothed in silvery wool, American representative of edelweiss. Also a saxifrage; the name is proud, it means 'breaker of rocks,' yet this is a frail thing with only the unconscious strength of a child that will be born.

We could not linger in the pass, not even for the flowers. The snow, the granite, and the rare atmosphere made the blood run colder from the laboring heart. An ominous breath from above chilled the sweat of climbing at a high altitude. The sky, so near, which had been purest blue, closed like an eye as the clouds fell. Trailing dark rain, they met together; they clapped with a sound of great rocks tumbling around us. We were sent away, down from this too high place.

Below, beside one of those enameled lakes that lie at the finger tip of each long impressed valley, midsummer was a gentle thing again. We sat late, on our balcony of the long log hotel, in the northern twilight. The encircling summits slowly gave up the counterglow. This is not sunset, but that after-light above the dust of living which the mountain-tops alone, peering over the rim of the world, could still perceive long after the valley was deep in shadow. We were in the latitude of Labrador, of the southern tip of Kamchatka, and the Russian steppes. It was barely past the summer solstice, and at half-past nine I could still decipher the small print of the flora on my knee. But I did not read, nor did my wife and I have any need to talk. Before us glimmered the lake waters, and the big black triangle of the alp beyond lay reflected in them, making a block of darkness in the silver dusk. The stars were pricking forth, but the day, and the life in it, were not quite done. A single bird persisted in his song, a white-crowned sparrow.

The farther crests were now gone cold and gray. Lake and sky could still find some thin light. The bird sang on, in the deepening night, impetuous, unquenchable, confident that there was one who listened.

I looked into my wife's still face and saw upon her lips
the old wondering demand.

Where does the spirit go? It is the question cried under
the first blow of loss. It is asked over and over, in the
agony that comes when the numbness of that concussion
wears off. And it remains, in the wide aftermath, when
the absence lengthens out and out, and the great silence
deepens.

But of all circumstances under which to formulate that
serene thing called a philosophy, those of bereavement are
the most unpromising. It should have been prepared in
hours of happiness and good fortune, when thought is
clear and the heart steady. A sound philosophy can endure the shock of disaster.

Those, of course, who can accept as indubitable the
promises of the church are fortunate, for it makes the most
definite of all promises. Only when we too travel the one-
way road will those promises ever be verified, and many
who are grief-stricken seek assurances requiring less absolute faith. Some ask the family physician; he is likely to
give a consoling answer, whether he believes it or not, for
it is his business to comfort the suffering. Others go to
spiritualistic mediums, and some who do so are able to

find comfort in the persuasion that they actually get in touch with the departed. And sometimes, I find, the bereaved turn to the naturalist, to ask, What happens to life when it dies?

After all, the business of the naturalist is to understand life. He has learned to analyze it and control it and predict its actions. In the laboratory he can perform sundry curious feats with it. He can keep a chicken heart beating long after the poor fowl's carcass is no more. He can graft life onto life; there is a rumor abroad that he will some day synthesize it, though no genuine biologist has ever claimed that he was in sight of such a miracle. One thing is certain: the naturalist's business is with life, and since death is a part of life, he should be willing to face the question of life after death and try to answer it according to his science. If mine will not provide me with a philosophy able to endure the shocks and tests of our common lot, then it is not worth the years it cost me to acquire it.

Science does not, like religious faith, give absolute answers to the unknowable. The belief of science is confined to earthly evidence. This is the limitation of the whole scientific viewpoint. It is also what makes a scientist's statements trustworthy. When an astronomer predicts an eclipse, to the minute and half-second, at some date a hundred years from now, nobody doubts it will take place as predicted, though we shall none of us be here to verify it. Adhering religiously to its own tenets, science has earned this trust placed in its utterance. It will not tell even a small and very white lie. Not even to comfort the suffering. But science is not disbelief. It never destroys a truth. In truth, it could not. It states what it knows, and it dares to suggest those possibilities which evidence makes probable.

The natural sciences, of course, are not so simple as astronomy. The forms and deeds of life are neither so precise nor so permanent as the behavior of the stars. Whatever life is (and nobody can define it) it is something forever changing shape, fleeting, escaping us into death. Life is indeed the only thing that can die, and it begins to die as soon as it is born, and never ceases dying. Each of us is constantly experiencing cellular death. For the renewal of our tissues means a corresponding death of them, so that death and rebirth become, biologically, right and left hand of the same thing. All growing is at the same time a dying away from that which lived yesterday.

The life of the race as a whole is a perpetual moving forward and upward. The living coral on the summit of a reef is founded on the bones of its ancestors. In half a billion years or more, however, life has been continuous in the race of corals. For a million years or more, it has been continuous in man. Part, at least, of our immortality is in our children. As it is a biological law that life comes only from life, so each generation just touches the next, with the God-like finger of procreation. Our children are our very selves, miraculously extended out into the time stream, where our own mortality cannot touch them. To the naturalist the 'continuity of the germ plasm' is a very real kind of immortality. Heredity is a cord which runs without a break down the ages, while the individuals are but beads strung upon it. The beads, brought into existence by a rapturous instinct, inevitably fall from the cord at last, by inexorable law. The cord alone remains, and is greater than any one bead, or the sum of all the beads.

So the son who may lose a parent need not ask, 'Where has my father gone?' 'Where is the bright and loving spirit that was my mother?' They will be in good measure, and for the most practical of all purpose, in himself. Their spirits, their hopes, the aim and end of their lives, their very flesh and blood will be their boys. So too are more remote ancestors. We go wondering about immortality, unconscious that we are ourselves immortality.

From afar we can see the place where the rainbow comes down to earth, and we speak of the end of the rainbow as the place where all the gold must lie. But those who are in that spot cannot see the heavenly color. They see no more than that the sun is shining through the rain. So I think we are all in the rainbow of human immortality, and do not appreciate it.

This earth and all upon it, this material world, is known to be composed of some ninety-six primary chemical elements, just as the alphabet has twenty-six letters. The combinations of these letters into words, the combinations of words into meanings, is infinite. So life, which is perpetually disintegrating, forever recombines its elements. Of all this material of living there is no loss anywhere, only a great cycle, an overturn, an equal sharing. The leaf of yesterday is the flower of tomorrow.

True, the elements are not themselves alive. The life force is an intangible thing that dwells in the material. We can measure the amounts of material in any living organism. We have, admittedly, no yardstick for the life force, neither can the Bureau of Standards weigh it with the most

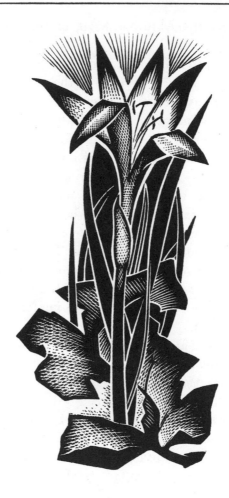

delicate instruments. But this much the naturalist knows:
the quantity of life in the world has never diminished.

Peering back into the misty beginnings of time, he finds
that, a billion years ago, there were just a few organisms on

earth. They were the lowliest, most unthinking, unfeeling, and primitive living beings imaginable. Very slowly at first they increased, gaining hard-won mastery over the lifeless environment. With every age the abundance, the variety, the beauty and strength of life have all increased. Life is like a great chorus, whose melody begins with a single slender voice that is joined by one singer after another, until at last it swells out in a tremendous, irresistible anthem.

But what of the one human voice listened for, longed for, not heard now any more in all that chorus?

Again I attempt only a biological answer, without denying other beliefs. Life is energy — perhaps a unique sort of energy or perhaps only an intricate, compactly impounded, domesticated form of the one great solar energy on which we all depend.

Half a billion years ago tremendous charges of energy leaped out of the sun, just as they are still doing, and were absorbed by the fern forests of the Coal Age. The plants fell where they had rooted, but the energy that went into their lean height and their spreading fronds was locked up in storage, under the rocks. Today the powerhouse burns that coal and sends that ancient energy through the wires, to light, let us say, a study lamp. There one might think it was finally expended. But I am not sure of that. If the light slants into a bacteriologist's microscope, if it illumines the page of a minister composing a fine sermon, if it is concentrated on the manuscript of Doctor Einstein's next book, who will say that in a new form, light is not shed again, perhaps down the ages?

Life, after all, does not take death for an answer. Of all

things the most natural, life has all the qualities I would look for in the Supernatural.

And still one who has called good-bye into the dark must ask, Where did it go, that unique individual life? To what unthinkable destination?

A human life has been compared to a burning candle, of a length definite but mercifully unknown when it is set alight. The flame burns its way down through the fuels supplied to it. But the flame is not the wax, and it is not the wick. Finally the candle must burn out. The wax went up in smoke. The wick turned to ash. But the light from the flame did not turn to ash and smoke. Where did it go?

It has radiated away where our poor eyes no longer see it. 'How far that little candle throws his beams!' said the wise Portia.

In theoretical astronomy, if I understand rightly, once light has begun to travel, it travels on and on. Once a light from earth has quit the earth's short cone of shadow, it is merged in the great flood stream from the sun. As it came from the sun in the first place, from the source of all energy, all life on earth, so it rejoins the great radiation. And the tiny heat of that candle, which warmed the hands that cradled it from draft — that too has gone where I take it you and I are going, into the common fund of warmth and light.

For one, for two of us, this was not cold comfort. To another, it may seem to be hedging wide around the problem. Do I, or do I not believe in the survival of personality?

I do.

The only woman I ever loved as much as I love my wife took in her last breath in a sudden gallant gasp some years ago. But her personality, which deeply influenced, surely, a thousand people, is just as vivid today as when her quick step sounded, the candlelight looked out of her eyes into mine. I hear every month from someone who loved her, often a stranger, who writes to tell of some witty thing she said, some kindness she showed, some wisdom she let fall. People who knew her only long ago remember her voice and her gestures, even her costumes. Her personality lives for them, as for me. She is more alive to me at this moment than are half the people I see and talk to. Yesterday someone asked me how long my mother had been dead. Dead! Is she dead?

If I go to see a friend still here in the flesh, he may be away from home; he may be out of humor, asleep, in the company of people I do not care for. Not so when I visit those who have been transposed. They come out instantly to meet me, vivid, radiant with all the qualities that made them dear. If it is a gentleman who loved a jest, I find that he is always dryly twinkling over it. If it is a child who loved to run over the grass, she is forever running ahead, with flying hair.

Then is it only I, with my loving memory, that re-creates her? Is she only in my heart? I know that I will never again see the sun laughing in her four-year-old curls, and yet I cannot, with scientific certainty, say that she is nowhere any more but in my heart. In all things little and gay and innocent I find again the feet like rain, the laugh like brooks, the eyes like gentians. Life, it would seem, is at its old trick of escaping, changing, transmuting into some other lovely shape an imperishable element. At least, what is gone does not, either to my reason or my instinct, seem really gone. I offer this evidence for what it is worth to you.

13

DOWN

FROM HIGH PASSES

LONG after the sparrow was silenced and darkness was complete, I lay awake in my bed, feeling the upthrust of the mountains around me, and the distance I had attained. For the arid eastern face of the Lewis Range, looking out across the starlit sagebrush toward the morning, is nearer to Hudson's Bay than to the Gulf of Mexico; it is nearer to the delta of the Mackenzie, where the golden plovers nest, than to the gentle Appalachians that were home to half my childhood. Its other home, that old house on Lake Michigan, lay distant from me now by one of the greatest open plains on the planet, great

as the steppe between the Tian Shan Mountains of Tibet
and the Caspian Sea. From here, I thought, you could fly
by plane to Teheran, via the North Pole, faster than to
Paris via New York.

But we would be turning westward, in the morning.
And between us and the open Pacific lay seven mountain
ranges, the Lewis and the Flathead, the Mission and the
Bitterroots, the Wenatchees, the Cascades and the Olym-
pics. More peaks than ever shut the barbarians from Italy.

So that here, high under the northern border of my
country, I felt remote, as I had never felt with all the Atlantic between me and the scenes where I grew up. In
those days an American in Europe had merely come home,
after all, on a visit to his ancestors and to a domicile that
no longer had room for his young length — as you come
back from college and jackknife on the sofa beside the
Christmas tree. If he had had familiarly around him the
evidences of his European heritage, he discovered a recognizable color and warmth, even coziness, in continental
life. And those of us who went to France in the twenties
and thirties found spread for us the last grace and ease of
the Republic. There for five years I was at home.

They were not years of travel. At fifteen with six other
boys I had traveled in Europe, chiefly afoot; we took our
picaresque pleasure in city and village, cathedral and port,
and nowhere staked a claim or left a shadow. At thirty I
lived in Europe. With my wife, I made a home there; I
saw one child die there and two born there. I worked
there, mining in darkness for the undiscovered lode. I
tasted sheer lotus-fed bliss there, and the hard, painful joy
by which powers come to birth, and desperate fear. The

fear that sends a man to walk the streets alone at night,
till they will let him into the hospital room again, where a
cold wind out of eternity kept two thin flames of life
whipped level for four weeks. The streets I walked were
twisted and narrow, full of antique smells and dark-
skinned people talking a patois, and though a month before I had loved this for home, I cursed the dirty cobbles
in my longing to hear an American ambulance come clanging over them to carry those two to some twentieth-cen-
tury safety. I loved the people too, until at the end the
pretty courtesy of merchants turned nasty as they saw us
in trouble, and fear came back again — the fear, this time,
that grows as a last fund of money dwindles.

On that old sod steeped with all human joys and terrors
I knew beauty too, a deep-dyed beauty that is Europe's
own. Of olive groves the Romans planted two thousand
years ago, of snowy Alps seen across a bight the color of a
peacock's breast, of Dauphiné's alpine meadows, Savoy's
lakes, and of Provence once more, and the welcome of an
old song floating out of the farmyard of the *mas* across the
valley from our own low roof. I had nightingales in my
garden there, every day in April and May, and the soft
bells and baaing of flocks going by on the road. And later,
at our villa down on the coast, I had friends, German,
Russian, French, English, and their talk in the warm darkness under the yew tree, with the lap of waves on the
promenade to fill good silences between. It seemed to me
in that Riviera city that I was someone visiting an old
mansion by the sea, filled with wonderful and difficult
characters, and I wrote about them, novels of outside
looking in, at Europe in the twenty years' armistice. Some

of the sharpest pleasure of my life went into the struggle to
write those books. It was not till foreign life was put behind me that I recognized that its complex story was not
mine to tell.

The end, the reluctant, wrenched, and desperate end to
those five colored years began in fall. Only they never use
that hickory-bark Americanism there. They say autumn,
or their version of it, from *autumnus* of the elegiac Roman
poets, that has the sound of the tomb in it. That is when
the fading leaves of the plane trees drift sodden in the
pessimistic avenues, and women in black veils hurry
through the streets with their chrysanthemums for soldiers' graves.

I was as far now from succeeding at my chosen task as
when I came here, or more exactly, I was five years more
of a failure. My wife, cradling a child who kept alive on
will and love, had even less health than she had brought.
Money was gone, markets remote and indifferent. The
older little boys had solemn faces that shocked me with a
sense of what might lie before them. Walking beneath the
purpling grapes in the long arbor by our seaside house, I
heard the autumn song of the famed European redbreast,
a wistful whisper like talking to himself. And, God, I
thought, will I never hear an American crow again? Raucous and bold as Andrew Jackson, black as Uncle Tom,
wise and full of pranks as Old Abe himself? I wanted
safety in blue distance, illimitable, uninhabited. I wanted
that thing there is no room for in all the treasure box of
western Europe — the grandeur of free solitude. I wanted
to smell Wisconsin north woods again, odor of sunburnt
grass and balsam boughs, raspberries cool with the woods,

lake water icy to the wrists. I wanted to breathe Canada
in the wind, the American wind that peels the clouds down
to the horizon and tucks them under the belt of the world,
that skies every hardwood leaf, and dries the air till
Labrador comes clear from Belle Isle.

'I should think,' remarked the frank and handsome
stranger who, on the strength of a liking for our books,
had asked us to a polite luncheon in Monte Carlo, 'that
you two would be wanting to go back to America, these
days when there's a war scare every week.'

She had hair the color the maples would be turning, and
eyes you would not lie to, and though we had never seen
her till we shook hands half an hour before, my wife looked
up and quietly said we had just francs enough for another
week's food. The maples flamed, I thought, a little redder,
and the inquiring eyes cleared off like an October sky. For
an American like that, even a hard thing does not seem to
be too hard to do; even a long shot was worth believing in.
And money lent as she lent it, paid back as I slowly paid
it, rings true as the purest gold two people can traffic in.

So, in November, our storm-tossed, homeward little ship
made port. Malcolm and Mark, stout-hearted sailors in
round navy caps, trotted before us down the gangplank.
My wife followed, with the terrifyingly light bundle that
was Noel. At her heels I crossed over that last strip of
uneasy water, and came home.

But in the dawn, on the train, I woke, and I have never
felt so utterly remote. The borrowed money had sufficed
to buy us tickets to the prairie grove where loving welcome
would not fail. Now in the first gray light I shoved up
the stiff curtain and looked out upon the midlands where

I was to live. There lay my country, cold, bald, flat, and bleak. No snow had fallen yet; no leaf was left. The land was a closed fist, showing me its knuckles. The farms and small towns, obdurately ugly, gave at this hour no sign of life; the roads were rutted, icy, and untraveled. But here my lines, apparently, were laid. I pulled the shade down and tried again to sleep. In that next hour I felt a drearier distance from my own climate than I have ever felt in a lifetime spent in many places.

Remoteness I had discovered early, on my mountaintop down in the Blue Ridge, a loneliness the wood thrush reverently underscored. Only in that gentled way is the south lonely, like something forgotten and well content to be. But, for the solitude I used to ache for over in Europe, one must go north, as far north as these Montana ranges where twilight fades so slowly that a sparrow likes to sing at ten o'clock. The light so long drawn out increases the purity and the strength of isolation. Time itself seems rarefied, as if there were a drop of vacuum between each tick of the seconds.

Here at the top of the map, amid the glaciers, we had reached the high point, the halfway point, of our expedition. Now we must go down, and away. For a place like Glacier, which you wait years to see and ardently spend strength and money to attain, is somehow centrifugal. Or, like a great swell of sea, it lifts you, gloriously, and then rolls you out and off, down onto the beach.

So we set out upon the homeward way — a long way, seventeen hundred miles by the route we were taking. As far by mileage, in climate, in feeling, as the Green Mountains of Vermont from the everglades of Florida. But with only three cities starring the long road. And almost every mile of it, from the lodgepole pines and Engelmann spruces on the arid eastern slope of the Lewis Range, to the redwoods and Monterey pines of the San Simeon country only three hours from home, would lead us through forest. As the first half of our trip had been all across the deserts — creosote bush in the south, sagebrush in the north, greasewood desert in the alkaline basin — so now we were never for long to leave the trees. Our car, at the top of the continental divide, stooped like a prairie falcon for a descending glide, and we swept between the boles of giant canoe cedars scattering light from their flat sprays. White pines, pagoda-shaped, hung the shadows with their glimmering tassels. Larch trees taller than the tallest sailing mast closed in about us with their feathery deciduous foliage. We had entered the aisles of the greatest forest on the planet.

There are forests wider, like the Siberian, but that is low, monotonous, and thin. There are forests of more fabulous variety, like the Brazilian, but though it spawns two thousand five hundred species of trees, one valuable tree to an acre is often the best that the *caatingas*, the *gapo*, and all the other Amazonian forests have to show. And not one of them is a sequoia, or a sugar pine, sweet-sapped, giant-boled, soaring a hundred and eighty feet in the air, king of all pines anywhere. Nor yet a Douglas fir, the most valuable tree in the world, second only to the sequoias in height and age, and seeming with its columnar strength to support the half-hidden sky. It was a jackal, as I remember my Aesop, that twitted the lioness about having only one whelp, whereat the great cat answered, 'Yes, but mine is a *lion.*'

No trees in the world rise so tall as these. Nowhere else grow so many kinds of conifer; one half of all the pines in the world are found in America, the greatest of them in the West. Besides the sugar pine, it boasts the ponderosa pine, in whose stems are locked up half the pine timber reserves of the whole continent, and the western white pine, white-fleshed and smooth of grain and bole. This is the homeland of fragrant firs and tall somber spruces, of the incense cedars, and the big-cone pines whose wooden fruit weighs two pounds. A single redwood tree will furnish forth three hundred and sixty thousand board feet, enough to build twenty big houses. In the Great Forest — for it deserves no lesser name — are seven hundred billion board feet of merchantable timber. That counts in only the commercially valuable trees; it does not include seedlings and saplings, nor superannuated giants with hollow hearts, nor woods too soft for working. There is no forest on earth so dense, so solidly one vast vertical lumber yard. All Europe, without Scandinavia and Russia, is not so great as the terrain that these trees possess.

The Great Forest begins in Alaska. It runs south in two parallel chains which gradually fork wide apart. Inland spread the mountain forests of the Rockies, in which the pines and junipers predominate; along the Pacific coast ranges the tideland forest, made up for the most part of conifers other than pine, of spruce and fir, redwoods and cypresses and cedars. Together they make the Great Forest, wishbone-shaped upon the map, each prong over a thousand miles long.

Trees over the rest of the world clothe the land lightly, as the deciduous forests of eastern North America and central Europe spread dappled and luminous shade in summer and drop their foliage in winter, letting in the sunlight, displaying their clean nakedness and detail. But to walk at the bottom of the Great Forest is to go benighted. The trunks stand battalion close. A fleck of sunlight on the forest floor is a gold piece. This is a discrete world, like the ocean or the desert. Trees are a power in the Northwest. Directly or indirectly all the wealth, all the luck and fortunes and misfortunes of Americans there depend upon the woods. Before you can turn around to live — to make a road, plant a crop, build a house, walk, sit down, or strike a match to light a pipe — you have to consider the trees.

I came a stranger to these softwood giants, a stranger intimate with their historic family lines. 'Softwood' is the lumberman's name for the timber of the conifers, for soft they are to the teeth of the mill saw, and smooth to the carpenter's plane. In the eyes of the logger they are perfect, for their habit of growth — a single mast of a stem rising straight from root to tip, putting forth branches in tiers (in which they differ from the forking ways of the hardwoods, the broad-leaved trees). More, in such dense stands do they grow that they find light and air enough to branch only at the top, so that their boles may be clean of knots for a hundred feet or more. They are sappy, too,

with lakes of pitch and turpentine and resin, amber still
unpetrified. The softwoods of the lumberjack soar in
serenity exactly to his pleasure, and he loves them for
their clean limbs and their smooth wood living as flesh,
and he tumbles them with a shout of conquest.

But to a plantsman who loves trees for the rooted life
in them, which the exploiting axe profanes, the great
conifers are not soft, but hard and male. Their bark is
rough, their needles harsh, and this evergreen dress they
never put by, but stand forever ready in it, armored, bole
to bole, chanting in unison, like the soldiers of Xenophon
crossing the mountains to the sea. When they must
perish, they go down all together, in the elemental con-
summation of a forest fire. Or when one alone is felled,
the concussion shakes the ground like a quake, and the
wind of the heroic fall is a gale. As timber the cone trees
do the work of the world. No temperate hardwoods,
tropical teak or rosewood, sandalwood or logwood,
mahogany or lignum vitae can compare in value with the
conifers, whose band of pines and spruces is flung about the
pole in a green zone, whose cedars are on Lebanon and
Atlas, whose kauris rise upon New Zealand alps.

I had been well informed, for a long time, upon the
conifers of the Northwest, and I had never seen them until
now. My knowledge of them was compiled of botanical
facts. Now at last, on a wild mountain-side some nameless
place in the Idaho pipestem, I stood up to these trees,
walked deep in the wood and faced their legions. And my
headful of facts was scattered on the wind that breathed
from the Bitterroots and commanded the army before me
into the gestures of triumphant life. The differences be-

tween many of the spruces and the firs are subtle; the profusion in the Great Forest is overpowering — some sixty
sorts of conifers, all told. I could not name this deeply
plated bark, that glaucous cone, the pine tassel with a
fragrance of orange rind, and I was tortured by this in-
ability, because in theoretic systematics I had known it
all so well, upon a time.

In Coeur d'Alene I went into a store with a red front; on
its counters I would find, I knew, a booklet that would
unriddle for me all this grandeur and mystery in five
minutes. I was confident of this, for the good reason that
the little book was written by myself. It had been lying
on the ten-cent store counters for some years now, like a
benignant practical joke, waiting for me to need to buy it.
Reminding me, when I put down my dime and slipped the
handbook in my pocket, of my hungry pleasure in the
writing of it, that first winter of our return from the south
of France, when we came back to Kennicott's Grove.

The trees at the Grove, in their curtailed, deciduous,
hardwood way, are old and honorable. These prairie
groves, these wooded islands risen on long low ridges out
of the aboriginal grass sea, are links in the long history of
Illinois. Indians, voyageurs, first settlers made straight

for them, like the passerine birds on their migration. The
land whereon our France-bred sons set eager foot, sixth
generation of its seed, had for a hundred years been home
to their forebears. In the year when by treaty the Pota-
watomies moved off it, the Kennicotts raised a log cabin
here.

What woods, I wonder, out of their virgin hardwood
forest, did these pioneer gentlefolk choose for the founding
of their home? Did they set axe to the oak, for its dark
brown heavy timber? The burr oaks that stand at the
Grove today are venerables, three hundred years to half
a century in age. They have grown old and stout, but
with a muscular grace; their lowest branches sweep out
and downward till sometimes they rest upon the grassy
ground, as if the tree leaned on one elbow in benignant
power. The native hickory, I think, must then have been
put to many uses; it grudges wear and will not split under
the strain laid upon wagon wheel and barrel stave and
axe-handle. The hickory trees at Kennicott's Grove are
legend. Women now old who used to gather in the nuts as
children every fall tell of the mightiness of that harvest.
As a boy there, I heard a scattered fusillade fall on the
roof of the cottage where I slept, all through October.
But the rich meats are part now of the vanished abundance, for a borer has got into the shagbarks, and when I
came back to the Grove from Europe, many a friend I
knew among them was a sapless corpse for woodpeckers
to nest in.

The trees you see from farthest off, when you come
toward the Grove in winter as I did, shine with a delusive
nobility. They are cottonwoods, tall with a height that

is not strength, for only on the impoverished western plains is their lumber worth using, so subject is it to warping, cracking, and decay. Out where there is nothing better to cast even a short shadow, where drought is the common law, the cottonwood is welcome for the lake of shade it makes, the sound of rivers in its twinkling, turning foliage. At the Grove it is a favorite only of the flickers.

For the Grove people are rich with trees, a heritage set out for them a hundred years ago. When they had raised their first roof, the Kennicotts began to plant. Not for their day alone, but for my sons'. Osage and walnut, Scotch pine and red pine, Norway spruce and arbor vitae, apple tree and pear — they grew as the family grew, and sheltered new doorways, shaded lawns merging without borderlines, and friendly walks between house and sister house. The bulbs set out a century ago spread, until spring brought a pool of squills to bloom, a meadowful of jonquils and narcissus to blow in the warm May wind. There were children always, many children, to find all the flowers over again each spring, to climb in the spruce trees, and pick glistening resin from the Scotch pines to chew. In the swing that hung from the stoutest ash bough I had swung Louise, her brown curls flying, and gently pushed my baby daughter. I had known the Grove at the height of its flower, and when its fruits were sweetest.

And then from the gaudy-bright Riviera, I came back to it again, in the stripped frugality of the eleventh month. The trees were there, the stout, indigenously rooted oaks, the walnuts and the ash with the dangling swing rope on it; they were naked and steely as fact. Time and the worm

had had their way with most of the hickories, and the
spruces and arbor vitae were gone. But the wall of the
wood still rose, smoke-colored with bare bark, crested with
ragged faggots where some winter crows lifted, distantly
jeering. Scant flakes were falling from a stone-gray sky;
the air, to lungs that had breathed five years of the chari-
table south, cut the throat that took it in.

The house where my wife was born, where we had read
from one book behind the old oil lamp together, was only
a charred cellar hole. Another, a modern house welcomed
us with warmth, but it was new to us as though we were
strangers here. Gone was the genial host of the Grove in
my boyhood. Gone were the handsome horses from the
stables; the hay blew with a comfortless rustle along the
dusky loft when I pushed the big doors open a crack and
slipped inside. There were no swallows now; only a mouse
ran out of the shadows across the dusty beam above me
and vanished, a spectral flicker.

I heard my children shouting in the gathering fall of
snow outside, first snow, that they had never seen before.
And I gave earnest thanks. The ground beneath their
running feet was frozen and prairie flat, but it was solid
ground. I heard the cow, sole occupant now, save for the
mice, of the grand old barn, as she ruminated clumsily in
her corner, and I thought of her milk and gave thanks
again. The wind shuddered with its own cold around the
barn corner. My wife, I knew, lay safe in bed in our warm
little chamber, lovingly tended. With all my heart, I said,
I am thankful.

So I went out again into the wintry field. The wind
came up behind me and knifed me between the shoulders.

Not enough snow had fallen yet to hide the colorless decay of a summer gone long ago to seed; the flakes stung sharp as sand against my cheek. The boys were out of sight; not even a junco flicked a wing to make the rusty field, the slaty sky come to life. I stood and looked at winter, at my America. I had gone away not so much to escape these as to grow certain seeds, secretly, in a climate that should favor them. Where were the golden fruits they were to have borne?

Still to put trust in me, I thought — of the women who did — was to perform more than I ever had yet. I tramped December fields and woods that showed not one indulgence, beyond the due of this starveling season. Even snowfall this year was scant; the prairie had no more to clothe it than the rags of summer, dingy now and threadbare. Yet the skies forever threatened. Against them the cottonwoods reared in flimsy loftiness; in another month or two they would begin to whiten with a pale premonitory shine. The burr oaks looked dead; they early drop their leaves and grudge to put them out again in spring. If there is any tree you have to take on trust, it is that one. How slow it is to grow! These stalwarts had been here for several centuries, and looked good for more. The cottonwoods had for a life span less than a hundred years, at best; and how they sucker, spread shallow roots and drop untidy litter!

I believed in the oaks. I knew that in their own time the sap would rise in them. The conviction I had got at majority, that was a staff with which to walk in personal darkness, rang still stoutly on this frozen ground. Nature was certainly not beguiling, in this place and season, but its law and order underlay all things and prevailed above those economic dicta by which I stood convicted.

As the faithful, in another orthodoxy, step out of the troubling street into the great stone calm of a cathedral, I used to go in to Chicago and drop into Field Museum. Upstairs, around the herbarium, I had acquaintances. Some I had known in Washington; some had aided me in my seven years' preparation of a *Flora of the Indiana Dunes*, which the Museum published while I was in France. It is a strictly systematic work, a leached skeletal imprint of months spent in those hissing hills of sand beside a fresh inland sea; half a page of it would send anyone but a botanist off into a drowse. Yet that does not explain, I think, why this bleak volume used to lie upon my mother's bedside table. She could wring romance out of a stone.

One day when I was haunting Field's herbarium, a botanist friend there told me that a publisher who sold to the ten-cent trade had inquired of the Museum for somebody to write him a handbook to the trees. Did I want the job? It would be hack, I was warned; the specifications were for exactly ninety-five pages, no more, no less, for not over a hundred words and just one picture to each page. The pictures had already been selected; the editor had found a set of old plates; what was asked was a neat hundred words for each.

Did I want the job! Does any poet grumble that a sonnet has fourteen lines? Were the Renaissance painters unwilling to paint because the demand was for more nativities and annunciations? And would Linnaeus himself have spurned a chance to write about the trees of North America? In the Depression who, when royalties were not offered, declined a flat sum in payment?

So I fell to work. The chosen plates, I found, were by none other than Redouté, the greatest rose painter of all time, a friend of Audubon; originally they had illustrated Michaux's work on the American sylva. I was in mighty company. I was back in the world of science. I walked in a wood where the trees, being archetypes, are forever green and stand forever. The winter could not touch me now. The library yielded all the books I needed, and in the herbarium I pored over specimens. Of tupelo from the cypress swamps of the South, where I had seen it in more carefree days. Of piñon pines from New Mexico, that brought back an instant breath of their incense blown to me through the sharp mountain dusk when, as a weary convalescent, I once rode toward the lights of Santa Fé. Of white spruce from the White Mountains of New Hampshire where I had tramped in college days. And, from out of the West, of Engelmann spruce of Colorado, big-cone pines of the Sierra, quaking aspen, Oregon maple.

The wind of January whistled around the cornice of the building; out there Lake Michigan, black and spiritless, slowly heaved its ice floes and dropped them again awash.

I fed my eyes upon these stiff herbarium sheets with a
hunger only whetted. How long ago some of these western
specimens had been gathered! Back in the days when
that country was first opening to exploration. The
scientist-adventurers who had found them, after the hard
plains journey in the saddle, the rattling climb among
the crags, were long dead. But the trees were there, from
which these cones, these needles, had been gathered.
They had but grown older and taller, imperceptibly in a
grandeur aged before the white men came. They would be
waiting for me always. Would I ever come to them?

14

FALLING WATER

THE man who came to discover for Europe the treasures of the Pacific coastal forests was David Douglas, to whose name the greatest of the firs is monument. He was a Scot then in his young twenties, the mark of promise on him. William Hooker had seen it, at Glasgow's botanical gardens where he found David, risen from a modest beginning as gardener's boy. Hooker took him botanizing through the highlands, and in the sturdy frame, the fresh enthusiasm for all things that grow and are green, the quick intelligence of Douglas, Hooker recognized a great plantsman. That is how, no doubt, the Royal Horticultural Society came to send Douglas out, when he was only twenty-five, to America to search for New World beauty for Old World gardens. In the eastern United States he visited gardens and planters and then, in an eight months journey, he rounded the Horn and at last came to the mouth of the Columbia River.

I see him gazing out from the deck of his ship, his little Scotch terrier barking excitement beside him. What young Douglas saw was a pristine and giant forest marching down to the sea, mounting up on the hills, receding into incalculable distance swept with the trailing veils of rainy mist. It rained straight down, and the conifers spired straight up, as though the mighty downpour had raised that forest by its power, every shaft growing up to the rain as a root will grow in a vein of water. The height of a tree is indeed a 'function,' as mathematicians say, of rainfall. The greater the precipitation, the greater the forest. And though there are lands where more rain falls, as in the tropics, their sucking heat offsets the fall. Nowhere else in the world is there so high a precipitation with so low a temperature as here, where in triumph the titan conifers therefore rise, and living wood becomes a natural force, like wind on the prairies and waves in the sea.

From Alaska down to San Francisco Bay this coast, in 1832 when Douglas sighted it, was one of the least known to white men of all the shores of ocean. Russia had reached a paw for it from the north, and the Spanish caravels were coming up from the south to thwart her. On Malaspina's vessel, in 1789, had been the naturalist Luis Née; he it was who took first specimens of the giant canoe cedar, the arbor vitae of which the Indians made their long canoes that held fifty warriors. England claimed this coast, as

mistress of the seas; and Captain Cook had beheld the
somber legions of the trees and recognized that among
them unnamed captains stood. Then came Vancouver
under the Union Jack, with Scotch Doctor Archibald
Menzies, aboard the *Discovery*, in 1792. Menzies saw what
today we call the Douglas fir and the western hemlock and
the Sitka spruce, before the *Discovery* up-anchored and
sailed away. Then, under the stars and stripes, came
Captain Gray, Boston merchant, hunting for furs, laying a
claim upon the Columbia. Thereafter Jefferson, scratch-
ing with a decisive quill at his desk far away to the east,
opened the way to the Pacific by the Louisiana Purchase.
Now, seriously alarmed, Britain reached from British
Columbia a hand for the Oregon country. She scattered
John Jacob Astor's fur-traders, and put in her own Northwestern Fur Company. It built Fort Vancouver; the
commander there, good John MacLaughlin, was ready to
be host to David Douglas, when he leaped ashore from the
landing boat, with his terrier at his heels.

For seven thousand miles, for three long years, Douglas
was a traveler through Oregon and Washington. Lonely,
sturdy, cheerful, friend to himself, he navigated his canoe
or tramped afoot, swimming, when he had a deep river to
cross, on his back with his clothes upheld in one hand to
keep them dry, and in the other his specimens, inkstand
and precious diary. Sometimes he had Indians for guides,
but they were thievish, and since they could not speak
with him save in signs, his nights were still solitary. He
had nothing to read; by the light of a pine torch, he would
write and write in his journal. 'My rifle,' he set down, 'is
by my hand day and night; it lies by my side under my

blanket when I sleep, and my faithful little Scotch terrier, the companion of all my journeys, takes his place at my feet.' At first he slept in a tent, but gradually learning to do without, he would roll up in a blanket and sleep on the ground, rain or hail — and there were always these, or fog, save for the two or three months of summer. As he slept like the Indians, so he learned to eat like them, bitter-root and camas bulbs, salal berries and wapatoo, the roots of the swamp arrowhead. They called him Man of Grass, because everywhere that he went it was his purpose to collect what grew.

So in those first years there fell to his glory the first definite scientific recognition of many uncrowned forest kings. He found the rare and beautiful Pacific yew, of whose elastic wood the red men made their bows and paddles. He distinguished that grand tree the lowland balsam fir, which towers up two hundred and fifty feet bearing aloft its big erect cones into the rain. He came on the contorted little beach pine, and the ponderosa pine, and constantly he heard tales of another, surpassing all other pines in height and girth and splendor, whose long cones ran with a sap that the Indians ate for a sweet. Far in the Umpqua valley of the interior he found them, the fruits of the soaring sugar pine.

> These cones are, however [says his rain-soaked diary] only seen on the loftiest trees, and the putting myself in possession of three of these (all I could obtain) nearly brought my life to a close. As it was impossible either to climb the tree or hew it down, I endeavoured to knock off the cones by firing at them with ball, when the report of my gun brought eight Indians, all of them painted with red

earth, armed with bows, arrows, bone-tipped spears, and
flint-knives. They appeared anything but friendly. I endeavoured to explain to them what I wanted, and they
seemed satisfied, and sat down to smoke, but presently I
perceived one of them string his bow, and another sharpen
his flint-knife with a pair of wooden pincers, and suspend
it on the wrist of the right hand. Further testimony of their
intentions was unnecessary. To save myself by flight was
impossible, so, without hesitation, I stepped back about
five paces, cocked my gun, drew one of the pistols out of my
belt, and holding it in my left hand and the gun in my right,
showed myself determined to fight for my life. As much as
possible I endeavoured to preserve my coolness, and thus
we stood looking at one another without making any movement or uttering a word for perhaps ten minutes, when one,
at last, who seemed the leader, gave a sign that they wished
for some tobacco; this I signified that they should have, if
they fetched me a quantity of cones. They went off im-
mediately in search of them, and no sooner were they all
out of sight than I picked up my three cones and some twigs
of the trees, and made the quickest possible retreat, hurrying back to my camp, which I reached before dusk.

Such a cone, gathered one summer in the High Sierra,
hangs on my study wall. I keep it for its foot-long pendant grace, and as much in memory of David Douglas.
Nor do I forget his little terrier. From California Douglas
went to the Hawaiian Islands; there one day in 1834 the
dog sat a long time guarding a bundle that his master had
dropped on the ground when he stepped forth upon further
discovery. In those islands and times a custom existed of
digging pits, covered with boughs and leaves, to catch
wild animals. Into such a trap Douglas had fallen. When
at last the anxious terrier could draw attention to the spot,

and Douglas was found, the life had been trampled out of him by a bull, his savage and frustrated fellow captive.

I came toward the coastal forests from a direction opposite to the seaward approach of David Douglas. Spokane was hot; there the thought of deep green shade seemed delusive. On a glittering morning we turned south and west, for the long sweep down to the coast. We knew that we had a gantlet now to run as, early in the journey, we had run the searing reaches of the creosote-bush country, hundreds of miles in a day.

For between the two forks of the Great Forest, up near the crotch of that mighty wishbone, lie the badlands of Washington and Oregon. They are the last and northernmost tapering extension of the vast desert basin which runs from the Gulf of Mexico north to British Columbia, where the Rockies and the Cascades come together like two tidal waves that collide and mingle in upthrown white crests.

The badlands were not always treeless. Sequoias grew there once; the first recognizable pines and spruces and balsam firs grew there, ancestral to our living species, evolving out of queer and primitive conifers at which we can but guess from the mute hulks of their great trunks

that lie as shattered stone in the wastes called the Petrified
Forest.

But in Miocene times, some twenty million years ago,
the earth began to buckle. Alps, Andes, Himalayas,
Rockies, and Cascades arose, two miles into the sky and
more. The Cascades cut off the rains from the Pacific;
the Rockies blocked all moisture from the Atlantic. And
then the earth opened in tremendous fissures and vented
its lava upon interior Oregon and eastern Washington.
Three hundred feet deep, it poured out, three thousand, in
some places five thousand — almost a mile deep of sple-
netic gush from earth's interior, that chilled to black rock.
In this tide the antique forest was overwhelmed. It never
has come back; it never can, till the wall of the Cascades
is worn down and the sea wind, laden with fog and rain,
sweeps once again across the sagebrush plains.

So we had one more taste of desert offered us, of earth's
dry crust. It can be downed in half a day, if speed is all
your thought. It seldom is mine. I may stop ten and
twenty times a day, to get out to watch a bird, tramp a
mile just to get the dust of the country in my boots, scale
a hill, or lie an hour in grass or under trees till even my
shoulders know the feel of the land. So the jalopies that I
pass, pass me again, as the tortoise passed the hare. Even
so, I call this superficial travel. Better to stay a week, as
we did on Fish Creek in Wyoming, set up as a citizen, however transient, with a bed and kettle of your own, learn the
look of the world from your doorstep, and loiter over buying groceries at the country store for staple talk with the
neighbors.

But in the badlands, I confess, I cut and ran for it. If I

stopped to swing my glasses at a hawk overhead, or gather
a harsh cull of the roadside flora, the blast of the badlands
hit me like the back of a hand across my face. On that hot
gale rode stinging sands derived from the lava and from
the dunes of the Columbia; they dingily obscured the
whole scene at a mile; they pitted the sheen of the car with
a lasting defacement. You would say nothing would please
to grow under such a lash as this. Yet here in my curious
hands lay western bee-plant with its heavy odor, and a
blazing-star fierce itself with prickles, its countless stamens a sunburst of gold. They came of origins alien to me,
the caper and the loasa families, very western, desertic,
and untamed; they were not to be called just pretty, any
more than was the red-bellied hawk whose nest, if I could
have found it, would be of sagebrush lined with pine
needles brought from the mountains.

So we slanted down to meet the Columbia, aquamarine
whipped by the wind to silver tips. I swirled to a stop at a
gas station for fuel, and shouted at the cheerful grinning
boy to ask if it blew like this often? His hair licking up
from his scalp, he laughed back that it blew this way every
day in summer. And in winter, I wanted to know, what?
Why, bless you, then it blew from the opposite direction,
off the snow fields.

We fled on, taking the way the river took; it was making
straight for the Cascades now, for the gorge it has sawed
through solid rock to the sea. So it had cut these terraces
on either hand, and the wind had scoured them wider;
coronet above coronet the bluffs receded. Like the river,
that flowed purpling over its shoals around the islands, we
passed between cliffs of basalt that had cooled to gigantic

crystals, up-ended and fitting together juttingly, trun-
cated at different heights. As if some unrecorded pagan
civilization once stood here, but all its columns had been
thrown. Nothing like our idea of a white Greece; rather a
Minotaur's land, like the Crete of mythology. The palace
roofs of jagged talus, black and furnace red and brown like
burnt out coke, collapsed and spilled down every canyon
and fanned out at the base in wide despair. Lichens on
these sheer rocks might have been fragments of wall paint-
ing no longer decipherable. And all-conquering time, from
benches a thousand feet above, poured out great open
sacks of sand, red, black, gray sand, spilling like a slow
hourglass, measuring out our Cenozoic era and the days
of man.

The West is abrupt. Its geology and climate have sharp
margins. So that, suddenly as pushing through a gate, we
found ourselves in late afternoon escaped from barrens like
those outside of Eden. Slant rays laddered the lofty shade.
That arid gale darkened with dust had become no more
than a fresh breath plowing steady as the trades through
boughs down-sweeping from the spires of giant evergreens.
It carried odors of well-watered fern, of cedar sap, of
needles smelling like tangerine peel, and a reviving
thought of the sea. Born of the sea, washed through a
million resinous leaves, this wind was dustless, colorless,
pure as belief in an invisible God after an age spent with
dancing demons. Dusty ourselves and blown to confusion,
we felt forgiven as we skimmed along through the long
light and the shadows. We felt rewarded, beyond reason,
when we were shown to our room in a fine old hostel (one
of the few on our journey; we use, like everybody else, the
West's excellent motor cabins).

The room was a corner one, on the top floor; it was pleasing as a chamber in one's own home. But more than airy curtains and white beds made it fresh. There was a presence here that I have known caught in an old stone springhouse, or on the under sides of willow leaves. It was both a light and a sound. Across the ceiling fled constantly the ripple marks of sunshine on a current, and when I flung the window up the breeze washed in the singing of a waterfall. There just below me it plunged, arched over by leaves. The room, like the inside of a violin belly, resounded with its voice. Tired, I lay a long time listening, under the billow of the light curtain, watching the ripple marks follow each other like the years of a happy man's life.

Now when I find a waterfall right outside my door, a fall with a rainbow in it, I will tell any man I have come home, and if he wants to see me he can follow me there to find me. If he has something better to say than the cascade, let him say it; otherwise he may hold his peace.

So next morning I went to meet my falls. I forget time, both the fullness of an hour and the briefness of life, when I walk into this spell. For the pulsing flight of a cascade is hypnotic; it forever passes and never changes. Not alive, it is nevertheless a picture of life. Every flung drop in it is individual, come flowing out of remote springs in the mass of the mountains, and drawn inevitably into this eddy. For one moment the onrushing stream is caught and wrought into a shape; the next instant that water which shattered the light in a prismatic arc has vanished into oblivion, down and away to the ultimate inertia of the sea bottom. More water forever enters and leaves; the form of the eddy alone remains, veering a little on the wind this way and that like a dancer, but always righting to the norm. Yet it has no existence apart from the drops that compose it.

And like a living body, this waterfall is a sudden outburst of energy. Not primal astronomical power which is terrible and eternal, but an earthly revival of it on a scale human as things go in the universe, a definitely shaped impounding of a great current strength, a kinetic expression of it, with a niche in space of its own. And you can, if you wish to harness it, turn the spilled energy into light and warmth and driving purpose, as you may burn a great tree, or set a man to thinking. Or you may leave it free to dance, and still its power is not wasted, any more than it is wasting solar radiation to lock it up in the shape of a fern which no one ever discovers. In being itself, the bracken is its own end and reason.

So, content, I watched the lovely water fall and fall, leaning just over the plunge with my elbows on a sheer stone wall. My wife came out, perhaps to tell me that we should make haste for something, but she forgot what, folding her arms on the wall beside me, watching the water, finding out how there was, after all, plenty of time. We all have time for what we want in this life. Or we should have, God knows, for we shall not want it long. A young man can make the time for a girl; a good woman always has time for a child. And a naturalist will take time for a bird, as long as the bird will stay to be watched or let itself be followed. It is not surprising that one of the last naturalists to see a passenger pigeon pursued it through the woods of North Carolina a whole day. Or that there is at present one man who spends his entire time watching what may be the last thirty-four California condors left in the world. True that he has a subvention for so doing, with the high motivating purpose that study may yet save the largest and most unlikely bird in all America. But penniless ornithologists have done as much, without money or appointment for it, and for birds less rare. That is how we all know what we do about Nature or anything in science. Newton resolved a problem in physics, so he said, 'by thinking of it all the time.'

Now into the narrow field of my concentration flew the bird which is the very fellow of such falls as this. The water ouzel, called the dipper, is never seen apart from just such foaming rapids and singing cataracts. As the sanderling is the bird of the shoreline, skittering forever back and forth in the drifting castles of foam, as the stormy petrel is the embodiment of mid-ocean loneliness, having no spot to rest save on the seething hills of brine, so the quick dipper belongs to the rush of fresh waters. Even a petrel must come to land to nest; it cannot, like the fabulous halcyon, rear its brood upon the sea in the unnatural calm that follows the equinox. Dippers fit with the most exquisite precision into their habitat; they live

and die within a mile or less of the spot where they were
hatched. Their world is a linear one, only a few feet wider
than the mountain stream that they inhabit. Even in winter they migrate only so far as the nearest hole in the ice.

And perfect as a dipper seems to find his life, he is oddly
made for it. Though he has not the long legs of a wader,
he spends his time a-wading. Though he has no webs between his toes, he can swim; chunky, he yet can dive like
the streamlined grebe, and without long wings, still fly
under water like the loon. Short of wing and stumpy of
tail, round of middle as a wren, with short legs and long
slender toes made as if for perching, the dipper is a land
bird by every anatomical feature. But by an incredible
plasticity, by sheer defiance of function over structure, by
an adaptation that looks like will, he is an aquatic bird.
He loves what I love — 'white water,' forest depths. He
loves a stream so pure that a man can drink of it thought-
lessly, a child can see each grain of hornblende and pyrite
on its bed. A river in its freshest youth, where caddis
worms and stone-flies and dobsons live. And over the
singing of all such western waters rises the dipper's voice,
in wild contentment.

But the voice I heard above the fall this morning was a
frantic baby peeping — the call of a hungering youngster
who sees his mother's approach. At the roots of a fir which
the water laved just before it toppled into the cascade,
teetered a top-heavy fledgling dipper, craning hopefully
over the perilous foam. And at the moment I perceived
him, a light shadow, a swirl of slate-gray wings returned,
the parent with a long aquatic larva dangling from its bill.
The cries of the starving child redoubled, its dipping

motion became a frantic *tic*. This is a continual rhythmic
genuflection, and it is said that a dipper can 'dip' as soon
as it can stand. For one instant mother and child curtseyed
to each other; then with a running flutter she rushed to
him, crammed the food into his spread beak, and disappeared with the flying spray.

Surprisingly, the young one began to forage for himself.
He turned over a twig, found a tidbit, swallowed it, waded
a little into the stream, found another, and to my horror
hopped right into the flume almost at the brink of this
cataract ninety feet high! I ran along the parapet and
looked down the fall for his mother. She was nowhere in
sight. The spot where her youngster perched was slippery
with algae; it was gusty with the down suction of the imminent plunge; the current was gathering momentum
there like a millrace. My wife clapped her hands in terror;
she called aloud to the child bird. He heard no voice to
which he would respond, but waded out to his knees in the
water, two inches from the brink. We clutched each other,
parents both. But the happy birdling probed, got something, took another step, thought better of it, turned
around, came back to the fir roots, and began playing a
game that I suppose would be called 'pick up sticks.' You
grasp a twig in your bill, shake it, think about it, drop it
in the current, and find another one — if possible, a difficult bit of wood to extricate. This went on for many
minutes. Sometimes, with luck, he found a caddis worm
and gulped it. Unsure though his short wings still obviously were, he acted quite the worldling, as though long
ago he had forgotten the nest. And yet it might have been
this morning he had left it.

In the Yosemite I had seen that nest, a dome of moss carefully erected yet looking much as if it had been accidentally washed into that wedged position on a great boulder in midstream; the entrance is, uniquely, at the bottom, and I watched a dipper there come flying through the rapid waters for a little space and flick up and into the aperture bearing a worm for some invisible mouth within. That was the first time I had ever seen this bird, for I had just come out to the West. And in all of Chapman's *Handbook of Birds of Eastern North America* you will not find even the name. Other western birds turn up in the East — western meadowlarks on the prairies west of Chicago, marbled godwits south of it on the reedy lakes of the Calumet district, western willets on the Lake Michigan dunes. But never by any chance a dipper, for it cannot cross the great plains; it will not follow the muddy rivers; it has never been seen east of the Black Hills of South Dakota where the outposts of the western forests begin, with ponderosa and limber pines.

So dippers have never reached the Appalachian system, more's the pity. How they would love, I think, the terraced sheet of falling water in my Tryon glen! Or that other falls, the tall, wild, shouting one that plunges from the mountain of my childhood; I used to hear it, playing in the woods, before I knew they called it Shunkawakin.

Audubon himself never saw a dipper alive; he painted from specimens. Wilson did not know of it, I believe, to the day of his premature death. Major Long's expedition to the Rocky Mountains turned up no dipper, though surely the naturalist of the party would not have missed it had he seen it, for he was Thomas Say, discoverer of such new western birds as the cliff swallow and the linnet, the lazuli bunting and rock wren and seven more. Warren's expedition to the headwaters of the Missouri and the Yellowstone brought back no word of it, and even Elliott Coues, stationed for years as an army surgeon in Dakota and in Arizona, never saw a dipper but once in all his life.

But long before eastern ornithologists had more than a few skins for their edification, and not a nest or an egg or any knowledge of either, beyond the continental wall dippers and men had made acquaintance. For this is a frank and cordial bird; not the fret of a mill nor the presence of man affrights him. And both the dippers and the Forty-Niners wanted something from the stream bottoms, so that many a bearded panner knew the liquid chittering song, while ornithologists of Boston and Philadelphia were writing 'nidification unelucidated' and other dignified admissions of ignorance.

But since those days the ouzel has grown more retiring. Irrigation has stolen away his streams; pollution has disgusted him with them; deforestation has deprived him of his solitude. Yard by yard and mile by mile the dipper has lost ground, and territory he has abandoned he does not reclaim.

So that I knew that it was a fugitive bold beauty that I saw when the mother ouzel flashed back from the valley below. Up she came in a flight dark and silent as a bat's but with no such stagger; straight she came, graceful as a swallow but never gliding, beating her wings up, up, right into the glittering furious heart of the falls, up through the plunging water, to her eager child.

Be it set down, to my folly if you will, that in a world

racked with war and worm-eaten with despair, I could
somehow take an entire day and devote it to the doings
of two dippers, and the dance of one slender cascade. I
do not know how to justify my way of life, any more than
I know how long it can continue. I can only say that this
too is reality; this too is truth, this also is the business of a
man, and its own wage.

15

HOW THE

DROUGHT BROKE

I FELT in the Cascades that I could never get enough of the great conifer forest, of the straightness and strength and down-bending generosity of these trees. But I have heard how men who did get their fill ached to get out from under that brooding darkness. The evergreens can be relentless, as deciduous boughs are not. I remember a letter that was written in 1862 by Robert Kennicott from the desolate tundra, the monotonous muskegs of La Pierre's House in the Mackenzie country.

I never fully knew how much I loved trees till I found myself made melancholy by thinking of the bonnie oaks and other trees I remember so well at The Grove, while passing through some of these almost treeless wastes, or everlasting forests of spruce. I used to like evergreens best, but I fear the too constant view of spruces will give me a distaste for them. And oh! how I long to see even the bare branches and shaggy bark of the hickory.

A century before I returned to the Grove, this most famous of its sons came to it, a year-old babe in the arms of his mother, her lady skirts light over the wild tangled grass as she carried him into the log cabin just raised for them by her husband, the planter and patriarch.

It happened that that was a great passenger pigeon year; they passed over the oak and hawthorn glades, a wind, a thunder, a darkening cloud. In the not distant village of Chicago, consisting of less than a hundred houses around the mouth of the sluggish river, men sang in reckless parody to a hymn tune:

> When I can shoot my rifle clear
> At pigeons in the skies,
> I'll bid farewell to every fear
> And live on good pot-pies!

That was a marvelous autumn, one of those midwestern falls when the Grove seems held in an iridescent bubble. In the woods the Carolina parakeet still lingered, and under the fiery sumach leaves the wild turkeys gobbled, each gobbler lord of his harem. There were prairie chickens in the high grass then; timber wolves and deer listened, deep in the forest, to the faint sound of the axe. Buffalo had just gone; their wallows in the woods reflected blue sky in untroubled waters. That year the Potowatomies were taking their appointed departure. The white men, the Kenni-

cotts, held this land now by government grant. The unrecorded aboriginal era was over in the Grove; this autumn
saw it go. Across the sky was scrawled new title, written in
smoke that rose from the hearth where the baby played.
That boy, Robert Kennicott, had less than thirty years to
live and far to go. Far to the north, to the unknown headwaters of the Yukon, to the nesting ground of the wild
swans upon the bleak Delta of the Mackenzie. The arctic
summer is brief, the night long. It is not widely remembered now that in Kennicott we had the beginning of an
Audubon, a Humboldt; we had an ardent and greatly
American scientist.

With the Grove for his book, he grew; the irk of ill
health kept him from the classroom. But the physically
hampered child turns inward for his resources, and in the
frail years of his childhood, Kennicott taught himself science, languages, literature, self-discipline and the out-of-
doors. The fields, the woods, the hidden sloughs wherein
the bittern nests — all this familiar ground to me is ground
that he made classic in his time. Before he was seventeen
his observations drew attention from the learned. One who
knew him then wrote of him so:

> He often visited the city with little discoveries he had
> made and almost always called at the office of the writer.
> There would be a knock, the door would open, and he would
> begin to talk before he closed it, and talk his way up to the
> table and talk himself out of doors. It was a flower, a bug, a
> bird, a quadruped. He was full of plans to help others to
> see as he did. He bristled with facts. His mind was luxuri-
> ant. He had a love for natural science 'passing the love of
> women.' He read in concentric circles from his boyhood
> home farther and farther until he read the state of Illinois.

He explored its Delta, that queer region with tropic traces, that is bounded by the Mississippi and the Ohio. He brought out its plants, caught its butterflies, unearthed its reptiles. No hardship was too severe if only he could add some coveted treasure to his cabinet. Slight in frame, he would be brave as a lion if anything for his darling science could be gained by it. What a companion he would have been for Audubon!

Before long the Smithsonian made a place for him. He came to its rococo-Gothic, red sandstone halls like a western wind; his youth, his bubbling sense of fun, his enthusiasm and fine courtliness made him the darling of his associates. Between his zoologic labors there in Washington, he would hurry home, now to found the Chicago Academy of Sciences, now to give young Northwestern University a natural history museum, and at last to turn north, to seek out the last refuge of the eastern mammalian fauna, into Manitoba.

That first cold, stinging whiff of the North went to his twenty-two-year-old head; when he turned southward again at last, laden with bird and mammal specimens, it was with a backward look and a promise to the land rolling a thousand miles and more away to the arctic sea, that he would come to it again.

So in April of 1859 he set out from Chicago by the lake steamer *Fountain City*. His destination was Fort William, on Lake Superior, and I mention it only because I well recall my own brief hours there, and the feeling that pressed upon me that nothing then lay barrier between me and the pole. In canoes of the Hudson's Bay Company, Kennicott and his partner started for Lake Winnipeg. Like

Linnaeus's immortal journey to Lapland, this great trek
to the North outran the late arctic spring. Through melting ice jams, with the wild geese and swans flying overhead, Kennicott made his way to Great Slave Lake, and
descended the Mackenzie among the migrating *foule* of the
caribou. Wherever he passed he acquired languages, Indian and Eskimo and hybrid tongues without lexicons, the
lingoes of the guides and trappers.

There he wrote home of his longing for the trees that
gave the Grove its name. Nothing, save Captain Scott's
accounts and the Lapland journal of Linnaeus, has
brought to me, as do these pages Kennicott sent back, the
tundra, the huskies, the devouring cold, the awful white-
ness of the arctic. He writes of the difficulty of breathing,
in that ultimate winter, so that my own chest is con-
stricted. He describes how the moisture of the breath
freezes upon the air until the moving dog train is enveloped
in a crackling fog. He tells of the coming of that reluctant
spring, when the wild flocks fly crying overhead, the ice
breaks up in the rivers with a roar, the barren tundra becomes enameled with sudden flowers. Of the dread return
of autumn, the loneliness of Christmas in the empty
wastes, when he smokes his last cigar as a salute to all the
bright faces around the table at home. For three years he
is lost in that outer North.

It was not until the spring of 1862 that a mail packet got
through to him, and he read that his country had been at
war for two years. He broke camp and started home with
the intention of taking up arms. But enlistment officers
look upon only the best physical specimens as fit to be shot
and rot. Kennicott went instead back to the Smithsonian
with his collections, to work them up.

The results of his trip were enormous. In spite of the loss of many specimens by the upsetting of his canoe on two occasions, he had brought out the most astonishing materials and data that any single-handed American has wrung from the icy grip of the North. He had discovered the nesting grounds of scores of our migratory birds whose ways had hitherto remained mysterious; he had seen the unknown bridal plumage and heard the mating songs of others that never descend to our latitudes. A wealth of ethnographical material, of mineral specimens, of data on fisheries and fur-bearing quadrupeds were but a part of his spoil. He had prepared lexicons of the unwritten tongues he had mastered. He had discovered the headwaters of the Yukon, and mapped hundreds of miles that had never been traced before. Here was the work of a naturalist upon the grand, the classic scale.

Perhaps it will never be possible to make the public see that this sort of arctic exploration has more meaning than dropping the American flag from an airplane upon the hypothetical pole. But even in the uproar of the Civil War, the rumor of Kennicott's accomplishment rose to fame. And the Western Union Telegraph appointed him naturalist to their survey for a line to be run to Russian Alaska.

His passport, treasured in the archives of the Grove, lies before me as I write, in English and in Russian script, stamped with the double eagle of the Tsars, that once put the resources of an empire at his command and now is as historic as a coin impressed with the head of Tiberius Caesar.

He sailed from New York at the beginning of 1865 for Greytown, Nicaragua, crossed the isthmus, and continued by boat to San Francisco and Sitka. Red tape, wrangling, hampering economies leveled on the scientific branch of the expedition, and personal jealousies and disloyalty hindered the start for the interior. Working himself to death, Major Kennicott struggled to get on, all but pushing the sledges himself. A premonition must have come upon him; he wrote directions for continuing the work in case any-

thing befell him. On a May morning in 1866 he stepped out of the fort at Nulato, spoke a few words of Russian to the guard, and was never seen alive again. Death took him younger, even, than it had taken Douglas.

They found him lying with his compass beside him, and indications for his map-making of the surrounding mountains drawn in the soft soil; he had been still at work when his heart failed. A cross and tablet was erected there, where his thirty years were ended. 'Kennecott'(*sic*), the copper range, listed every day under mining stocks in the newspapers, is named for him. 'Fame,' said Lord Byron, 'consists in falling on the field of glory, and having your name spelled wrong in the dispatches.'

It was in winter that his body came back to the Grove, to lie there, on one of the coldest of January days. They say the birds, the chickadees in particular, looked from the trees, and when the coffin slowly sank into the grave, the quail called — not their 'Bob-white!' whistle out of happy summer, but the minor note they utter when the day is over and the flock is to be gathered together against the final dark.

By January of the winter of my repatriation, I was sick for spring. That year was strangely without snow. Day after day went mildly by, breeding in one who knew this continental climate the pessimistic feeling that what begins too well must soon end badly. I walked the woods without need for a topcoat, the weak sun caressing my hands, and found the ponds, where once the buffalo may have wallowed, floored with cracked marl. Since we were spared blizzards in their season, for lack of them the shallowly hibernated batrachians were exposed to cold.

After the little book on trees, more writing for the ten-cent trade was offered me — a history for children (since republished handsomely), then three wildflower guides. They were worth doing as well as I could. I was at least a breadwinner.

'Do you know what that is?' I asked my six-year son who trotted at my side.

'A man who writes pot-boilers,' Malcolm said with gravity all too polite.

In April the last of my novels was to issue forth upon the lists. I had concluded it in the final racked months upon the Riviera, and it was all about a White Russian wonder-child — of all unnatural phenomena! — and the flotsam of fallen empires. It was not possible now to hope much of it, but it would have been impossible not to hope.

In March the black winds began. They gave a scathing whistle through the leafless trees; from the bald earth they called up malevolent afriti, all the drear débris of winter, powdery leaf mold and spores of fungi, and gray ash from fields the stupid farmers had burned off. Snow fell then, contrarily, a dry snow hissing on blown dead leaves. The first meadowlarks began to whistle, as men do to keep their courage up. The wind came back, with a long thirst at the back of its throat, licking any moisture. What rain fell, the parched earth sucked instantly. When the red-winged blackbirds came over, they caught no heliographic welcome from the swamps, and they passed the Grove this year without descending to nest. The sun went veiled. In Nebraska, so it was told, dust lay piled against the fences like snow in blizzards. In Illinois, where tons of dust made twilight of the noon, the prairies were Mon-

golian with the whine of the hydrophobic wind, and the
grit of everything beneath the fingers. The story of the
Wunderkind appeared, and disappeared from public notice. This was spring by the publishers' lists, by the few
cowed squills in bloom here at the Grove, and by blown
and withering jonquils and narcissus. The birds sang all
their old songs; they have the stoutest hearts among us.
The climate went through all the impish transformations
in its bag of tricks, consistent only about drought. In the
daytime one was not aware of what the essential lack was
in this harried season. But when the twilight fell, and the
winds died, you knew. Out of the greening woods came no
sound. The pools and marshes with their poor cracked lips
were mute. And in the dark my listening ears would ache
for the sweet eerie trilling that every year tells of the
awakening of life.

Here on my desk in California I have the journal I began in March of that year of no frogs. It speaks of aspen
catkins out, and the first kildeer, and when honey bees
appeared again and where they may have got their nectar
so early. This was a Nature diary; in it is recorded a cycle
of the Grove and not the season of a thinking man. What
sang and bloomed and nested I put down, with the dates,
but nothing of my wife's long tortured illness or the
thoughts I had all day save for the little time I took to
write my journal up. 'Elm buds now large and red,' I read
now. 'Saw a golden-crowned kinglet, an occasional migrant here.' 'Pistillate flowers of pussy willow in bloom.'
Once, I see, I wrote, 'This day most heavy of heart.'

And I remember that in those days I was like one listening. Listening ... The frogs were still; there was no reas-

surance coming out of the woods. I was feeling for a pulse.
Almost I had lost it. Five years I had been away, in another land, preoccupied with an endeavor to understand
things other than the thing I listened now for. Once, over
there in France, only once I had heard it, felt the throb of
it. That was when my mother wrote to me from Tryon in
Carolina that the glen I loved there, with tall trees and a
waterfall in it, was to be sold up for its lumber, and what
had I to say to that? So I sat down, in our Riviera villa,
and wrote about everything that grew there, the tulip
trees and sourwood and dogwood, the maidenhair and
trillium and trembling saxifrage, and the birds and mammals and insects, and about the falls itself, that leaps forever with a pulsation like living. This report my mother's
friends took to the richest man in the small town, and he
bought the glen for them. The women have paid him back.
The trees are there still, and the dewed maidenhair; the
red birds call 'What cheer!' there, and any time I like
I can listen and hear the pulsation of the falling
water.

At the Grove, in the year of drought, I was trying to
hear like that, a heartbeat. Once it was loud in this place;
it thundered with the hoofs of the buffalo; it drummed with
the wings of the grouse. There was a great serenity then in
which to hear America live. I mean the America that was
here before we Americans came to it, and will be here for
our posterity and beyond. You can hear it as surely
as ever today, in the small strum of insects among the
summer grasses; it persists in the voice of a single vesper
sparrow singing late into the dark.

I caught it; I was sleeping in a tent now, with my wife,

for greater quiet, for the coolness that came out of the
empty woods at nightfall. I wrote on June fourteenth:

> Last night in our tent I heard the vesper sparrow singing
> not merely in the twilight, as is usually reported, but up to
> midnight, and again near dawn. Like many of the spar-
> rows, this bird has a song that consists in one syllable only,
> without difference in the pronunciation of each note; not
> only that, but the song as I heard it was a monotone, with-
> out change of pitch. Yet it is most flexible and, as is the
> way with the sparrow tribe, fine and of piercing sweetness.
> The whole performance succeeds by accent and rhythm —
> the length of time he holds a note, the running together of
> rapid notes, not to mention volume, the effect of diminu-
> endo and crescendo, and the expression poured into the
> phrases. With this economy of means, this almost severe
> restraint, he sang so that I lay long awake to listen.

Yes, I heard. By dawn all the birds were noisy, out
there on the fringe of the woods, orioles, song sparrows,
field sparrows, mourning doves, robins, black-billed
cuckoos, meadowlarks, catbirds, flickers, thrashers, and
the cardinal that will mean to me always the suburban
woods beyond Cherrydale in Virginia. Celia knew him and
his whistle before she was three, and early every March
morning reported him to me. I was hearing the beat of
living surely now, the measure of my days as I had lived
them, according to my creed and training as a naturalist.

I had begun to write about this, not caring if it should
satisfy any others but myself. Only a page at a time, as I
had done my first Nature writing for that Washington
paper. Once I got out the flimsy carbons of those short
newspaper pieces and glanced through them. How thin
they were! There was the sparrow I began with; he was

there, all right, but the man who listened heard so little
then! I put away the carbons and began instead to remember, and listen, and write down what I wanted to
find out, about the cycle of the year and the time of a
man.

The summer went, with drought and heat and the rapid
fading of flowers as they came to their season. The entries
in my Nature diary are fewer now, for I was busy. September, I see, brought sweeping rains and the restorative
smell of mushrooms in the woods. October was a triumph.
There was balm like honey in the sun; the skies were high
and bald; at last the mercury shot down overnight, a gale
stripped all the trees but the red and black oaks. 'Three
nights of frost, each harder than the one before,' I find
recorded. 'Not a living insect seen, but some Orthopteran
stridulation heard from a single creature, and a dead clover
yellow butterfly found on the road.'

Then in November, it appears, we had that tardy gift we
like to think the Indians bequeathed us — a last ghost of
summer. Upon the twenty-first I noted a flock of Lapland
longspurs; so the journal ends. The other journal I was
writing, out of the total of my years, strung on the thread
of a life I could best examine because it had been cut off,
was going well, was growing in a pile of manuscript. My
mother came from Carolina for a visit. Again, at my desk
on the balcony over the drawing-room, I heard from below
the tapping of her typewriter, that sound which seems to
me to have ushered in my very existence. What she typed
now was the almanac that I was writing. I never heard her
typewriter again; this was the last time that we had
together.

It was a good time, and the winter, though it was harder than the one that brought the drought, was a good one. There was plenty of snow; the drifts piled against the house; they would be filling up the ponds and swamps, I thought. When I went out I had to struggle for my walk, and almost liked it. The air rang like a bell; the boughs of every tree were rich with their soft burden; the pathos of an empty sparrow's nest was buried under a cocked white turban. And at night the glorious winter constellations rode high in the vast prairie sky, Orion following red Aldebaran, and heeled by the Dog Star.

The nature of this season is essentially thoughtful. There is provocation to thought in the first flake you catch upon a lifted finger, one of those earliest flakes that, endlessly repeating the plan of a six-sided crystal, are fretted to a Gothic intricacy. Faster and faster they fall; the wind takes them and hurls them like a flight of arrows through the woods; the crystals are broken, rounded, polished by the wind of stinging bullets. Ice too is worth thinking about, the primordial great grinding power of ice that has carved us out much of a continent. The mind demands then whether our modern human life is not impermanently builded between two eras of the glacial period. It raises fundamental biological queries, as to the power of spores to withstand the inconceivable frosts of outer space; the possible origin of life upon other planets; the drifting of the earth away from the sun into the cold hells of universal night.

Deep in that winter *An Almanac for Moderns* was finished; March twenty-first was set as publication date. On the first of March I took up my Grove diary again; there-

after are recorded thaw and floods, rising winds, freezing,
thaw, and blizzards again.

March 17: Light snow fell last night. The morning blew
off clear and cold. A naked sky all day, wind very sharp off
the snowbanks and ponds. Bird voices coming clear and
sweet through it all.

The pond is half sheeted in extremely thin ice; presum-
ably at zero centigrade now, water and ice deadlock each
other. But it *is* water melted for the first time to the bottom, and actually swirling, driving in ripples before the
wild warm damp wind, for all the world like a liquid! There
are reflections of the bushes in the water. Only we who
lived through the dust storms, insufferable heat and drought
of last year, can imagine the beauty of water.

March 18: Arising this morning at about two o'clock, I
heard the first singing of frogs, species as yet unidentified.
To me it had a very eery chromatic vibrato. The effect is
shimmery — sad, high, thin, weird yet pleasing, and at that
deeply cheerless hour, secret.

I remember that secret, as I held it, leaning from the window with the chill of spring in the night blowing against my breast. It is a secret never to be unriddled, the secret of life itself as the frogs seem to know it, uncomplicated at their primordial amphibian level. They proclaim it to intelligence that cannot understand. A man could well spend his life trying to understand, trying to report accurately. I wanted nothing better. I knew that now. I was clear at last as to the work I wished to be allowed. But that this appointment should be given me was much to ask.

March 21: This, by the calendar, is the first day of spring. With the ice melted in all the sloughs, with the sky a soft blue flecked with puffs of vague cloud, with pussy willows and aspen catkins bursting, frogs trilling, and the first migrant birds singing, this may well be accounted spring's birthday. It is also the birthday of my *Almanac....*

How good fortune came to be awarded this book of mine, the *Almanac*, in such measure that all my wish was granted, I find it more suitable to tell as a story to my children, the younger ones who like a tale to end 'and they lived happily ever after.' This story, following an admired precedent, began with an invitation, though not to a ball. It was large and stiff, and in its handsome engraving the directors of an association for the production of fine books requested my presence at a breakfast in the Jade Room of the Waldorf-Astoria in New York, 'the occasion being the first award of the Club's Gold Medal' to an unstated author. A telegram explained the rest.

At dusk of a November day a train slipped out of the ugly yards at Chicago; it was one they called 'The Rainbow,' and there were two people aboard who could really hope to find gold at the end of it. Over the dingy roof-tops one of those heroic winter sunsets died its early death; we were very quiet, feeling nameless and lucky, these two in all the world when it might have been two others.

So we approached New York, that port which we had entered last as refugees retreating from a personal defeat, that city where in my ungrown first manhood I could find no foothold. Now I shall always be absurdly wistful for Manhattan Transfer, where the train came to a long premonitory pause. I shall never stand at just that point again to look upon the city rising, towering, glittering, and untaken, beyond the girders and power lines, bridgeheads and freight smoke, beyond the melancholic and serene marshes full of reed-grass bowing obedient to a small seeking wind.

We lodged at an obscure hotel, the kind that has grown dingier since Sydney Porter wrote about the variety of people who used to stop there. Before noon my agent came as courier; he is a man who has outgrown nothing of what is worth keeping and is so easily lost, and, handing my wife into the yellow taxi, he gravely told her that it really was a pumpkin.

Even the reception hall of the Jade Room holds a great

many people; there were a hundred talking in it now, mys-
tified and guessing at whose luck this was going to be.
Nobody talked about me, because nobody knew me. And
I don't think any but a few had read my book.

So that their ultimate kindness took me on trust. The
kindness of the judges I like to look upon as a challenge
rather than a reward. I am grateful, most grateful to all
the people who, by granting me a living for it, permit me
the work I choose. I have called it an appointment, but of
course it is one made with myself. I have arrived at it, it
seems, partly because I never found another I could well
fill. I have called myself a reporter, and I acknowledge
that the field is one of battle, and that to be a soldier is a
braver thing. God knows I would probably make a very
poor one. But I would like to be another sort than I have
called myself; I wish that I might be, for some at least, a
water-carrier. This is a light task, but the human thirst is
very great. I understand this from the many who call, out
of the fighting.

In the end every man of us must fall, but there is no one
who need die of thirst. The waters are infinite and, hidden
within the rock, they flow with the greatest of all strength.
They leap into the sunlight, and when a man sees them he
beholds that life is worth fighting for. That last day in the
gorge of the Columbia when I came in the Cascade Mountains of Oregon upon seven waterfalls, one after the other,
was a Sunday, and there were people come out from the
city, come from all over the country, to look for them. I
watched these visitors coming. Men and women, careless
young people and children, they got out of their cars chattering, laughing or arguing; they seemed then as common-

place as most of us look on a fine summer Sunday, when a human with his queer garb and gear is the least lovely thing in the natural world. One by one they would start up the narrow path that climbed to the falls; I stood and watched them coming. The voices died as they approached through the shafts of light slanting through Douglas firs and hemlock, toward the perfect singing arc, the purity of the perpetual wind carrying spray across the curtseying maidenhair. The people walked slowly, hardly looking now where they set their feet, not noticing me as I searched their faces. They came with lips parted in listening and wonder; they saw only the waters. And in their eyes I saw a reflection. I hope to keep that always before my own eyes.

16

SINCE WALDEN

THERE comes a time in any journey, no matter how far or near its end, when the mind turns homeward bound. If it is a holiday trip you are making, at that moment the holiday is, in essence, over; the prime exhilaration of escape is gone. Instead, if you are now refreshed, your thoughts run ahead, outstripping the wheels, going to meet the task that lies at home, awaiting you.

So, as I packed up on Monday morning in the room above the falls, I felt the wind change. I felt at my back the country I had traveled, Utah, Wyoming, Montana, Idaho, Washington and part of Oregon — they lay behind me. I set my face toward the sea, for I was going home, home by the long run down the coast, into California.

There, in a rambling hillside house in an overgrown

garden looking out upon blue sea, stood my desk, with my
chair drawn up ready. Beside the chair stretched the long
window that reaches from floor to ceiling, giving on the
little patio where the juncos hop under the fig tree. On
the giant Monterey pines, beyond the patio wall, where the
horned owls roost and hoot at night, and, beyond the
pines, on the shining steeps of the Santa Yñez Mountains.
All my books would be standing silent, eloquent, in their
places on the shelves around that room; the fire would be
laid upon the hearth. It was vacant, that study I loved;
the desk would be lying broad and bare, the paper on it
unwritten. Here was I, in the gorge of the Columbia, with
miles and miles to go. The ripple marks of light from the
falls waved me farewell over the ceiling.

So, when we started out that morning, for the first time
I did not see what I was looking at, not for a good many
miles. Thoughts that weeks ago I had in weariness put
from me were thronging back. Once more I was thinking
about my job.

This Nature writing is a curious business. Judged by
scientists, it has sometimes been accused of amounting to
no more than science diluted, uncreative, retold, the picking
of great brains. One might fear that it would correspond
to some sort of corruption of great music — as if one
should first cut, let us say, the César Franck D Minor symphony, then partially de-orchestrate it so as to bring out
the sheer melody, then arrange it for popular instruments
like the saxophone, clarinet, and snare drum, syncopate
it, put words to the tunes, and thus get it going on everyone's lips. Thereby leaving it an open question whether
it would not be better that great music should remain in-

comprehensible and inaccessible to the many, but still great and pure for musicians at least.

If the popularization of science always fitted this comparison, it might well be a worse than useless endeavor. At its worst it has been exactly that, I fear. At its worst it is guilty not merely of certain slips of fact (a fault as serious as the slip is large or small, yet not intentional treachery to science), but some popularizations have committed the high crime of deliberate misinterpretation. Scientists are justified if they do not forgive a writer who sets out knowingly to distort their meanings for effect. They have reason to be grateful to the expert journalists, such as George W. Gray and Waldemar Kaempffert, who faithfully translate their technicalities into the language of Everyman. Still more to the rare few, like Thoreau and Maeterlinck, who give to accurate reporting the luminosity of poetry.

For poetry and scientific writing aim at a same goal. The winged word, which is the poetic word, gets there fastest. Unfortunately, for many at the moment, the language of poetry connotes a vague and high-flown mysticism. This is due to the afterglow of nineteenth-century romanticism. No such fear of the poetic existed to trouble the minds of Virgil's readers, when he wrote of animal husbandry and the harvesting of crops. Aristotle employed the power of poetry in his cosmology, and was not accused of weakness of mind. Lucretius showed no fuzzy thinking when he thus popularized the atomic theory of his master, Epicurus (who learned it from Democritus):

> And all the pageant goes; whilst I, with awe,
> See in its place the things my master saw;

See in its place the three eternal things —
The only three — atoms and space and law.

. . . .

No single thing abides; but all things flow.
Fragment to fragment clings — the things thus grow
Until we know and name them. By degrees
They melt, and are no more the things we know.

Globed ꞌrᴜᴍ the atoms falling slow or swift
I see the suns, I see the systems lift
Their forms; and even the systems and the suns
Shall go back slowly to the eternal drift.[1]

It is the verdict of history upon Lucretius that though
he added nothing new to the atomic theory, he kept it alive
for a thousand years, against the hatred of the Church and
the opposition of the schoolmen, till Giordano Bruno discovered it in his pages, and restored it to the heritage of
mankind. I think it is not too much to say that it was the
majesty of poetry that preserved the atomic theory when
almost the entire didactic writings of Democritus have disappeared, and the chill and lofty skepticism of Epicurus
degenerated into the amorality and hedonism of epicu·
reans like Nero.

Less scientist or poet than reporter is the writer in the
field. He takes us with him, through the gate he holds
ajar, into living Nature. There he learns from the event
even as he teaches — how to follow through on an unknown bird, how to listen, how to memorize its song, to
note its habits, to find its nest. If he knows too much, he's
no friend of ours. We prefer sometimes to see him
stumped; we don't mind if he scratches his poll in public.

[1] Translated by W. H. Mallock.

Better that than a fellow in an out-sized wig, handing down decisions.

We want no professors, either, to lecture at us out-of-doors, and the writing naturalist may not so much instruct as kindle enthusiasm. For this, his own enthusiasm is boundless. He wants no less than to get everybody thinking his way (modest ambition!). To pipe even the asphalt slaves out of the streets, over the Weser, and into the hill.

So far as I can think, such was done for the first time in English literature by an ironmonger — a hardware retailer, as we would say now — with a shop in Fleet Street. He was a quiet body, a man who had given great stakes in life, and lost them — a wife and seven children. He was pious, too; he went every Sunday to St. Dunstan's to hear Doctor John Donne preach. He was a friend of Ben Jonson's, and a minor poet in his own right. But as a Nature writer he was our first, and comes dangerously near to being the best. In proof of the inimitable stamp of his genius, I have only to quote one line of his to have him recognized, as the only possible author of it: 'I envy nobody but him, and him only, that catches more fish than I do.'

Walton, like a south wind in March, unlocked all the brooks for us. He is the ouzel among writers, never found far from his stone-flies and chubs. If, in his discourse, he has to go overland, he is like the eel who will cross land, slipping through the dew film to keep his skin wet, until he comes to the next pond. And it has been said of him that he has won to his way of thinking countless thousands who have never put a worm on a hook, much less that frog, for bait, of which he urges us to 'use him as though you loved him, that is, harm him as little as you may possibly, that he may live the longer.'

The English language was to wait more than a century for another Nature writer of his caliber. When he came, it was in the age of Danton and George Washington, yet no bruit of arms disturbs his tranquil pages. He lived in the times of Linnaeus but was little of a systematist, in the day of Buffon, who was undertaking a Natural History of Everything, yet our author never wrote anything but a sheaf of letters to two other gentlemen almost as retired as he, and his subject was the natural history of one sleepy Hampshire parish. Nevertheless, to the history of ornithology, his quaint and quiet lines ring in modernity:

> Selborne, *Jan.* 15, 1770
> To the Honorable Daines Barrington
> Dear Sir, — It was no small matter of satisfaction to me to find that you were not displeased with my little *methodus* of birds. If there was any merit in the sketch, it must be owing to its punctuality. For many months I carried a list in my pocket of the birds that were to be remarked, and, as I rode or walked about my business, I noted each day the continuance or omission of each bird's song; so that I am as sure of the certainty of my facts as a man can be of any transaction whatsoever.

The bird census, now so widely promulgated by the Audubon Society, was the invention of Gilbert White; he was the original exponent, as far as I know, of the close seasonal observation of Nature, a branch of science known to the pedantic as phenology. He was the first to perceive the value in the study of migration (then a disputed fact) and of banding or ringing birds, though it was Audubon who

first performed the experiment. No professional ornithologist ever did so much to widen interest in birds; from
White's pages they cock a friendly eye at us, and hop out
of his leaves right over our thresholds. Since the appear-
ance of *The Natural History of Selborne* in 1789 there has
been a fresh edition of this classic on an average of every
two years, so that not only is White to be considered as a
pioneer but as a continuing influence. For he was — he is
— above all things the prince of amateur naturalists. And
natural science still has room for the amateur. White
lends him his countenance; he shows him what he can do,
even at home; he raises a hope — so admirably fulfilled by
other amateurs like Darwin and Fabre — that one might
become a very Humboldt of discovery by traveling around
his own back gate.

Half the charm of the letters lies in their effortless drift
from topic to topic, yet scientifically White is all the while
getting somewhere. Through all his pottering and gossip-
ing you will perceive that he is out for nothing less than the
biota of a sample area in the temperate zone — to use a
terminology that he would not understand if he could hear
it. He is, with admirable modern spirit, taking up the
larger problems of biology as they occur in his experience
and on a small scale — migration, hibernation, instinct,
habitat, adaptation, distribution, life histories, and animal
psychology.

It points the rising significance of the Nature writer to
observe that though there was only one great one writing in
English in the seventeenth century, and one in the eight-
eenth, this curious sort of bird began in the nineteenth to
flock and sing in a chorus. Note too that those who con-

tributed most to this realm of English literature were
either born in the New World — Audubon in Haiti, Hudson (whose father was from Maine) in Argentina, Thoreau
in Concord, Burroughs in the Catskills, and Hornaday in
the same state as Riley, who was the best of our Nature
poets — or they did their great work in the western hemisphere, Alexander Wilson and John Muir (Scotsmen by
birth) in the United States, Humboldt in Brazil, Thomas
Belt in Nicaragua. For the nineteenth century was the
heroic age of natural history and of the exploration and discovery of Nature in the Americas. And while other men
were founding their fortunes on the exploitation of natural
resources in the New World, the Nature writers were
recording and defending the primeval treasure.

Like the poets of the nineteenth century and even its
scientists, Darwin, Bates, Wallace, Haeckel, its Nature
writers were romantics and, essentially, moralists. Sometimes mystics. Their romanticism found its extreme expression in Thoreau's withdrawal into the woods — a
style he all but imposed upon his followers, so that Burroughs left his wife to do it, and occupied one eremitic
cabin after another where, since he lacked the man of
Walden's vestal inhospitality, he sociably entertained a
string of visitors. The mysticism of the Victorian Nature
writers comes out in an unforgettable passage of Thoreau's, in which he prefers astrology to astronomy, which,
he considers, does less to reveal the secrets of Nature, and
not so much for human kind. It reaches absurdity in
Bronson Alcott's refusal to eat any but 'aspiring' vege-
tables; earth-bound tubers, he felt, exerted the wrong
influence. This mysticism is rationalized in a vague hos-

tility, found in almost all the romantic Nature writers, to science, as if it were blind, and blinding, to some higher truth and would, just as Wordsworth feared, desiccate something fresh and lovely.

In Emerson is expressed the moral tone of these men and this era. It is a manly tone; for him the value of Nature is as a bracer to ourselves, toward naturalness, self-help, sincerity, and a well-grounded optimism. How Thoreau wielded the bright axe of this morality is too familiar for discussion. In Muir, it took the practical form of a burning indignation against the despoiling of western Nature, which resulted in the establishment of Yosemite and Sequoia National Parks. Hornaday turned his blade-like pen to the defense of vanishing wild life. Burroughs in America, Hudson in England took up the cause of the birds.

I hope I have made clear my feeling that at its best the morality of the Victorian naturalists was all for the good. That the romanticism of those Nature writers was not only understandable in the light of their times, but in itself a precious contribution. There is something even in mysticism — when the mind which entertains it is of a great enough simplicity. If I acknowledge all this, may I then be permitted to say that the whole romantic pattern for the life, thought, and style of a Nature writer is not binding upon a man of the twentieth century? That a new attitude toward Nature must be allowed to grow, to meet new hungers and new truths?

I drew a deep breath, with something fresh in it. The sweeping conifers still thickly screened the view ahead, but I glanced at my companion to see if she had sensed what I had. Her head, I saw, was tipped back a little, her eyes were half-closed, and I knew by the smile on her lips what she was tasting. Like flying insects obeying a tropism, we sped toward the highest concentration of this diffused appeal, until at last we caught a genuine tang of salt, and met again the vast invisible presence of ocean.

For the ocean does not wholly stay in its bed, and is not confined to sea level. It takes the air, as flung spray for many rods from the shore, as a salt mist for many miles, as a breath of moisture from the great well-head of all moisture, that may reach, refreshing, restoring, a hundred and fifty miles up the Columbia gorge where first we had seen the greening grass upon the hills, then the spires of conifers again, then the living brooks and the cataracts that give the Cascade Range its name. It was the ocean, really, vaporized, freed of salt, and recondensed, which brushed the chain of extinct volcanoes with their mantles of frost and snow and ice. We had seen them shining — Mount Hood, Mount Jefferson, Mount Saint Helena, and, once, we thought — or perhaps we only hoped it — a faint trembling star-prick of light upon ice, that might have been Mount Rainier.

For it is one of the unique properties of water — almost without parallel in the chemistry of things — that it can quit the liquid state for that of a vapor without being brought first to a boil. Molecules of water at ordinary temperatures are forever jumping out of the ocean into the atmosphere. And they do not drop back into the hydrosphere. They scatter, suspended; they may rise miles up, and from that altitude diffuse far.

Well for us that this is so; else would a waterless desert come down to meet undrinkable brine. But as it is, the ocean (to speak of it as the chief bank of water on the planet) in invisible veils sweeps around the world. It softens the blue of the skies, makes winy the sunsets, enshrouds, sweetens, sustains. As it is essentially the ocean, in crystals of frost, which tips the cones of Oregon, so it is a drop of water, once in the sea, which just upholds and spreads abroad the small pride of each frail petal in this lush and tender flora — rhododendron starring the woods to remind you, with dogwood and trillium, of the Appalachians. Or this bear-grass and Missouri iris and camass which recall the Rockies. And everywhere by the roadsides, in deep ferny glens, the eye was startled by spires of foxglove, looking native as the maidenhair, yet foreign, by origin, to Oregon as the drug-shop of Hans Sachs or the *Märchen* of the brothers Grimm.

With every mile, as we approached the Pacific, the feel of ocean intensified. The Columbia, for one thing, had broadened now to a great estuary, a glittering tide that rose and fell with the pull of the sea. With every mile we saw more gulls, wheeling in the softened light over piles of stranded fish. And flocks of other water birds, too far out on the river to be distinguished, swept by, going up and down steadily on maritime affairs of their own. There multiplied jetties, and barges, and far-off funnels, and near-by forests of masts in little harbors. The fisherman and his business, the sailor and his, were evidenced still miles from blue water. Roads, and railroads, and skid-

roads came down to the river shore and stopped, as all
land things stop at the sea's edge. The last long bridge was
passed; the river, at last, reached its destiny; nothing now
could separate it from the ocean; no thread could span it.
It was merged, like a soul bound outward that has not
quite departed yet cannot be called back.

But there was none of that gradual, spiritless flattening
out of the land one feels on the east coast, in the South and
Mid-Atlantic states, a sinking away into marshes, endless
marshes that shut off the sight and might of the sea. There
is beauty in that, a melancholy, monotonous beauty; I
have loved the Low Country, with its pensive egrets and
crying fish-crows over the slant, salt-stiffened yellow grass
and the barrier dunes behind which brine in the air turns
balm. But it is the glory of the Pacific coast that the
mountains come right to the combers, and that the forests
march down to the very shore, swinging their boughs in
the salt wind. Until the shoreline, we were still swooping
up and over fine rocky ridges, down into shadowy, misty
vales with rushing brooks in them, flashing through the
barred light and shade of the Douglas firs, and tideland
firs, Sitka spruces and pines.

So that when we swung into a long curve, up, over,
down, around, and suddenly out — and there was the
ocean — its finality and spread, the surging voice of it, the
chill of its open breath, its thousand glittering eyes, and
the proud step of its white chargers upon the shingle, called
us up like a band marching round the corner. As the road
bent southward — the first time we had seriously taken
this direction in all these weeks, but the only direction
henceforth, for a thousand miles — we had at first an ex-

hilarated impulse to race the ocean. I let the car show its
paces, mile after mile, shouting a song over my shoulder,
laughing at the high skidding of gulls, at the mincing grace
of waders, the strings of snake-necked cormorants streaking out in black flight formations just above the spume.

But in the end we drew up by the lonely sand. You
couldn't race the ocean, after all. You were impelled to
stop, to give this majesty a long deep homage. We got
out, walked down the beach, and watched the water, all of
a plouter and spew, come foaming in with heavy rhythm,
the meter of an elemental poet. We watched the wan
glitter on the thin last lips, that spread out, curl behind the
sand-girt stacks of rock, meet, kiss, bicker a little, merge in
overlapping arcs, like one petal behind another. Then we
lay down on the dry shore, on our sides, close to the incoming surf as we dared, and looked seaward, and laughed a
little, because it is terrible to see the ocean like that,
higher than the land, to see that off there, between us and
Japan, there is a great moon-lifted bulge that has got to be
compensated, satisfied for hours upon the body of the
shore. And that there where your head lies now, your
wind-whipped hair, your open eyes, your nostrils drawing
in sweet oxygen, the green sea water has to come, and with
it all its creatures, its children and demons, waving gills,
staring from long-stalked eyes, crawling on jointed spidery
legs, clinging, sucking, scavenging, retiring at the will of
the satellite to wait again out there in the depths.

On the Oregon coast there is often little peace in the
Pacific, and no blue about it, and what you feel in the air
is the Aleutian Islands, Kamchatka, the Kuriles. Not too
hard to remember that the Russians were early on this

coast, Captain Kotzebue in the *Rurik*, with the poet-bota-
nist Chamisso aboard, and later the Baron (also Admiral)
Wrangel. This is the faunal province of the seals and
whales; this is the rough cold water where the diatoms,
those glass boxes that are microscopic plants, are plenty.
This is the kingdom of the giant brown kelps, their chloro-
phyll all masked with dusky pigment, the bobbling sea-
otter's cabbage, the slashing strops of oarweed, the big
bull kelp, the bloated rockweed.

Offshore, I thought, there should be little kittiwakes
twinkling on the wing, shearwaters cresting up over each
hissing wave and down into each yawning hollow, rolling
in their flight, one wing up and then the other. Long-
winged albatrosses would be following the ships, stocky
fulmars fishing, and parasitic jaegers hawking the royal
terns. There must be petrels out there, I knew, gray as a
nimbus sky, surf scoters and hardy scaups, arctic terns,
perhaps, upon migration between one polar sea and another, guillemots like sea-going pigeons, murres riding the
swells, ancient murrelets and rasping auklets.

Here, anyone will note, is scarcely a familiar bird name
in the lot. These offshore birds have less to do with the
western land birds, the varied thrush, the priestly solitaire,
the domestic linnets and wayfaring blackbirds, than with
the avifauna of New Zealand.

For he who comes down to the sea, and has business
with the waters, enters another world of life. A world,
even among birds, most remote of all from his own. The
offshore birds have, many of them, almost never seen a
human being. Even trees they know as a dark fringe upon
that useless and hostile thing, the land. In all their lives

some of them have walked but a few steps, at the most. On the land they have to be born, but you would say they seem ashamed of this weak necessity. When they rest, it is on the waves; when they live to the full, it is on the wing. To them, a gull must be a landlubber, a scavenger of dead fish, who can neither really dive nor swim. A curlew would be a complaining knock-knees who hugs the shore like a Greek mariner, and even a tropic-bird might seem a fair-weather sailor.

Out there in the thickest smoke of the ocean's battle with the rocks I noticed sea-palms growing. Which are not palms but algae, seaweeds unlike all others in that they stand up stiff as little trees, a foot high, or two at the most. And it is their preference to grow nowhere that the surf is not forever beating them. Half their lives — I mean every other moment — they are emersed, they are standing clear of water, breathing free oxygen, exposed to desiccation, forced to hold their palm-like foliage aloft. The next instant a ton of water, enough to break the spine of any swimmer, descends upon them. For a long moment, two, three — time to drown a man — they are submerged in the insanity of lashing water. They are twisted, torn by the roots, lifted by the hair. In vain. For as each wave draws back again, sucking in its breath, swallowing the foam of its own mouth, for another bite, the little sea palms rise up again into the gasp of air. They shake the brine from their heads as if they laughed, in the strength of all life which is stronger than the rage of ocean, and longer than the staying power of rock.

Once, on the Monterey coast, I collected some, at my peril. I put them in my vasculum, not knowing it was an elf-gift I locked up there. I meant to press and dry them on the first sunny day — and on that peninsula you may have to wait long for that. But in two days the fog cleared off, and I opened my box. The sea-palms had simply deliquesced. Out of the fight, they died; they turned to slime and ink. Without woody tissue, they had nothing to preserve; like all life, they were not much more than a thin membrane surrounding a little water. Torn from the surf that beat the life into them, life leaked out of them. Life — whatever that is — was all that had kept the sap within from joining the sea without. I threw the limp waste of them back into the brine. Tomorrow, Lucretius, I thought, it will be again the living form, the fighting thing, the sap, the membrane, and the leaf.

The tide now was coming in faster; soon it would cover the spot where I lay. I rose, and drew my wife up, and we turned our backs on the sea-palms. They only show a little more plainly what is as true of the twinflower or the rose.

> Observe this dew-drenched rose of Tyrian grain —
> A rose today. But you will ask in vain
>   Tomorrow what it is; and yesterday
> It was the dust, the sunshine and the rain.[1]

Long ago I had forgotten the consideration of my work,

---

[1] Translated by W. H. Mallock.

which had preoccupied me that morning, the plans for
what I should do at my desk at home, when I arrived there.
All this light-filled and spray-hung day I had been living
Nature, not contemplating it. Now, swinging the car back
into the road, I began out of a sense of repletion, of gratitude, to think again about what I have called my appointment.

I have said that I am a reporter by profession, and attempt to be also a water-carrier. By this I mean one who

fetches refreshment to those who do the fighting. And
that, I fear, is not bearing a full share in the war. A woman
could do it; a boy could do it.

But certain essentials are required of even a water-carrier. First, he must know where the water can be found,
and that it is fresh. Second to nothing, he must have a
bucket which really holds water.

Finally, he must be quick about it. And he must know where the troops are, and how to reach them.

Apply these rules to the profession of a popularizer of science — or, in the language of Emersonian times, a Nature writer — and you find the discipline I must obey.

To know where the water is to be found demands, in the case of my calling, to have a trained sight. Slipshod observation, dilettantism, feelings of intuitive spiritual superiority in the literary ambler through the woods over the 'grubbing scientist' and his 'materialism' may once have been tolerated. But in the blood and dust of today they will not go down. Nor will tender moral lessons drawn from the blossom and the bird by analogy and not by fact. That isn't water, that's rosewater. It would leave the throats of the troops thirstier than before. Only the real thing, the sky-juice, the leak of the mountains' ribs, will do. Pure out of the granite.

I have said that the water-carrier must have a bucket that will really hold water. In the case of my profession, this means an argument built of reality. My bucket has been sawn and shaped and hammered together for me by the multiple labors of science. The hoops that bind it are the iron laws of Nature.

I remember listening to a bishop, once, who told us that astronomical law implies a Lawgiver. He said astronomers tell us that, despite the inconceivable multitude of stars in the sky, not one collides with another. And that therefore a Greater Intelligence must be waving the stars on or holding them back. Like some celestial traffic cop, I imagined, drawn by William Blake.

I didn't have the pulpit then, and I haven't the space

now, to point out all the fallacies in the bishop's thinking. It will be enough to say that astronomers do not suppose that there have never been any accidents among the stars; at least, as I understand them, they postulate not a few accidents in the memory of living men. The laws of the astronomers are not like human edicts for behavior; they are only descriptions of the order of events. There is no evidence that they were given by fiat, or that intelligence of any sort exists outside the animal kingdom. Or, be it noted, that intelligence is certainly the highest of all imaginable powers.

I am not making an assault upon Divinity. I am asking that Divinity shall not be made incredible by calling false testimony on its behalf.

The most reliable witness we can get upon the stand is science. So far as Nature is concerned, at any rate, science sees where all was darkness before; it is the new ray; it opens a new dimension and, with telescope and microscope, crucible and vacuum tube, it performs the modern miracles. Allowing for the human fallibility of the scientists themselves, science is the proving of truth. It is the new belief. Almost every one believes it, at bottom, for even those who decry it and deny it live practically by it daily and count unconsciously upon it. And anything that science begins to doubt has begun to die. The people will it so. The people today believe; they now accept the findings of science. There are those who still rouse the rabbles of superstition and prejudice, but here in America these do not prevail, for we are the people who say, 'So what?' and 'Show me!'

And we have a fine thirst on us, so that a water-carrier

must run his best. He has to remember that old city-room story about the famous newspaper editor who gave but one piece of advice: 'Be interesting, and be damned quick about it.' Scientists may go slowly; they must go slowly, making their tests over and over, reserving conclusions till these are watertight. But their interpreters must be wide awake, and wake up the rest about these matters. For, after all, the purpose of science is knowledge, and everyone has the right to know. What science has discovered is common property, and should be made easily available to all. This is not always remembered by a great many scientific writers who have never spoken outside of classrooms where attendance and attention are compulsory, never written a book which they could not order their students to buy. If the scientists practicing inside the college close are not always and widely understood, they may not be always and widely supported. They take that support for granted, along with their intellectual liberties. They had better look across the seas and ask themselves just how secure they are.

To be secure, our scientists must be so understood and admired that the whole people will allow no one to molest a hair of their heads. I am not saying that all academic wise men should try to popularize their works; I am saying that these works should be as widely popularized as possible by those equipped to do so. Sometimes these are the wise men themselves, like Haldane and Julian Huxley, Wells, Beebe, Hogben, Jeans and Paul Sears. Nobody knows as well as they what they are talking about. And these men are all interesting, and damned quick about it.

Yet there is no one who strolls so much as your man of

the natural sciences. It is sometimes the fastest way for him to get where he is going.

I seem to have been strolling, through red Utah, wide Wyoming, high Montana, green Oregon. But I have been searching for the waters. Four thousand miles and more I have gone flying over the roads. Running, with my empty bucket, for the springs. I have quenched my own thirst — I, who did not need water. But I have not forgotten that others parch in agony. All this time, all this way has gone along with me the bleeding Thing with its face torn out of it. I have never got away from it. I wouldn't try.

For a water-carrier, I have said, must know where the troops are. I hear, above the soft rush of the waterfall, above the hushing of the tall trees and the calm pulsing of ocean, the distant battle that comes each night a little nearer, the flashes mounting up the skies. I hear the breaking of men's bones, and the tears of women who gave everything in vain. I have been listening from the time I started; I remember how on the desert I would go out with my papers on the porch, planning to go to work — and would sit and stare at the vanishing snows on the mountains, and see nothing all day but the gash in the side of a nation I have loved like my own.

But that is not filling the bucket.

To be just too old to be worth shooting, just too young to expect to die before I have to see the outcome, to be nothing more than a water-carrier who does not know if he can reach even one man on the firing line — it's not a noble figure to cut. The water, at least, was dipped from a good spring; the bucket may just possibly not leak faster than I can run. There might be a few drops left — if I knew the way.

17

ROAD

WITHOUT END

THEREFORE we ran straight southward down the long coastal highway that does not leave the sea, save for a few miles a few times, from Astoria on the Columbia River all the way to the Redwood Empire. All the way we ran beside the ocean, and all the time the surf was coming in to meet us, green-blue curlers arching, glinting, breaking at the summit of their proud perfection. We drank the air, the misted salty sunshine that is Oregon's, in long breaths; the spinning wheels reeled up the mileage hour by unbroken hour.

We had to stop, of course, to eat, to sleep, but never out

of sound or sight of ocean. And once we stopped for the sea-lion caves. The ocean lay like a vast platter of glittering light below the cliff-top, and we went down to meet it, zigzagging down a path through thrift and bright figmarigold and blowing grasses, till we had nearly reached the ultimate level. There you descend into earth.

The ice-green caverns are a chain of domed rooms under the cliff, connected by a long tunnel, opening each to the sea by an arabesque aperture. A single kingly sea lion reared and swayed and bellowed on a rock throne in the center of the swirling cave waters. There was a flash of bird shapes, a skittering flight that broke out into a black-and-white pattern; by their pink feet I knew the pigeon guillemots. It is always strange to see a bird, a creature of air and light, inside a cave; strangest of all to see them washing in, just ahead of a comber, and settling on the cobbles with the contented snuggle-down of rock doves. Over that monstrous barking I could hear their wild chitterings, rising nervously, sinking away, echoed and megaphoned by the vault of the cave, drowned in the clangor of an incoming roller. Waves in a sea cave sound not at all like honestly liquid water with its rustle and lisp. They are like falling metal; they crash with the shattering clank of iron gates that close a catacomb.

Climbing up from this nether cauldron, I could look out, through chinks in the ascending shaft, at the sheer face of the cliff above. There I saw what looked like stumpy parrots standing about on horrifyingly narrow ledges, waddling a little, toeing out. A number, upon seeing me lean outward, launched themselves down the face of the precipice and spread their legs apart like a falling cat. I thought for an instant that they were flightless birds that I had frightened to their deaths. At the last minute, as it seemed, they broke open the short fan of their wings and lumbered away over the waves in a heavy flight.

They were my first tufted puffins, and they were in full breeding plumage, with long silky streamers of yellow feathers sweeping back from the ears. Enormous vermilion bill, vermilion feet, black back, pale belly, and white face ornament, a squat figure fit to be carved into a totem pole; so it bespeaks the north, the upper regions of Alaska where it ranges.

But we were racing south again, and south; I could feel
California, I thought, coming out to meet me. Up at the
border, in Del Norte County, its air is just as sharp as
southern Oregon's, but it seemed to me I caught a smile in
it, a personality familiar, easy-going, eyes humorously
narrowed a little against an intolerant sun.

It has been too much praised, this state in which for the
present I am living, for all the wrong things. Its sunshine
has been oversold to forty-seven other states tired of hearing about it, and no one has told enough about its rains,
those long green soaks that slake a nine-months thirst.
Too many people come out to it and see nothing of it, and
then go back across the country talking about all in it that
is foreign to it, the palms and the palmists, the pepper
trees and picture business, the whole synthetic Garden of
Allah effect.

But look upon the map, and you will see California as
she is, as she has been from the beginning, incorruptible, a
state shaped like a torso breasting the Pacific. Upon the
map of our country the outline of this state is like a figurehead under the bow of a mighty ship, the ship of states,
America, plowing westward. Fragmentary yet perfect,
her figure has for backbone the High Sierra; all the fertility
of the Great Central Valley lies within her belly; under her
breast, which is Cape Mendocino, pressed against the sea
like a proud swimmer's, lies her deep heart. Into it we
entered; we came within the redwoods.

This is time, made visible. This is the past, still standing. Laying the finger of a long shadow on the lips, saying
Hush ... and *Still* ... and *Slowly*. This is thousands of
years alive, and it looks every day of that. This will be

here, these identical trees, when men have forgotten where
your grave is. When children shall speak of the *Luftwaffe*
as they do of the Armada, as something long ago and hard
to remember.

I have talked no little about the trees of the West, and
they are all slight beside the Sequoias of Bull Creek Flats.
Anything I can say about them must also be slight. Just
at first you can motor through the redwoods as if they
were merely a forest; you can exclaim, even chatter excit-
edly. But when the soaring boles get closer and closer and
always taller than before, when the sense of time begins to
creep over you, and the hush falls like a shadow, you can't
go on. You draw to a stop, shut off the motor like a pro-
fanity, and get out, to go into the wood and worship.

Wherever you step into the redwood forest, there is a
crowding of great fluted columns as in the nave of Rouen
Cathedral, or Lincoln; there is the incense smoke of fog
drifting between the colonnades, smitten with the long
shafts of sunlight shining through it; there is a deep
gloom and internal quiet that is nothing sorrowful but
only peace. No footfall sounds; ten centuries of needles clothe the earth. It is a forest spacious, cleanly
empty, because there is little undergrowth in the redwoods, only sometimes a bit of azalea, commonly great
ferns, wide-spaced, serenely spreading. There are no lower
branches in a mature grove. It may be a hundred feet to
the nearest branch of foliage. At two hundred feet and
more the crowns expand; the needles, like those of yew,
grow in a ferny spray; they make at last a close canopy.
A bird, up there, is invisible from the ground. Even his
voice, his little soliloquy, barely descends to you. What-

ever impious noise or gesture you could make would be too
far below the bird for notice; he would not quit his small
foraging.

Touch the base of his tree; put your hand on it, and try
to believe in it. That's a thick armor, the bark itself so old
that it is all hung, in every crack and interstice, with the
close tremulous cobweb of spiders who have dwelt there,
mother and child, from the time of Charlemagne. Knock
upon a redwood. There is within as much life as there is in
you. More. For nothing in the animal world is of a rank
to address these trees. Not one of us can trace a lineage so
far back as this one existing life, not one of us has so little
rot in him or is less likely to burn, has the stature, or the
strength, or the straightness or loftiness. None has such
hope of a green old age, or of heaven. The redwoods have
attained it, rooted though they are in earth. From their
unseen upper branches, so high they reach into clear sunlight and still are growing, there falls a kind of mercy upon
men far under them.

The Great North Road of the Pacific Coast is U.S.
Highway 101. Motorists call that 'going up the coast,'
though most of the way they are fifty miles inland, shut
away from the sea by a high mountain range. Beyond this

wall lies another road, a narrower thread that for something like two hundred miles hugs the lonely shoreline where the white fog clings, and in fair weather or in foul the buoys toll a slow cling-clang.

This is the coast that no one comes to visit. This is the outline of the figurehead's lifting breast and of the lean rib under it. It is Cape Mendocino, California's farthest west, and the wild, fog-rifted shoreline beneath it all the way down to San Francisco. The railroad skips it, motorists overlook it, the mountains have it well hidden. Though a hundred and forty years ago the Russians colonized it, though it boomed in the fifties and sixties of the last century, today it is that part of California that even California has forgotten to boast about.

Twenty years ago, talking in the Gray Herbarium to Professor Jepson, the veteran western botanist, I conceived for this narrow region one of those place-passions that burn unquenched by the utmost improbability that they can ever be satisfied. Now on a summer morning I was turning out of the so-called 'Coast Highway' just where the greatest redwood forests diminish, into the beginning of Route 1. The car, I fancied, rather shied at the whole proposition. This was a rocky unpaved road that twists up over the intersecting mountain chain through wooded gorges that were still full then of purple rhododendron, white azalea, and the airy, plumy heads of that big forest herb called ocean spray. The sea, as we crossed the range, came forth in the air to claim us. On this old once-Russian coast the crowding mountains shut away swiftly all sense of the sweetness of land life, the sun-steeped days, the dusty sunsets, the warm confident warbling of the

sparrows. The crying of shore birds blew to us; the moil
and brine of the sea swept far up into the creeks' mouths.
It is a region that has turned its back to the continent. It

speaks to the sea only, in the voice of its whistling buoys, and by its lights it signals vigilantly to the ships.

It lives by the ocean, that strip; it lives by the fog, for it is only in the fog belt that the redwood will grow. And this is old lumber country, so old that it is strewn with dead or half-dead lumber camps, wooden ghost towns, the roofs of the planing mills lying on their floors. The logging railroads have been abandoned; their rusted tracks hang out over banks undercut by the streams that come streaking out of the mountains to gnaw away the steep earth and die themselves in some meandering estuary shut in by a sand spit from the tumbling Pacific. This was the timber stand that was first exploited, soon after the gold rush, the greatest stand of valuable timber in the world, found growing close to a chain of small harbors where the planks could be loaded on coastwise ships, or the unplaned logs be lashed into rafts and towed to wood-hungry markets. Those were the days, almost a century ago, when the government was giving away the redwood empire for the nominal payment on a homestead claim! When Norwegian sailors just off the ship in San Francisco were nabbed by timber companies for 'straw entrymen,' to enter a claim and sell it next day to the buzz saw for a five-dollar profit.

So they cleaned out the most available redwoods; they felled the giant canoe cedar, the precious Douglas fir, the Sitka spruce. Later they went after the magnificent Port Orford cedars, a fine-grained, aromatic wood demanded by Japan and China, and finally they got down to trees nobody had bothered with in the first boom days — lowland white fir, western hemlock. A second growth came in, and

that was cleaned out too. Now there's a third growth,
fire-blackened in many places, swept through with the
grave, eternal fog.

And still it is a beautifully wooded country. Because
one redwood, even a young redwood, is worth a hundred
other trees. Because what a lumberman would call a
cleaned out stand of hemlock and cedar and fir is, on this
coast, by other standards still a dense growth (so much is
the fog the friend of trees). Still the Douglas fir is dark
upon the crests, the hemlock spreads its ferny sprays, the
Sitka spruce is tall again, the lowland fir is fragrant.

And the lumbermen never touched the somber little
yews, or the tree alders that have mottled smooth boles
like eastern beeches and the same emerald shade. The
big-leaf maple too brings in the brightness of deciduous
forest to compensate for the coniferous gloom; the leaves
of California laurel glitter; their spicy, peppery clean
aroma sharpening the air. There is still some exploitation
of the buckthorn for its bark — I saw signs advertising
good prices on cascara bark; but nobody touches the wind-
twisted cypresses on the headlands, and the knotty prickle-
cone pines are free to take over the abandoned farms and
pastures.

If there is any place truly haunted, it is one that men
have discovered, lived in, left, and forgotten. That's what
gives Easter Island its hold over so many who never will
see it. The old Russian coast, this bygone lumbering
country, is thus possessed. It is old whaling and sealing
country too; there is something to remind one of Maine in
the sternly neat white mansard houses and meeting-
houses, in the lilacs — rare in this state — hanging heavy

heads over picket-fences. It is the kind of place that Americans of English stock early and courageously settle, individualistically exploit, then half abandon. Where, after them, come Italians and Portuguese, gleaning closely where their predecessors have despaired of the fisheries, sowing their dark-eyed children to mingle with the blue-eyed youngsters on the school playgrounds and to rove with the freedom of natives all the wild headlands and long sand bars, the caves, the rocks pierced by ocean, the brooks with trout in them and woods with deer in them.

Even on a calm day the Pacific off this coast is not really calm. All up and down the shore you can see the breakers smashing on reefs and rocks, shooting geysers twenty feet into the air, and everywhere the salt smoke of the endless battle between sea and land drifts in. Through the smiling sunlight in wraiths of spume that drench the sea-thrift, it goes trailing among the cypresses that grow with their backs huddled toward the sea and their arms flung up on the slopes for succor. Even when the sea is an exquisite silken blue and looks level half a mile from shore, still the tide, striking the jagged shelves of the continent, gathers itself into a long slow breath of determination. You watch that grow to a wave that topples to a mountain, that curls, in an accurate geometric green arc, and suddenly fumes with a backward tossing of white mad locks and opening of awful jaws where the seaweed for a moment appears to struggle for life. Hurling itself on the rocks with the momentum of uncalculated tons, the wave bites at every resistant particle, wrenches every loose thing from its hold, batters the sea-palms, dashes seething into the tide pools and plunges into unseen caves beneath the cliff. And then, while every barnacled rock is running with salt rivulets, and the gasping gravel is sucked back, comes the collision of the trapped force inside the cave, a final sound like the slamming of a great door.

Already out there, the ocean is drawing in its next breath, its clean tremendous anger, growing green with it, going white with it, smiling like a proud killer, lifting hundreds of pounds of rushing kelp, clattering shells, and whistling gravel. Then the long *punch!* in the sea caves. All day, like that.

All day the rocking buoy, raggedly tolling with a sound of church bells. A sound like summer Sundays, to make you think of kneeling girls and sevenfold amens, and old dates on mossy headstones. Like that, but, of course, not anything like that. A mockery of that, a tinkling, enticing, come-hither-and-die sound. A sound you remember from Cape Ann, from Great Orme's Head, a sound to go with the mewing of gulls and the skimming of shearwaters when they come wandering up this coast, after breeding in New Zealand, in the summer that is our winter. Something to make you think of fresh lobster and old wrecks. I saw one such — for we had left the car to stretch our legs by the strand — the wooden bones of a small craft that were sucked dry now of tragedy by the sun of many summers. A brown pelican was sitting cosily under the hulk as I passed by. I could have touched him with an outstretched arm, but he did not fly. Instead he settled down on his feet, fluffing out his feathers, flashing the milky blue nictitating membrane over the friendly big jewel of his eye, listening while my wife talked to him, and for answer clacking once taciturnly his great bill.

Only once again, after this, did we pull to a stop and get out, for we were bound to make San Francisco by nightfall. So the miles of bleak coast fled by us, till swinging around a bend we saw rise on the barren downs the fragment of stockade, the commandant's house, the incredibly Muscovite outline of the little wooden chapel that together are called Fort Ross.

Out of the vast salt air of the Pacific we walked into the little holy building where still the ikons hang, speaking of Europe and European man bringing his God and the Son of his God and that Son's Mother, all this way. All across Siberia. Down through or along Alaska, past Vancouver, Cape Flattery, the Columbia's mouth, to this lonely spot.

Moscow was burning as Napoleon's soldiers entered it, when the walls of this little church went up and its two squat towers were lifted. At that time the Spanish had not yet completed the northernmost of their missions, San Francisco de Solano. Russia was reaching down from Alaska for what is now our America, pushing south in the fog belt, hunting sea otters mostly, Pribilof seals perhaps, aided by her allies the Aleut Indians who came in their wonderful long canoes built of arbor vitae, launched in the fjords of Alaska, sent south to bring death to the gentle otters. Meanwhile the Spanish were pushing northward in the sun belt, in the inner coastal ranges, padre and don, hunting for souls to save and gold to dig. Russia come halfway around the world from the east, Spain halfway from the west, passing each other warily, with a mountain range between them.

Even the Spanish had been doing some business in sea otters as early as 1784. California Indians, stimulated by beads and scrap iron, knives and cloth, would bring in any number of otter hides. These were handled by the Spanish wholesale, being sent to China, where the furs were exchanged for quicksilver, needed in the Mexican gold mines. But the thin pelts from the warm Spanish waters never fetched the big money, and the Spaniards and Californian Indians never really got the hang of the business. It was the Russians who knew the game, and the Aleuts who were the terrible sea-hunters. In five years they took fifty thousand pelts. Two hundred thousand of the animals were destroyed between 1786 and 1868, when the hunting of them constituted the only really profitable industry of the California coast.

I must use the past tense, in general, in talking about the sea otter. It was a creature always found near rocks, wherever the sea bottom was rocky. It foraged usually in twenty-five fathom of water, and the resting grounds were beds of floating kelp, mostly the sea otter's cabbage whose tips, like the heads of small seals, we had seen bobbling and sinking and rising all this day, off shore.

The rate of reproduction was slow — normally one young at a birth. The mothers were noted for their solicitude. When traveling a female would swim on her back with her young clasped in her forepaws. If pursued she would seize the pup in her jaws, by the nape of the neck. Young otters could not swim, and when their parents plunged into the depths they would leave the babies floating on their backs. The cries of the baby otter have been described as a mewing sound, like that of a cat, but others said this resembled the crying of a human infant.

This is the animal whose exquisitely soft dark brown fur,

shot with a frosty tip of light on each hair, brought the
Russians all this way, to this tiny settlement on the
westernmost fringe of wilderness. But in a few years' time
they had skimmed the first cream of the sea; their Aleuts
had cleaned out even the Farallones of sea otters. When
the plunder was done, Russia surrendered its claims to this
coast without a struggle.

Off there where on the track of the Japanese current the
fog lies forever banked ready to roll in at the wind's command, the earth was tipping darkly soon to swallow the
sun. The long run was almost over. Not many miles ahead
there must rise the towered hills of San Francisco, looped
with necklaces of light, the shipping lying at its feet in
bays that would be swimming now with the wine tints of
sundown. Behind me lay vast realms of desert and forest
and oceanic wilderness, and over me swept an appetite,
sudden and fierce and happy, for the city to come, and all
my brothers in it. In mind I stood, as presently I would
stand, at the high window looking down from Nob Hill
upon the lights, the purple dusk, the moving glitter of ships
across the bay, hearing the lusty urge of traffic up the
steep streets below, and in the room behind me the whisper
of my wife's evening gown going over her head. There

would be dinner preparing for me in some favorite restaurant, and in my hand a glass; my ears would still be ringing from the warm voices come over the wire, of my children at home. I could taste that moment pitched to perfection between satisfaction and eagerness, a full hour before it came to me to live.

And I knew just how at sunset of tomorrow I would go down to Fisherman's Wharf, when the big sea-battered boats come in trailing a cloud of gulls, and how, amid gulls wheedling, sharp planks and tackle gently creaking in the subdued unrest of harbor waters, I would talk to the fishermen about the Farallones, and jokingly cajole the grinning sons of Genoa and Oporto to take me to those wild rocks forty miles out at sea. I know that nobody ever goes to the Farallones now. They are the most marvelous bird rocks on the coast, where the murres and puffins and cormorants, the guillemots and auklets and petrels once came in incredible numbers to nest, but man has worked himself out of his welcome there. First the Aleuts killed off the sea otters. Then, when in the gold-rush days eggs in San Francisco were fetching prices high enough to buy the golden goose itself, the egg hunters came to the Farallones. They killed the parent birds; they robbed the nests, and wherever they went the cruel gulls came after, breaking the eggs the hunters missed. For forty years and more this slaughter went on, until the ornithologists got the government to put a stop to it. Now even the ornithologists can't get permission to land on the islands, not in nesting time, at least. At the breeding season the chief of the Biological Survey himself couldn't persuade the lighthouse authorities to let him land. For myself, I always carry with me a letter granting me the Coast Guard's permission to land at any other season but the nesting time — if I can get there. So that's why I go down to wharf and talk to the swart men just in from blue water, pretending to myself that I might go, where the fishermen go. They know me now, and joke me about how seasick I would be, pretending they might take me. It is good, I think, to have some islands in your cosmos that you long to visit and only by some miracle might reach.

The light was failing; I switched on the headlamps. They picked up a tawny form loping ahead, but the wildcat did not break for the bush. Instead he raced me, running just ahead, down a long piece of the road, in a burst of easy speed beautifully coordinated of muscle, leashed of power, as if he could do twice this time if he chose, though the feral heart must have been pounding in the furry belly. I had enough manhood to be ashamed to pass him by the easy cheat of stepping on a pedal. Suddenly he sprang in one lion-like leap up the bank and vanished into darkness. It was my last taste of the wild, for this trip, and I knew it.

The great release that wilderness had brought me was almost over; I was going back to mankind, and my place in it, and I was glad to go, glad of my place. For that place, whether in cities or in desert or forest, is in Nature, inescapably. Nor do I think, in spite of the history of the sea otters and the redwoods, even in spite of bombers over Europe, that we have wholly disgraced our station in the scheme of things. I thought back to the little memorial tablets I had seen among the greatest of the Sequoias, bits of lettering that promised that these trees would stand unharmed forever, promises bought by the dollars, even the pennies of people some of whom might never see the trees. But they had seen a taller thing, a value higher than any tree that grows, even a redwood. And they believed in a future for which this value should be preserved.

Any faith that is to support mankind today has to be strong enough to stand proofs grueling as those a test pilot gives a plane. We will not put our trust in any method that will not demonstrably work. What is the force, the discipline, the brotherhood bound by vows to the pursuit of incorruptible truth, which proves every step, is forever returning to verify, will abandon any cherished tenet the moment it is not completely convincing? What is it that works all the modern miracles, has put the practicality into compassion for suffering, has unchained men from their superstitions, has endured persecution and martyrdom, and still knows no fear?

I am not proposing science as a new religion. It is not worthy of that yet. It has not yet assumed the responsibility for man's soul and conduct that a true religion must assume. Possibly sound science is by its very nature delimited from such an undertaking. Or perhaps science has not yet found the courage to become admittedly a moral force. I only point to science as a method, a way of thought on which all men can well agree. For it sheds a light of clarity and certainty. By it, beyond it, we may, I hope, behold the faith which we all need as we need our daily bread.

For not many of us, in this modern day, are still believing that the world is a pattern all beautiful, and that its seeming imperfections are only the flaws in our vision. We cannot say that either among the stars or in the affairs of men are events directed with justice unless we call that justice inscrutable. But thinking men of this generation will not accept even a God they may not scrutinize. This may be the gift of modernity to the world — the reconciliation of science and religion.

For superstitious ages they were considered enemies. Men were afraid to find out; they tortured Galileo and Bruno; they cursed Darwin. But the faith of science is so profound that it is not afraid of anything it may discover.

And its discoveries have served to strengthen the religious faith of men who love the truth. Ideas that struck at first as destructive have but cleared the way to viewpoints more splendid. Knowing life better, a man will worship life more. The surest, serenest men I have ever met are the biologists, the astronomers, the physicists who have looked most deeply. Of all men, those absorbed in scrutiny of it are the most loyal to life.

What is it, this life, this relentless cataract that dashes an instant into human form, sparkling and fresh and, fated, seeps away through all the pores and cracks of mortality? The thoughtful have been trying for centuries to discover its nature. They seek its origins, aware that the origin may well be the same as the force itself.

The seeking brain of man has not been bettered since great minds functioned in the old Greek stoa, but it is better equipped today than ever before. The method of experiment is new, the tools and processes of science are new and growing. The whole world is a common field of research. Life is under the lens. And the great cannon-shape of the telescope is swung upon space. They have pushed their search, the scientists, beyond the world.

For as they try to see life from every side, so they attempt to outline its boundaries by a careful scrutiny, too, of that which is not life. They find that not-life is almost everywhere. There is not life in the sun, nor in the three jewels studding Orion's belt. There is not life only three miles overhead, and not life even one mile down in the earth. Swiftly frozen, instantly consumed in the fires, life is spread out in a thin, thin film on this minute and temperate planet.

Here we must live it, a giant task in common which men struggle to master. The desperate instinctively look to the sky, to the stars, in query. And science, the reporter in the battle, has this to say: that life itself is not separate from the matter of the universe. Cosmos was its womb. The earth was wrenched out of the sun. From that birth were derived the elements of which all that inhabits the earth is made, some ninety-six primary elements which are the alphabet of this planet. And when the spectroscope is turned upon the stars to find what they are made of, it cannot discover any element beyond the ninety-six which are the stuff of ourselves and our planet home. The whole of Nature is made of one matter, from Aldebaran, its light, to Zoe, her young body. At the nuclear core of each molecule of her blood is an atom of that same iron which, simon pure, comes hurtling down in meteoric stone, out of the depths and the heights. More, every atom has a structure like that of the planetary system with its central sun. So that the structure of the elemental units of matter, the very pattern and force of that unit, are kin to the revolution of our solar system. And if there is no proof, there is also no reason to doubt that in the island universes runs the writ of comparable law.

Yet vain, utterly vain, to cry to the stars for help, when the battle goes against us! The human race, however, has never given up the fight, even when the enemy seemed to be winning. In any war, when the soldiers sicken at heart and desert their posts, it is because a rumor is running that the supreme command is gone.

If by 'supreme command' I may express an order in Nature that a man can understand and revere, then that command, that order has always been there. In fact, it is Nature itself, revealed by science.

So that when we go through the world touching a flower and taking the sunlight on our hands, we are not beholding a shallow illusion of beauty having no relation to ourselves and our troubles. Those troubles are disorder, and subject to alteration. The immutable order of Nature is on our side. It is on the side of life. For life is a particular case of Nature. Its structure, whether in a leaf or a starfish, is so complex that only the most rigid laws could sustain it, and they are the same laws that we read everywhere in matter. Perhaps only this planet in the universe supplies the right conditions for life. Or just as possibly its elaborate problems are being worked out elsewhere than here at home on earth.

The farther men gaze through the telescope, the vaster and more enigmatic does heaven appear. The closer they stare into the microscope, the more valiant, adaptable and conquering does life, mortal life, reveal itself. Science can give you today the chemical formulae for the cells in the leaf or the starfish, but the life in those cells remains unknown, of an unguessed origin. Perhaps it will always remain so.

Enough for us, while we live this life, that it is the unexpected and dazzling flower that sprang out upon this rock of earth. It is the manifestation of some long, slow will to victory that is held up to the sky and the stars. It is the signal in universal language that, to the firmament executing its glittering and faultless movements, answers back: Here too are order and supreme command.

And here, also, is the intelligence of man which, entertaining now these evidences, dares both to question and believe. To such an intelligence there is no longer any gulf between the conclusions of science and tolerant religion. For the discoveries of science are due not to the greatness of man but to the awesome greatness of the order. That order is not inscrutable; it invites to exploration like a beautiful corridor. But this leads not into a labyrinth like the Minotaur's — a tortuous whim of madness where dark things are done — but into a vast, an infinite temple. Man is born into the order; he is always a part of it, and whatever indignities he suffers, that order cannot be outraged.

THE END